GRAND PLANS

GRAND PLANS

Business Progressivism and Social Change in Ohio's Miami Valley, 1890-1929

JUDITH SEALANDER

THE UNIVERSITY PRESS OF KENTUCKY

Scholarly publisher for the Commonwealth,
serving Bellarmine College, Berea College, Centre
College of Kentucky, Eastern Kentucky University,
The Filson Club, Georgetown College, Kentucky
Historical Society, Kentucky State University,
Morehead State University, Murray State University,
Northern Kentucky University, Transylvania University,
University of Kentucky, University of Louisville,
and Western Kentucky University.

Editorial and Sales Offices: Lexington, Kentucky, 40506-0336

Library of Congress Cataloging-in-Publication Data

Sealander, Judith.
    Grand plans : business progressivism and social change in Ohio's
Miami Valley, 1890-1929 / Judith Sealander.
        p.   cm.
    Bibliography: p.
    Includes index.
    ISBN 0-8131-1653-8
    1. Miami River Region (Ohio)—Economic conditions.   2. Miami River
Region (Ohio)—Politics and government.   3. Dayton (Ohio)—Economic
conditions.   4. Dayton (Ohio)—Politics and government.   5. Business
and politics—Ohio—Miami River Region—History.   6. Business and
politics—Ohio—Dayton—History.   7. Progressivism (United States
politics)   I. Title.
HC107.032M477   1988
330.9771'73041—dc19   88-4237

Contents

Illustrations follow page 104

For Willard Gatewood

Acknowledgments

Our discipline emphasizes the product, not the process, of scholarship. When that product is a monograph, it very often has one name attached. This monograph bears my name alone, but, like most historians, I could not have written it without help. It is a pleasure here to acknowledge that fact.

First, two institutions gave me timely financial help. A grant from the American Council of Learned Societies allowed me to take a six-month leave of absence to conduct research. My own institution, Wright State University, was also generous with research support. Under the aegis of the University Research Incentive program and the College of Liberal Arts Research Committee I received help with travel and manuscript duplication expenses.

Friends and colleagues gave something even more valuable: their time. Several people at Wright State read parts of the manuscript, dug into files for answers to questions, lent enthusiasm or an ear just when I needed one or both. Dorothy Smith, Mary Ellen Mazey, Carol Nathanson, Charles Berry, Bob Adams, and Bill Rickert deserve special thanks. Other colleagues around the country kept the mails busy, making bibliographic suggestions, helping with grant proposals, reading drafts, and offering advice. Bill Chafe, Bill Tuttle, Don Mrozek, Don Critchlow, Marc Weiss and Sandy Beidler were especially supportive. As he has done for years, Frank Costigliola mixed enthusiasm and trenchant criticism most helpfully.

Steve Ward of the Patents Division of the National Cash Register Corporation took a personal interest in this project and helped me gain access to the NCR corporate archives, as did B. Lyle

Shafer and Marjorie Jones of NCR Personnel Services. I am very grateful to them, and to NCR archivists Eugene Kneiss and Bill West, for this generously provided help.

Nina Myatt of the Antioch College Library staff took a great deal of her valuable time to shepherd me through the as yet totally uncatalogued Antiochiana archives of Antioch College. The days I spent reading and taking notes at a long wooden table behind her desk stand in my memory as especially pleasant ones.

Although they have no idea of it, Roberta Julian and Fran James have for many years been role models, academic women whose grace and style have influenced me greatly. Also of great influence has been the work of Ellis Hawley and Louis Galambos. Though neither personally helped me with this project, their books leave me in their debt. I am most certainly in the debt of my editor, Jerry Crouch, whose good judgment and good humor helped me during many stages of this book's completion.

Finally, as I total debts, two people stand out. This book's dedication to Willard Gatewood stands as insufficient symbol of the value I place on his support and advice. Ed Melton knows the value I have placed on his judgments about this manuscript. He may not know the much greater stock I take in his friendship.

1

Business and Progressivism

In the late nineteenth century, Ohio's Miami Valley was still predominantly agricultural. A nine-county region in the extreme southwestern quadrant of the state, it contained numerous villages and hamlets that nestled along the hundred-mile-long watershed created by the Miami and Mad rivers. The average family lived on a farm and shopped for cloth, horseshoes, and other necessities in a little crossroads village, such as Harshmanville, Harries Station, Little York, Liberty, Union, or a dozen others. But the Valley's one city, Dayton, heralded the significant changes to come, not just to the region, but to the country, in the four decades between 1890 and 1929.

In 1851 the first steam engine and the first steam bakery appeared in Dayton. In 1889 natural gas supplemented steam as an even cheaper and more efficient source of fuel. Powered by steam and gas Dayton boomed. Factories specializing in farm machinery and wood products began to crowd the city's riverfront. People, overwhelmingly native-born whites from the surrounding countryside and from Indiana and Kentucky, flooded in. In 1870, Dayton's population was 30,473. By 1890 it was 61,220, by 1900, 85,333. The new prosperity brought by rapid industrialization meant that theaters, opera halls, and fine mansions appeared along with smokestacks and freightyards. Famous actors, singers, and speakers made appearances. In fact, to accommodate the community's desire to hear the period's eminent lecturers, city leaders mounted a campaign to build a huge new auditorium, able to seat 2,500.[1]

And Daytonians were not the only Americans in the late nineteenth century who made heroes of compelling platform speakers. Baptist minister Russell Conwell delivered his most famous talk, "Acres of Diamonds," more than six thousand times. Literally millions of people sitting in tents or town halls heard him thunder, "The opportunity to get rich, to attain unto great wealth, is here . . . within the reach of almost every man and woman who hears me speak tonight."[2] Certainly Conwell's vision of a country offering its citizens unparalleled opportunities was not unique. Dozens of writers, politicians, and business leaders echoed it. Tremendous national economic transformation, typified by the factory boom in Dayton, seemed to verify it as well.

But now, of course, the opportunities that beckoned were not the traditional ones so much a part of the American self-image. They did not stem from the greater availability of cheap farmland or land in the West. The farm labor force and land in farms had grown absolutely during the nineteenth century, as the nation had ballooned in size, but by the 1890s the expansion of land under cultivation slowed to a standstill. Twentieth-century technology would improve productivity but would not increase the amount of land being cultivated or the number of farms in the nation. Moreover, by 1890 the frontier was running out as well. The national census published in that year argued for the first time that a clear "frontier line" no longer existed. A nation that had rooted its mythologies in idealizations of the sturdy farmer and of the limitless possibilities of westward expansion now faced major changes. The diamonds Russell Conwell promised would come from the factory, not the farm. With farmland growth static and machinery increasingly able to replace human labor, America in the late nineteenth century began its historic shift from agriculture to industry.

Here again, change in Dayton was the prototype. Industrial America knew no limits during this period but rather enjoyed phenomenal annual growth rates far exceeding those of any country in Europe. Dramatic changes that established the foundation of the twentieth-century economy occurred rapidly during the nineteenth century's last three decades. An industrial sector almost wholly dependent on pig iron in 1870 had converted to steel by 1900. Wood, as late as 1870, provided about 75 percent of the heating needs of the country. In the next two decades coal and petroleum almost completely replaced it. As late as 1870, horsepower remained a literal concept: work animals still furnished more power than all other prime movers combined. By the beginning of the new century, coal-fired steam engines, not horses, supplied the nation's horsepower.[3]

Even more significant than the widespread application of new sources of energy was the completion of a communication and transportation system that unleashed the potential of the largest and fastest-growing market in the world. The railroad and the telegraph provided the tools necessary for the creation, for the first time in the country's history, of a truly national economy. And railroad and telegraph companies were the models for the new, enormous organizations that would soon dominate that economy. Such organizations introduced not merely changes in business structure; they started a revolution that altered the nature of capitalism and reorganized American society.

Railroad and telegraph companies discovered that they needed teams of managers to orchestrate the complex movement of trains around the country and to control the millions of messages sent over telegraph wires. The introduction of these managers stimulated basic changes in an economic system that had remained essentially stable for centuries. In fact, the sixteenth-century European mine, or bank, or trading company had remarkable similarities to its early nineteenth-century American counterpart. In each, owners exercised personal control over business decisions. They did not employ salaried hierarchies of managers. In fact, the real differences were not between the Medici Bank and the Hudson's Bay Company or the Bank of the United States, but between these institutions and the new organizations that emerged in the late nineteenth and early twentieth centuries. These new corporations made the production and marketing volumes of all their predecessors look miniscule in comparison.

The emergence of this new kind of "managerial capitalism" took place in a period of falling prices, stable or falling interest rates, and slight declines in the average number of hours worked per week. Moreover, American industrial workers saw their real wage rates rise slightly. These were, of course, relatively small gains. Only a few families acquired fabulous wealth.[4]

In such circumstances, the average worker at least did not lose ground, and a few founded great fortunes, but not everyone echoed Conwell's enthusiasm. In fact, many Americans, both leaders and followers, responded to the booming economy and rapid transformations of the late nineteenth century with a sense of foreboding. They anxiously asked questions. What would happen to a nation that idealized the family farm if the population of big cities, where foreigners or their children often constituted a majority, continued to grow three times as fast as that of rural areas? What would be the social costs of an industrial system that maimed or killed thousands of workers each year? Could the growing gap between rich and poor tear the country apart? Were the bloody strikes of the period a harbinger of just such a possibility, of another American civil war, this time based on class rather than regional hostility? Which traditional social, economic, and political institutions should be defended in the face of rapid change? Which should be altered?[5]

Americans, then, reacted to this period of rapid industrial growth, organizational formation, and accelerated social change with both excitement and doubt, optimism and fear. The combination produced a response labeled *progressivism* by contemporaries and historians alike.

Scholarly debate about the origins, character, and legacy of progressivism has been prolonged and fierce. Even the label *progressivism* itself has been challenged. In a much-discussed article published in 1970, Peter Filene denied that anything sufficiently cohesive to deserve the title had existed. Progressivism deserved an "obituary," not continuing analysis.[6] But few scholars have been willing to stand with Filene at the grave. Most continue to assert that progressivism, a real and significant effort to restructure society's institutions, occurred.

While most historians have disagreed with Filene, they have also disagreed among themselves, challenging each other's analyses of the character and spirit of progressivism, each other's profiles of the progressive personality, and even each other's chronological limits for the era's birth and death. Through the cacophony of interpretations, however, one idea has rung clear: that the business community acted as an important stimulus to progressivism.

The first historians to analyze progressivism not only admired what they judged to be a reform crusade, but they often wrote from the perspective of participants. Charles Beard, for instance, did more than write about municipal reform during the era, he lent his prestige and considerable energies to such progressive organizations as the National Municipal League and the Short Ballot Organization.[7] Historians such as Charles and Mary Beard, Harold Faulkner, and Benjamin Parke DeWitt saw progressivism as a struggle of the "people" against the "interests." Chief among the special interests blighting the United States was the business corporation. Having discovered that business interests often corrupted politics or neglected to maintain minimally safe and healthy working conditions, an angry citizenry united to demand reform, often in the shape of new state and federal legislation.[8]

The progressive battle, one pitting the forces of democracy against the forces of privilege, had ended in victory for democracy, a "revolutionary" effort by the people to create a more socially responsible society.[9] Of course, authors of studies contemporaneous with or slightly removed in time from events described could hardly be taken to task by later historians for lacking a long-range perspective. Not surprisingly, these historians tended to blame social and economic changes brought by World War I, not inherent defects in the movement itself, for the decline of progressivism.[10]

Historians continued to view progressivism as a lost crusade against industrial greed and business excess for almost two decades. But beginning in the 1950s some began to assign quite a different role to business. The business community, especially big business, still stimulated progressivism, but in a way very different from what the movement's first historians had suggested. Led by Richard Hofstadter and tied loosely into what came to be called the consensus school, historians began to see the progressives not as "the people," struggling for economic justice and social democracy, but as members of a far smaller group. They were the old nineteenth-century urban middle class: lawyers, teachers, ministers, doctors, journalists, and writers. The industrial boom had not left members of this group impoverished materially, but it had left them bewildered, fearing loss of their roles as community leaders. Rather than a mass movement to challenge economic exploitation by robber barons, progressivism was a movement orchestrated by members of an urban middle class seeking to maintain status in their communities. They could do this by leading a reform movement attacking the new corporate order.[11]

A romantic idealization of the traditional nineteenth-century values they sought to preserve in the face of rapid economic and social change hampered the effectiveness of this movement, however. The progressives correctly assessed some of the excesses and dangers inherent in rapid industrialization: filthy cities, dangerous factories, and unsafe food, to name only a few. But in their search for solutions, progressives employed an idealized version of a nineteenth-century system of morality and ethics. So, they sought, largely in the political arena, to reconcile the new corporate order with an image of traditional white, Anglo-Saxon, Protestant family and community values that had never really existed. Driven by this motive, rather than economic self-interest, progressives too often championed symbolic solutions, like Prohibition, to complex economic problems. In fact they sometimes lacked any real understanding of the massive social and economic transformations wrenching the country. Interestingly, Hofstadter and his colleagues such as George Mowry, Arthur Link, and James Timberlake still saw progressives as reformers fighting industrial and business abuse. Large corporate business was still the villain, the evil foil to progressive reform.[12]

By the 1960s numerous critics had challenged the "status-anxiety" interpretation of progressivism. Many demonstrated, often through the use of regional or state case studies, that Hofstadter's profile of a "typical" progressive frequently matched a profile of a "typical" conservative. Educated, financially stable, religious, "WASP" professionals in state after state also opposed progressive reform.[13] Moreover, by the 1960s, historians not only challenged Hofstadter, but they also produced new interpretations. What remained central was the same old idea: business was an important stimulus to progressivism. The relationships between corporate America and progressive reform, however, were dramatically altered.[14]

According to historians Gabriel Kolko, James Weinstein, Raymond Callahan, and William Appleman Williams, the leaders of top industrial, financial, and transportation corporations were not the enemies of progressive reform but the gray eminences behind it. Kolko, focusing on patterns of federal regulation, argued that prominent businessmen shaped these regulations to counter the more radical controls they feared states and cities might try to impose. Progressivism, then, was a "triumph of conservatism."[15]

Powerful business leaders, according to this interpretation, saw progressivism as a means of securing the existing social order, of, in fact, establishing a "corporate ideal" in the United States. That ideal valued efficiency, organization, and standardization. Corporation leaders, by adapting to these ends the ideals of middle-class social reformers and others, gained allies during the period. But they were the leaders of progressivism, the architects of innovations as diverse as city commissions or revised school curriculums.[16]

Business, then, still motivated progressivism, but it was the agent, not object, of change, reordering society to its own specifications. Figures from John Dewey to Theodore Roosevelt to Woodrow Wilson were either the dupes of or the front men for the real leaders of progressivism: J.P. Morgan, Elbert Gary, George Perkins, and their corporate colleagues.

Critics of those who saw progressivism as the triumph of conservative capitalism noted that not since the 1920s had serious scholars suggested that the progressives were revolutionaries. Indeed, historians had been pointing out for many years the conservative aspects of progressivism. Further, critics argued, Kolko and his colleagues had exaggerated. To describe progressivism as the monopolization of power by corporate America was to simplify excessively the phenomenon and the era.

The view of progressivism as business conspiracy has been roundly debunked within the past fifteen years, criticized as rigid, guilty of an almost complete lack of attention to all the other factors and powerful forces that might have motivated progressive actions. Many historians have argued that there was no business monolith in America during these decades. There was certainly no business monolith secretly orchestrating putative reform.[17]

Gabriel Kolko began his best-known book, *The Triumph of Conservatism*, with the question "What *really* happened in the past?"[18] While few scholars have accepted his answers, many echoed his question in interpretations of progressivism that cautioned their readers to look more carefully and skeptically at forces reshaping the late nineteenth- and early twentieth-century

United States. Two historians, Robert Wiebe and Samuel Hays, members of the same generation as Kolko, Weinstein, and the other scholars who saw the progressive era as dominated by big corporations, initiated another approach to progressivism. Once again the idea appeared that business had acted as a stimulus to progressivism. Hays and Wiebe, however, did not picture businessmen as puppeteers behind the stage, entangling politicians in their strings. In fact, the average small entrepreneur was also confused by the bewildering pace of change at the turn of the century. The small shopkeeper was not partner to some vast business conspiracy to control the United States. Neither, however, was John D. Rockefeller, Edward Harriman, or J.P. Morgan. These men and others like them greatly enlarged their business empires. The greatest of them controlled assets in excess of half a billion dollars. Yet *control* was a relative term. Corporations had reached huge size by the late nineteenth century, but their owners did not yet really understand how to integrate and manage them. Corporations, seen by Kolko as powerful enough to transform presidents of the United States into their waterboys, were in reality entities suffering "jerry-built organization, ad hoc assumptions of responsibility, obsolete office techniques, and above all an astonishing lack of communication among [their] parts."[19]

Business too faced monumental problems. It also had to fashion a response to the changes generated by massive national growth and a maturing industrial economy. Business leaders organized, both internally and externally, to form new types of corporations. In the process, they invented managerial capitalism. That response, a growing number of historians in the 1970s and 1980s argued, was of central importance to American history. Louis Galambos wrote, for instance, "The single most significant phenomenon in modern American history is the emergence of giant, complex organizations."[20]

But even with new systems of centrally coordinated management, the new corporations, separately, could not cope adequately with the developing complexity of new price and market networks. Together they could. A mature industrial system shifted economic decisions from relationships among individuals to contests for power among well-organized groups. The business community was the first to realize the implications of this new reality. Progressivism, then, was not a democratic revolution, a battle of the people against the interests, but an organizational revolution, led by business. And the United States, responding to forces spawned by industrialization and following a corporate model, emerged from the progressive era as a bureaucratic, modern society. In such a society, most people functioned within networks of organizations, both public and private. Geographic and governmental divisions mattered less; educational and professional divisions mattered more.

The progressives were systematizers who accepted industrialization but sought to control it through methods first invented by large-scale business organizations. The new organizational society they created was one in which businessmen and "the people" did not do righteous battle. Rather, something more complicated occurred during the early twentieth century in the United States. Society experienced "corporatization"; traditional lines between public and private blurred.[21]

No new school of history has yet emerged sufficiently powerful to dislodge the organizational interpretation of progressivism from its prominent position. That is not to say debate has ended. Nor is it to say that organizational historians share no conclusions in common with their predecessors. They agree with New Left scholars such as Kolko and Williams that corporate America reshaped politics and society in the early twentieth century. But they argue that reshaping was not conducted as a conspiracy, an effort by a cabal of big businessmen to retain power and wealth. What's more, they say, historians should focus on processes, not personalities, on the phenomena of bureaucratization and professionalization, not on the alleged machinations of the House of Morgan.

But that very focus on process has left organizational interpretations of progressivism open to attack. These interpretations, critics have argued, drained progressivism of its blood and its passion. Progressive reformers were not simply roused by inefficiency and the lack of order in society. Evangelical Protestantism, optimism, and faith in progress were also powerful spurs to reform. Their religious and moral beliefs impelled progressives to attack conditions that led to suffering, to demand that filthy tenements and firetrap sweatshops be eliminated. Their optimism and faith in progress convinced them that through vigorous effort, Americans could in fact improve their environments. In fact, keys to progressivism were not just processes, but ideology and personality. Some historians, in fact, even began again to emphasize an argument used by the first generation of analysts of progressivism: that antibusiness emotion was a powerful stimulus to reform. David Thelen and Sheldon Hackney, for instance, found that a new sense of public-spirited citizenship helped bring diverse groups of people together in Wisconsin and Alabama as progressives.[22] Progressivism was indeed motivated by a search for social justice and a desire to curb business excess, these historians argued, just as the first analysts of progressivism had asserted decades earlier.

Furthermore, at least one historian has tried to revive Hofstadter's progressives, those frustrated and alienated members of the middle class who opposed big business and sought to restore Gilded Age values. Albo Martin has argued that progressives were ignorant and fearful of the organizational changes wrought by business in the late nineteenth century. As a consequence, they saddled industry with unnecessary restrictions.[23] Once again, a half century later, a historian saw progressivism as an antibusiness movement, a movement of the people against the interests. Except this time the historian's sympathies lay with the interests.[24]

In what ways can an examination of business and progressivism in Ohio's Miami Valley between 1890 and 1929 contribute to this continuing debate? Even this brief review of the historiography of progressivism reveals that, decade after decade, historians have returned to one central idea: that business stimulated progressivism. Major economic change in the industrial sector in the late nineteenth century shattered old business organizations. The emergent new ones may have been labeled either monsters run by robber barons or archetypes of modern bureaucracies. The business sector may have been the enemy of progressivism or the genius behind it. But clearly no major interpretation of this most interpreted of topics has been able completely to abandon the conclusion that to understand progressivism one must understand business's relationship with progressivism.

And that relationship was a complex one. Progressives, even those working within the business community itself, may have simultaneously accepted the new corporate order and opposed its abuses. Crucial to progressivism may have been a complex, business-led reorganization of the public and private institutions of society. But also crucial may have been broadly based public anger and confusion, stimulated by these rapid and far-reaching changes, even if the changes themselves were only imperfectly understood. If too many members of the first generations of analysts saw only the public anger, too many in recent years have seen only the webs of structural reorganization.[25]

Even adherents of the organizational school agree that a focus on concepts like "malfunctioning pluralism," "collaboration in the private order," or "bureaucratization" has led to "murky" history.[26] Those less charitable might charge that it has depopulated history, emptied it of the colorful people whose fervent speeches damning corruption and industrial irresponsibility were not intentional camouflage. But no historian would be well advised to return to an analysis of progressivism that relies primarily on descriptions of colorful people or fervent speeches.

A case study of business involvement with progressivism in a limited geographic area undergoing significant change could integrate these two approaches. A study of the work of specific human beings and their reactions to specific issues could bring life to, as well as critically test, such concepts as "corporatization." The need for more case studies that seek to throw light on larger questions has been recognized. Ellis Hawley, for instance, has argued that crucial questions about the roles played by business during the progressive era and questions about the forces shaping what many see as that era's new social order "await more detailed studies."[27] In a review essay published in 1982 Daniel Rodgers listed areas in which he saw future research as most needed. "The [progressive] period," he said, "remains ripe for more enterprises like Carl V. Harris's fine study of Birmingham, Alabama, which—holding in abeyance preconceived notions of victors and losers—tries to ask which social and economic groups won precisely what."[28] In 1986, Peter Buck counseled organizational historians to "take time out from their rewriting of the nations' past and spend a day in the country."[29] Business historians, Buck challenged, still focused far too exclusively on change at the national level, on headquarters activities in big cities.

But any attempt to understand the complex nature of American society and the phenomenon of American reform activity between 1890 and 1930 must begin with a realization that, as late as 1920, there were still only nineteen cities in the country with more than 250,000 residents. The cities that probably were the real crucibles for progressive reform were not the few very large ones, but rather the medium-sized ones. In fact, the most rapidly changing urban areas were those that combined rural districts with one or two cities having populations that in 1910 fell within the 50,000-100,000 range.[30]

The Miami Valley was just such an area. It affords an ideal opportunity to "spend a day in the country," examining not just "what social and economic groups won what," but looking too into what ways, if any, business acted as a stimulus to progressivism.

If it is true that the rise of corporate business in the late nineteenth and early twentieth centuries led to major changes in American life, then the region was a fascinating microcosm. Perhaps in no other area of the country did so many pioneering features of business progressivism emerge so quickly and receive so much national attention. To use the words of one prominent businessman, "grand plans" had been put in motion.[31]

Between 1890 and 1929, readers of *Outlook, Literary Digest, Municipal Affairs,* and dozens of other national publications found articles extolling the "Dayton model." The articles discussed "practical" education, free vocational training for workers, company gardens and lunchrooms, commission-manager city government, "scientific" dam-building or "progressive worker-camps."[32]

This book will analyze four important examples of progressive experimentation instigated or heavily influenced by the area's business leaders: welfare work at the National Cash Register Company, the establishment of the Miami Conservancy District, commission-manager government in Dayton, and progressive education experiments in the region at both public and private schools. These examples help to provide the details lacking in the work of too many analysts of progressivism who have, through the decades, seen business influence as a crucial motivating force, but who have examined that force solely on a national level or have constructed fascinating new organizational syntheses populated largely by anonymous bureaucrats. Without this kind of detail business influence during the period, although almost universally acknowledged to be important, has been exaggerated. Business either stood as the evil, out to corrupt society and stifle democracy, or as the driving institution, molding America to new designs that enabled the country to modernize and adapt to industrialization without breaking apart. This study suggests a reality that lay somewhere in between, a reality in which business leadership and money could in fact powerfully shape and change communities but in which business interests very often faced opposition, forged compromises, and finally met defeats.

This study of failures, of successes, and of opposition to these four business-influenced "grand plans" provides an integrated examination of the connections between business and progressivism not found in the excellent but limited monographs of the last decade that examined just one aspect of the phenomenon: welfare capitalism, or municipal reform, or educational administration.[33] This body of literature raises crucial questions, but often business historians have written for business historians, labor historians for labor historians, political historians for political historians. Few of the works examining relationships between business and progressivism synthesize historical interpretations among these specialties or look at multiple environments for business-influenced change. Any attempt to answer questions about roles played by new business models in restructuring society should try to look at possible influence in many different arenas. If those arenas—be they local government, schools, civil engineering projects, or the shop floor itself—existed within the same community and repeatedly involved the same principals, who themselves saw interconnections between their various projects, a historian can with greater confidence generalize about relationships between business leadership and social change, business and progressivism, and about the society in which progressives lived.

Finally, an examination of these Miami Valley "grand plans" provides an opportunity to work within the most generous of chronological definitions for the progressive era. Debate has raged for decades about proper time demarcations. One historian has argued that progressivism began in 1907 and ended in 1917. While not insisting on such specificity, others have agreed that the decade, give or take a few years, which ended with the

American entrance into World War I marked the progressive era. Not all scholars accept that framework. For them, the progressive era spanned the late nineteenth and early twentieth centuries, certainly was in place by the presidential election of William McKinley, and did not completely decline until the arrival of the Depression of the 1930s.[34] The choice of the chronological framework, 1890-1929, of course, subjects this study to the criticism that it implicitly trumpets one particular interpretation of progressivism. One answer might be that such a chronology allows the greatest possible flexibility for investigation. Moreover, although they shared a general belief that progressivism, in some phase or another, lasted roughly forty years rather than ten, historians who have used this expanded chronological definition could scarcely be said to have formed one interpretive school. Finally, a historian who accepted the more narrow chronological definition while studying the political influence of business in California discovered that "the progressive era as a distinct epoch spanning the years between 1910 and 1915 or 1917 held little meaning for Californians, at least with regard to business legislation."[35] In southern Ohio, as well, such a narrow chronological framework would exclude important progressive developments that spanned the decades from the turn of the century to the New Deal.

Between 1890 and 1910, the National Cash Register Company created "welfare work," the first major program of corporate employee benefits in the country. Companies across the United States copied it for the next two decades. Before its eclipse in the 1920s, the NCR Welfare Department sponsored such programs as worker education, children's gardens, company parks, golf links, sickrooms, and insurance plans for workers.

After a devastating flood in 1913, a coalition of powerful Dayton businessmen, led by NCR's John Patterson, raised the money and hired Arthur Morgan, a Memphis engineer, to devise a plan for five massive dry reservoirs, to be known as the Miami Conservancy District. Not only was the dry dam plan a dramatic engineering innovation, challenging traditional river-channelization schemes for flood control, but the Ohio Conservancy Act of 1914 was also a legal innovation. It established a flood control district with appointed, not elected, officials and challenged local and county authority over disaster relief, definitions of eminent domain, taxation, and other matters. This coalition of businessmen did more than shape flood control legislation; these businessmen also, their opponents charged, used the 1913 disaster to reshape city government to their liking. Within months of its terrible flood, Dayton had become the first city of significant size in the United States to adopt the commission-manager system.

Finally, Arthur Morgan succeeded not only in making the Miami Valley known for a revolutionary new program of scientifically managed flood control. He also, during the teens and twenties, was one of several educators who allied themselves with the region's business community to make the Miami Valley nationally known for experiments in "progressive" education. Morgan established the private Moraine Park School during World War I, and then in the 1920s he revamped the curriculum of Antioch College, the small liberal arts school Horace Mann had founded in Yellow Springs, Ohio, before the Civil War. Furthermore, during the same years, the Dayton business community took an increasingly active role in public education. With businessmen dominating the school board, the Dayton public schools too won a reputation as "progressive" institutions.

So, from the 1890s through the 1920s significant change gained the Miami Valley national attention. Some contemporaries saw it as providing the rest of the country with models for practical, businesslike, progressive reform. Others warned that the Valley had provided the nation with models all right, but models of business tyranny that weakened individual freedom, challenged organized labor, and denied radicals a fair chance to participate in local politics.

This study seeks to shed light on the question that has over the decades emerged as central to any attempt at deeper understanding of the progressive era. That question, of course, is, what relationships existed between business and progressivism? In answering that question, this study will also attempt to judge the nature of what the business community itself called progressivism in the Miami Valley. Were the plans really grand, improvements over existing systems for the conduct of work, government, and education? Who gained? Who lost? What were the legacies?

This study of the leaders, programs, motives, and achievements of progressive business in the Miami Valley will, by its very nature, not illustrate every aspect of business activity in southern Ohio. Progressive businesses were, as was perhaps the case in many other regions, in the minority. Though a minority among business concerns, they were, however, tremendously influential, dominating and shaping the reform agenda in the area. Although a great deal more scrutiny of other areas is necessary before any generalizations about the entire country can be made, regions dominated by business progressivism may have experienced reform efforts striking for their simultaneous defense of traditional values and promotion of new, technocratic ones.

For instance, businessmen reformers in the Miami Valley quite consciously barred women from positions of real influence. Of course in cities like New York or Chicago, names like Lillian Wald, Edith Abbott, or Jane Addams were synonymous with progressivism. Even elsewhere in Ohio, especially in its two cities with populations over 400,000, women reformers played very significant roles. Women in Cleveland and Cincinnati were leaders of a wide variety of progressive campaigns.[36]

But they were not in Ohio's Miami Valley and hence remain, in important ways, absent from this study. Even in areas traditionally seen as appropriate for feminine concern, such as education and health care, Miami Valley business progressives made conscious attempts to reduce the importance of women's leadership.

Their firm belief that women should, in the best of worlds, be protected and in the home linked Miami Valley business progressives with traditional Victorian values. In a parallel fashion, so did their open worry about excessive reliance on government intervention and their efforts to create a better society based on voluntary organizations.

But cities like New York and Chicago, or even Cincinnati and Cleveland, the kinds of places where women progressives were most prominent and where more reformers talked about a necessarily greater social role for government, may in fact not have been as typical of progressivism as was the Miami Valley. Historians have built models for types of progressive reform, from the short ballot to settlement houses, based on more accessible evidence from large cities like New York, Chicago, Cleveland, and Cincinnati.

But these cities, unlike much of the nation, and unlike Ohio's Miami Valley, coped with unique problems. They were the first to experience significant black migration from the South. Throughout the progressive era, the Valley's one city, Dayton, had a black population that hovered around only 5 percent of its total population. Cincinnati's black population was almost twice that. While blacks in cities like Chicago or New York began to organize politically and to demand concessions from white leaders, blacks remained invisible to the dominant white community in Dayton, as they did to most white leaderships in most communities.

Dayton and the Valley, like most of the nation, were still populated by a majority of native-born residents. By 1920, when 29 percent of Chicago residents and 30 percent of those in Cleveland had been born in another country, only 8 percent of Daytonians were foreign born. In fact by the midtwenties, in cities like Chicago, New York, and Cleveland only about a quarter of the residents were native born with native-born parents. In Dayton, well over 60 percent still were.[37]

The Ohio Miami Valley between 1890 and 1929 led the nation with startling organizational and scientific transformations. Its progressive businessmen reorganized their companies in dramatic and widely copied ways. The region's inventions—from a significantly improved automobile with an automatic starter, to the cash register, the airplane, and numerous breakthroughs in hydraulic machinery—accelerated the process of change in twentieth-century America.

But at the same time, the Valley echoed the nineteenth century, when, even in urban areas, foreigners were in a minority, when the problems of blacks were easy for white leaders to ignore, when woman's role was to be a supportive and secondary one.

The four "grand plans" here examined reflect this central contradiction: the fact that their creators loved tradition and change. And they sought, with great energy and optimism, to fashion a new society that would allow them both.

2

Employee Welfare at National Cash Register

The Civil War spurred an industrial boom in southern Ohio. Within a decade of the war, Dayton, one of two major cities in the region, had emerged as a center in the Midwest for the production of agricultural implements and lumber products. Dozens of factories made iron plows, flour-milling machinery, hay rakes, wooden boxes, pails, and wagons. One company, the Barney and Smith Car Company, became by 1880 one of the five most important manufacturers of wooden railroad cars in the country, using more than 10 million feet of lumber each year. Its many buildings stretched over almost thirty acres of land; its payrolls included the names of one out of every five industrial workers in the city.[1]

It probably seemed safe to predict in 1880 with such a huge carworks and so many agricultural machining concerns that Dayton would continue for decades to furnish equipment profitably to railroads and farms. Instead, between 1880 and 1910 another industrial revolution swept most of these factories away. By 1913 even the immense Barney and Smith Company was in receivership, soon to fail entirely. Daytonians, no longer suppliers of items for a traditional nineteenth-century economy, acted in important ways as inventors of a new one.

By 1910 many of the agricultural implements factories were gone. They had been stranded by the swiftly changing currents of a market that had made their products suddenly obsolete or they had been swallowed by emerging giants in the industry, like the International Harvester Company of Chicago. Taking their places were plants making fare registers for streetcars, germproof water filters, electric generators, gasoline engines, automobiles, and, by 1909, the Wright aeroplane.[2] In few other places had the transformation been so swift and so complete.

None of the new industries, however, matched the importance of the National Cash Register Company, formed in 1884 and destined for the next three decades to dominate the Miami Valley. In 1879 James Ritty, a Dayton saloonkeeper plagued by what he suspected to be petty theft by his employees, took a voyage to Europe. Invited to visit the ship's engineroom, he was fascinated by the indicator that recorded the revolutions of the propeller shaft. Back home Ritty adapted the machine he had observed in the engineroom. His "cash register" consisted of a cabinet equipped with keys marked in multiples of five cents and containing a wide roll of paper marked with columns. When pressed, a key punched a hole in the corresponding column of the roll. The machine rang a bell and raised a small tin indicator showing the number on the key. At the end of the day, the owner of the new invention could unlock his cabinet, remove the paper roll, and count the holes punched in it to determine the amount of cash that ought to be on hand.[3]

One of the first to purchase the new machine was John H. Patterson, who with his brother Frank was a southern Ohio coal merchant. When the new device enabled the Patterson brothers to uncover employee pilferage at their mine store in Coalton, the enthusiastic John H. convinced his brother, always the silent partner, to invest most of their capital in cash registers. In 1884 a $6,500 investment bought John H. Patterson controlling interest in the National Manufacturing Company and the ridicule of the Dayton business community. Patterson owned a failing company and the right to manufacture a product considered insulting by clerks and unnecessary by proprietors.

Few believed Patterson then when he predicted that the "cash register business can be made one of the biggest industries in America."[4] A one-room factory and thirteen employees hardly promised greatness. Nevertheless, within two decades this cash register factory expanded to employ thousands of workers and eclipsed Barney and Smith completely as Dayton's major employer. Moreover, its influence extended far beyond Dayton. Its innovations provided models during decades when the modern American business corporation emerged. Hundreds of firms openly copied its management, sales, and personnel practices.

Many companies duplicated its "pyramids" of middle managers who operated separate departments with separate sets of books but were ultimately accountable to a single head.[5] The NCR pioneered systematic sales promotion and invented the guaranteed territory, the sales convention, memorized sales pitches, sales manuals, and mandatory training schools. By the onset of World War I, one observer estimated, no sales organization anywhere in the United States with more than twenty-five employees was without someone who had first attended a sales school at NCR.[6] Presidents and prominent officers of powerful corporations ranging from General Motors to IBM began their careers with NCR and transplanted its methods. Perhaps as many as one-sixth of all major corporate executives and sales managers in the United States between 1910 and 1930 had been trained at the NCR.[7]

Certainly the company was at the forefront of the organizational revolution some historians have identified as crucial to an understanding of progressivism. But the company's personnel practices, not its structural innovations, earned it the label of a progressive business from its contemporaries. By 1900, the company offered its employees the nation's largest and most completely developed program of employee benefits, or, to use the company's label, "welfare work." Its elaborate programs of housing, recreation, education, libraries, gardens and parks, health care, and profit-sharing and stock-ownership plans expanded a new approach to employer–employee relations first pioneered in Europe in the midnineteenth century by companies like the English cocoa manufacturer, Cadburys. An examination of "welfare work" provides this study's first vehicle for examining relationships between business and progressivism. Did NCR's programs of employee benefits reflect a progressive agenda? What did they accomplish?[8]

By 1910 numerous other American companies had instituted their own welfare plans. But NCR's system remained arguably the most ambitious and, certainly, the most long-lasting.[9] National Cash Register headquarters in Dayton remained for several decades a beacon for dignitaries like William Jennings Bryan, who chose the factory repeatedly as a perfect site for delivering speeches about capital and labor.[10]

Until his death in 1922, John H. Patterson utterly dominated the company he created. His son Frederick succeeded him as president but exercised little influence and allowed the real direction of the company to remain with its general manager, John Barringer, who closely identified with Patterson and continued his mentor's techniques. In that sense the company was still "identifiably Patterson" until its board of trustees replaced Barringer with Col. Edward Deeds at the onset of the Depression.[11] Certainly welfare work was identifiably Patterson, largely the personal creation of the company's founder. Patterson, who insisted that all ideas be limited to five subheadings, himself summarized the five NCR welfare objectives: "physical, mental, moral, social, and financial improvement."[12]

The physical improvements began with radically redesigned factory work space. In 1884, when Patterson acquired the then dubious right to produce cash registers, his production space, in an upper story of a former warehouse building near downtown Dayton, differed little from that of thousands of other small factories around the country. A fence of tall, unpainted, wooden palings surrounded the plant. Broken crates, cinder and slag heaps, and piles of rubbish greeted workers as they began and left their jobs. Small rattraps were a common sight underneath workbenches.

Moving the factory to farmland owned by his family south of town, Patterson inaugurated an architectural revolution in factory design. By 1905 he had constructed a complex of buildings covering twenty-three acres of floor space. In sharp contrast to prevailing practice, the new NCR buildings were glass-walled shells, "almost greenhouses." Steel construction allowed the supporting brickwork to be restricted to less than a fifth of all wall surface. Even the customary brickwork underneath the windowsills had been eliminated, with low sashes substituted. In summer, all the windows could be opened to provide every worker with cross-breezes. In winter, when workmen bolted and caulked the giant sashes to keep out the cold, an elaborate system of ventilating fans changed the air in every room completely every fifteen minutes. Fresh air was drawn from the roof, warmed, and driven through supply pipes to all departments of a building, while a complementary system of exhaust tubes drew foul air out to the roof. An inspector whose sole job was to make certain that no building became either too cold or hot circulated throughout the factory, checking all departments every hour.

Further, the factory was clean, with each shop and office swept daily, floors and windows scrubbed weekly. Special precautions meant that even normally very dirty or very hot parts of the factory remained far more comfortable than did comparable surroundings in other factories. Special fans cooled the brass foundry, for instance. A complex vacuum system in the metal-polishing rooms carried off dust from the buffing wheels. Rather than the usual whitewash found in American factories, interior walls in the NCR buildings were painted soft colors. Palms and potted plants appeared in the bindery and assembly rooms, as well as in offices. All interior partitions were glass, to enhance the sense of light and space granted by the hundreds of windows in each building.[13] Interestingly, the only parts of the complex that were "gloomy" were the wood-paneled executive suites.[14]

Included in the factory layout were baths, showers, lavatories, and restrooms for both men and women employees. The company furnished free towels, soap, and hot and cold running water. Employees could bathe as often as they wished before or after work. John H. Patterson, who habitually bathed five times daily, constantly exhorted his workers to use the facilities, offering as inducement the chance to bathe at least three times a week on company time. At a time when only the rich had bathrooms and when even a warm room and a tub were luxuries for the average working person, the NCR bathing facilities were unique. George Grove, a worker in the NCR brass room, reported at one company meeting a conversation between himself and a friend. Having heard Grove's reports about the NCR bathrooms, the friend had returned to his lodgings and asked his landlord for a bath, to which the landlord had replied, "You don't mean to say you are going to take a bath in the winter time?"[15]

NCR workers not only bathed in all seasons, they also ate hot lunches in company dining rooms at cheap prices. A typical lunch of roast beef and gravy, mashed potatoes, cabinet pudding, rice, and coffee could be had for a nickel through World War I. Such a meal would have cost two or three times as much at a café. Workers who scanned the company newsletters and magazines could find in addition to postings of daily menus for the cafeteria numerous articles about proper nutrition, some written by dieticians and doctors, others written by Patterson himself to promote his own eccentric theories about food. For instance, regular readers of *The N.C.R.* in 1894 would have received Patterson's cautions about drinking ice water, one item never available in the company cafeteria. Workers should, of course, "take considerable quantities of water," but it should be hot, or failing that, room temperature. Soft-boiled eggs were "most indigestible." Workers foolish enough to eat eggs at all "had better eat them with the whites beaten up into a froth."[16] Yet despite his elevation of fried mush, prunes, and dandelions to a trinity of most nutritious foods, even Patterson did not insist that these items replace roast beef in the cafeteria.

The company sought to maintain employee health not only through good nutrition, but also through providing medical care. By 1907 a separate department, known as the "health pyramid," had been created. By 1920 its programs included the construction within the factory grounds of a fully equipped hospital. The company employed full-time doctors, nurses, massage therapists, and dentists. Workers received these services, even surgery, free. A visiting nurse also traveled to the homes of employees without charge.[17]

Certainly not least in the list of improvements in the physical welfare of workers was a final important NCR innovation: the nine-and-a-half-hour day for men and the eight-hour day for women, at a time when the twelve-hour day was still common throughout American industry.[18]

Patterson also promised "mental" improvement through welfare work. The company emphasized education for its employees and offered all kinds of free classes at night, during the lunch hour, and on weekends. Colorado Judge Ben Lindsey summarized the views of many of the famous reformers invited to tour the factory: "Your work here is doing more . . . than any university which I have ever visited."[19] The term *industrial university* appeared in the national press.[20] Men could sign up for regular courses in English composition or salesmanship, as well as numerous free apprenticeship programs to learn trades such as molding, carpentry, and window glazing. Women workers could study cooking, sewing, stenography, languages, embroidery, and emergency nursing. The company promised that any

time twenty workers wished instruction together in "any subject" it would find a teacher for them and locate classroom space.
But in keeping with its view that women workers needed protection and a "homelike" environment, not chances for promotion,
the company did not allow women to take classes that were meant
as avenues into management, such as sales training. In fact, with
the exception of a few recreational subjects, such as dancing, NCR
classes were segregated by sex. They were also not open to the
few blacks the company employed as janitors.

Supplementing the classes was a factory library with thousands of volumes and hundreds of magazines. Every noon, li-
brarians pushing book carts traveled through the factory so that
employees could choose reading materials without leaving their
workrooms.[21]

The company also emphasized educating workers' children,
offering them special classes and activities. Many of these were
efforts to achieve Patterson's third welfare work goal: moral improvement. Reasoning that it was difficult "to change the old
people, so . . . let's change the little ones," Patterson hired a
deaconess, Lena Harvey, installed her in a small cottage on NCR
grounds renamed "The House of Usefulness," and told her to
devise a program of clubs, classes, and activities for neighborhood women and children.[22] Harvey organized a girls' cooking school, a neighborhood mothers' club, several clubs for
neighborhood boys and sons of NCR workers. The boys' gardens
won international attention. Beginning in 1897 the company each
year organized several hundred nine- to fifteen-year-old boys
into a boys' garden company. The garden company was a real
enterprise, properly registered, with an elected board of directors, a president, vice president, treasurer, and secretary. NCR
furnished the tools, seeds, instructors, and each boy in the
garden company with a ten-by-one-hundred-foot plot on company land. After learning how to plant and cultivate, the boys
competed for company prizes for "best beet" or "best crop rota-
tion system." They also sold their vegetables at local farmers'
markets. Some earned in excess of one hundred dollars per
summer, certainly a good summer's wage for a nine- or ten-year-
old, and helped their families, since they were to furnish fresh
vegetables to their homes before taking the remainder to sell.[23]

Harvey also established an afternoon Sunday school at the

factory for both children and their parents. Though her "Baptist training suffered a momentary shock," she acceded to Patterson's demand that the Sunday school emphasize morality and right living in a subtle rather than traditional way. The more than eight hundred people enrolled in the Sunday school, therefore, often spent their afternoons watching movies or listening to lectures about travel or landscape gardening.[24]

Patterson's fourth goal for welfare work was "social" improvement. He tried "to make them [his employees] social" by sponsoring a wide variety of clubs and organizations. The lines between "mental" and "social" improvements often became blurred. Were the cotillions at NCR educational, teaching men and women grace and poise, or social, giving them a chance to dance and court under company auspices? Of course, the lines between "physical" and "social" improvement were also sometimes hard to define. The company placed great emphasis, in its social programs, on strenuous, outdoor activities.

Beginning in 1904 massive company camping trips in the summer became a tradition. In 1906, for instance, twenty-seven hundred NCR workers and their families journeyed together by specially chartered trains to a wooded site near Michigan City, Indiana. With the factory shut down for ten days in July, employees lived in a "camp," complete with water mains, electric lights, 1,350 tents, and a dining hall able to accommodate one thousand people at one sitting.[25]

Patterson converted 325 acres of land surrounding his home into a country club for employees. By 1916 the facilities included tennis courts, baseball diamonds, golf courses, hiking trails, and a playground for children. For one dollar in dues per season, employees and their families could play games, attend dances held every Wednesday and Saturday, send their children to clay-modeling and kite-making classes, watch movies, or camp overnight in cottages on the grounds.[26]

In keeping with its emphasis on factory beautification, the company stressed improving the neighborhoods in which most of its workers lived, seeking through a variety of competitions and incentives to encourage employees to improve their own homes and to apply peer pressure to neighbors to join with them. The company offered prizes to employees for having produced the best shrubs, the best vine plantings, the best front- or backyards on their streets or blocks. But their neighbors had to participate as well.[27]

Finally, Patterson had argued that welfare work should offer workers chances for financial improvement. The company paid at or above prevailing wage rates. After 1897 it established a nine-and-a-half-hour day for all its male employees but continued to pay them for ten hours' labor per day. In 1917 the company instituted a profit-sharing plan. Any employee with more than a month's service was entitled to a graduated share in the corporate profits, his or her percentage determined by the length of time served and the company's judgment about the degree of responsibility demanded by the worker's job. By the midtwenties, the company distributed, as an annual average, a million and a half dollars in profit-sharing checks to its employees.[28]

This summary of NCR welfare programs makes clear that the company provided its workers with an excellent physical working environment and fair pay. Those facts by themselves do not illustrate automatically that the NCR and its leaders were committed to progressivism. Speculation about the possible links between business and progressivism shown by welfare work requires analysis of the motivations behind and results of the NCR programs.

No visitor to the NCR factory complex between 1894 and 1920 could have failed to notice the dozens of large, boldly colored posters nailed to the walls of company shoprooms. Their message, "It Pays," was the constant company justification for welfare work. Contented, healthy workers would be more efficient workers. Their improved production would repay the company for its investments in them. In 1917, F.O. Clements, a foreman in the Test Department echoed what had become a well-established company line when he described welfare work as good business practice. If the company took inventories of machinery and stock, it had a right also to take inventory and care of its human resources. In the same way that it sought "to cover up dangerous machinery" the company tried "to reduce the dangers of sickness."[29]

The company kept careful records of job turnover, concluding that its welfare plans helped attract a "better class of people" who did not "care to leave." In 1897, for instance, it judged that only five people whom it wished to retain had quit.[30]

If progressivism saw the rise of a managerial class concerned with "efficiency and uplift," certainly NCR officers belonged to that class.[31] NCR employees heard regularly about the need to maintain the human machine at peak working capacity. They were certainly increasingly subject to work processes that had been timed and standardized. In 1919 women members of one NCR club spoofed their company's concern with efficiency in a playlet titled "Hoover Wins." While "Mrs. Ima Thrifty" shopped "scientifically," meticulously picking up and examining each egg, her "daughter" balanced on a high stool, making a pie in one hand, knitting a sweater with the other.[32] Of course these workers were having fun at the company's expense. Nevertheless, that they were free to perform their play in a company auditorium, with props and refreshments furnished with company money, revealed a refreshing corporate sense of humor.

Despite their apparent willingness to recognize the program's potential for stimulating satire, did NCR officials intend welfare work as an elaborate form of Taylorism? Was it a calculation by the company that its expenditures for employee benefits would be amply repaid with loyalty, lessened absenteeism, low turnover, and increased efficiency? Clearly, as a company in the forefront of the late nineteenth- and early twentieth-century managerial revolution, the NCR tested and standardized its products, so that each new "class" of cash register would perform predictably and reliably. To some extent it hoped that welfare work would help in its efforts to enjoy a work force that also performed predictably and reliably.

But welfare work at the cash register plants was not simply a sophisticated form of scientific efficiency, even though the company did tend to blend what have been generally viewed by historians as two parallel industrial management trends.[33] Managers at the NCR talked both about improving the human machinery, as would followers of efficiency expert Frederick Taylor, and about cooperating with workers as partners in a common enterprise, as advocates of welfare work were likely to do. Probably some of the company's emphasis on "It Pays" was meant to deflect charges that it patronized its workers or treated them like charity wards. In 1908 the widely circulated national magazine *Outlook* published a series of "letters from a workingman" addressing such subjects as piece work, welfare work, and strikes.

They may have been editorial constructions. Nevertheless, the letters "Jim" sent to "Sam" accurately reflected worker skepticism about company welfare: "Somehow, it seems to the fellows that when a firm is too good about such things they must have something up their sleeves, and sooner, or later, it will come out. It's too much like a 'con' game, you know. Maybe we're wrong, but we have been taken."[34]

Were workers at the NCR similarly worried about being taken? According to Sherman Rogers, industrial correspondent for the same magazine, they were not. In an article describing the company's lush grounds and beautiful buildings, Rogers reported that when asked that question "the worker on my right . . . looked at me almost with pity and instantly replied, 'Anyone discontented here will never be very well satisfied this side of heaven,' and I found that that feeling existed throughout the plant."[35]

Patterson himself took a less euphoric tone. As he admitted, "Some people have said, 'We cannot wear your books; we can't eat your flowers and don't want them.' "[36] Minute books of company meetings reveal that some employees refused to take advantage of the benefits offered them. Mechanics, in particular, rebelled at the "opportunity" to attend night classes to learn from primers new techniques for doing their jobs. What the company saw as a chance for advancement, the mechanics saw as an attack on their autonomy. What the company saw as a nourishing, free, hot lunch, women workers initially saw as unwelcome charity. Only when it began to charge a nominal fee did the women's lunchroom fill. Despite the company's varied bill and the presence of well-known speakers brought in at company expense, the workers did not always flock to the frequent lectures and speeches. On one occasion they even stood up the founder himself. When he announced that he would deliver a lecture on landscape gardening, Patterson worried that the hall would overfill and disappointed people would be left outside. Instead hardly anyone showed up. The angry company president fumed, "Everybody in the factory, everybody in Dayton, could profitably have attended that lecture."[37] The company stated that it expected its welfare work investment to pay handsome dividends in employee efficiency and enthusiasm. Instead the exchanges between workers and managers at the NCR were considerably more tangled.[38]

In truth, Patterson's own explanations of "It Pays" often hinted at problems worse than employee disappointment or apathy should companies not adopt welfare work. He traced his decision to begin to improve conditions for his workers to a near-disaster for the company. In 1894 English sales agents returned over fifty thousand dollars' worth of cash registers as defective. The machines, Patterson suspected, had been sabotaged by his own employees. Companies that did not properly provide for their workers could face a grim series of threats: worker sabotage, violent strikes, radical politics. The NCR founder, in fact, argued that his adoption of welfare work had helped "prevent Bolshevism. . . . Mr. George Burba, editor of the Columbus *Dispatch*, told me a few years ago that if we had not put our welfare work into operation and forced it upon industry, that we would have seven million I.W.W.'s instead of seven thousand."[39]

Was welfare work, then, really motivated by fear, by a wish to deter strikes, unions, and radicalism among workers? That explanation has played a large role in the historical interpretation of the phenomenon. In fact, most scholars who have written about the topic have seen welfare work as the creation of business leaders spurred largely by dread of unrest and violence.[40] Certainly such a motivation would not necessarily disqualify business as a force for progressivism, especially if progressivism was a movement led by those eager to avoid social chaos or radical economic and political shifts during turbulent years of rapid change.

John H. Patterson openly expressed his worries about the grave potential of worker retaliation against employer unfairness or actual mistreatment. Moreover, his fears of political radicalism were not entirely abstract. During the late nineteenth and early twentieth centuries, socialism thrived in southern Ohio and exercised marked influence in local Dayton politics. But even though John H. Patterson openly expressed his worries about worker retaliation or "Bolshevization," his company's relations with the Dayton Socialist party were not notably hostile. Socialist candidates for city council actively campaigned in NCR shops; party leaders singled out John H. Patterson for praise when they reviled other Dayton business leaders.[41] Moreover, the NCR only gradually came to demand the open shop. Over the fervent objections of some of his shop supervisors and foremen, Patterson declared he could work with unions and did not forbid workers in the NCR brass foundry from affiliating with the Polishers, Buffers, Platers, and Brass Workers Union in 1897. By 1900 the company had signed agreements with twenty-one other unions as well.

Yet despite the company contention that bad conditions, not unions, caused strikes, the NCR shut down for two months during the summer of 1901, crippled by a bitter strike. The brass molders who led the strike challenged neither wages nor physical conditions. Ironically, they attacked one aspect of NCR organization that had remained traditional: the power of a shop foreman to hire and fire. In doing so, they precipitated the further modernization of the company's structure and its declaration of an open shop.

The molders rebelled against the tyranny of James McTaggart, a foundry foreman strongly opposed to unions. When McTaggart fired several men for union membership, the rest struck. The strike finally ended in a defeat for labor, even though the company capitulated and removed the hated foreman, and even though the nature of that defeat was not immediately apparent.

During the strike, Patterson, in concert with his board of directors, began to reorganize the company. No longer could foremen hire and fire without the express written permission of the Employment Department. And that department—hitherto an obscure part of one of the three NCR organizational units, or "pyramids," with a staff of a few clerks to record payroll information—became the only department in the NCR hierarchy personally controlled by the company's chief officers. The company announced that "in the future President Patterson, General Manager Chalmers, and Assistant Manager Deeds will take an active interest in the Employment Department. Mr. Deeds himself will act as its head."[42] By 1905 not just the NCR foundry but all parts of the factory complex had become open shops.[43]

If welfare work had been meant solely to deter strikes, it failed. But that was not its primary purpose, and Patterson assured his employees, "We want to continue to do more welfare work. I am more than ever convinced that it pays when properly directed."[44] In fact, the company went ahead with plans for constructing a huge "welfare hall: the biggest of its kind in the world," capable of seating two thousand people.[45]

Still, the 1901 strike was a turning point for NCR welfare activities.[46] Editors of the *Nation*, analyzing the strike in July 1901, prophesied, "Doubtless the managers will continue to take thought for the welfare of their workmen; but they cannot feel their former hopeful enthusiasm . . . they cannot take their former pleasure in their plans."[47] John H. Patterson, somewhat ironically, considering the changes taking place at his own plants, became by 1904 a leader of the National Civic Federation.[48] The federation, organized in 1900 to be a bridge between capital and labor, had among its members prominent business and union leaders, and its officers included men like Samuel Gompers and John Mitchell, as well as Mark Hanna and Samuel Insull.[49]

Many Dayton businessmen, on the other hand, made no attempt at all to be "organized labor's colleague." Rather, Dayton in the period 1901-5 became known for the virulence with which its business community fought unions. When John Kirby, owner of a Dayton company producing railway car fixtures, discovered in 1899 that the International Metal Polishers had begun to organize in his factory, he fired all the men in its polishing department. The ensuing strike against Kirby's Dayton Manufacturing Company was violent. Metal workers fought in the streets with newly hired strikebreakers and company guards. Kirby emerged victorious in 1900, more determined than ever to defeat organized labor. As part of that crusade, he founded the Employers' Association of Dayton and used its *Annual Reports* successfully to address a national audience. Thus, John H. Patterson was not the only Dayton businessman to achieve fame during the progressive period as a national business leader. By 1902, certainly, John Kirby had emerged as a rival, quite literally, since the National Association of Manufacturers, for which Kirby served two terms as president, was an organization condemned by the National Civic Federation as a group of "anarchists" among businessmen.[50] Without question, the NAM was openly dedicated to the complete destruction of unions, and it made no effort to negotiate. By 1903 probably the majority of Dayton business firms had joined the Employers' Association of Dayton. Many more joined or sympathized with Kirby's national association as well. The local

Employers' Association established a spy network, successfully infiltrating even the most militant of the unions, such as that of the metal polishers and wood workers. It established a blacklist, tagging not only union members but non–union members deemed to be "potential agitators." It circulated the list not only within the city, but also within the region, so that a worker unable to find employment in Dayton sometimes found employment opportunities slim in other cities as well. Between 1900 and 1903, in firm after firm throughout Dayton, workers opened their pay envelopes to receive company notices declaring that their factories would be reorganized as open shops and that to retain their jobs they must sign cards pledging to quit or abstain from union membership. By 1903 A.O. Marshall, secretary of the association, could boast, "Every strike which has been declared in Dayton has failed utterly."[51]

Dayton, then, was a city whose business community had earned a national reputation for hard-line antiunion activities. It was a city whose judges granted employers "perpetual" injunctions that forbade unions to "interfere" with employers' rights to conduct business as they saw fit. Unions were not to "boycott," "congregate," "loiter," or "picket." They were even forbidden to communicate with other unions.[52] In such a climate, John H. Patterson did not have to and did not join the Employers' Association of Dayton to succeed in declaring an open shop.[53] And he could reshape welfare work while retaining a national reputation as a model progressive employer.

Between 1901 and 1917, the NCR welfare programs became more narrowly focused. The company expanded its health care and recreational programs, but it softened its attempts to provide all-inclusive services. For instance, it discontinued some of its cafeterias when "receipts . . . have not been enough to meet the cost of the food and the cost of operation and labor."[54] Returning from one of his frequent trips to Europe, John H. Patterson decided to turn the welfare hall, not yet ten years old, into a riding academy for company executives.[55] The image of welfare work at the company itself experienced a subtle transformation. Like many other company magazines, the various NCR publications often printed photographs of employees and their families. The caption for one of W.H. Farley read, "This is W.H. Farley of the Welfare Department, but he is better known as the man who explains the pictures [in the NCR Hall of Industrial Education] during the noon hour entertainments."[56] Rather than retaining a Baptist deaconess, the company had a welfare director best known as the man who showed movies.[57]

The change from female to male leadership did not indicate greater prestige for welfare work at the company. The Welfare Department was known as the "Farewell Department" among company executives. Stanley Allyn, who began as an office clerk in 1913, working his way up to the presidency of the company by 1940, remembered, "One of the surest signs of being in disfavor with John Patterson was to hear one's name mispronounced by the boss. In this way he let an employee know there was little value in him. And if he pretended to forget a name, the executive could be fairly sure that his career at NCR had ended. The victim was ripe for transfer to the Welfare Department."[58]

The company, moreover, increasingly warned workers that benefits carried with them responsibilities. A pamphlet about company profit sharing told employees that they must do their part: "If business lags, if production costs soar, if sales fall off, some employees say, 'let the higher-ups worry, that's what they are getting paid for.' But that is far from being true. All of us are responsible, all of us must proceed on the theory that we personally and individually owe a responsibility of trust and fidelity to the Company."[59] And, of course, if workers did not do their share for the NCR "family" their own share of the profits would be in jeopardy.

By the early twentieth century, probably as early as 1903, Dayton had become a city whose unions were in retreat. If NCR had created welfare work only to thwart unions and deter strikes, there would have been little reason to maintain any programs at all after that date. Clearly, the company envisioned welfare work as more than a deterrent to strikes or threats of worker violence. After 1901 the NCR restricted some of its efforts to mold a new kind of work force through welfare work. Specifically, it back-pedaled in its attempts to achieve Patterson's goal of moral improvement. Group activities were more likely to feature tennis tournaments than company Sunday schools.

Nevertheless, after 1901 welfare work may actually have played an even more important role in company affairs. John H. Patterson's widely publicized efforts for the National Civic

Federation may lead one to assume that his company generally earned admiration and accolades during the progressive period. In fact, by 1913 national news coverage of the NCR was more likely to be announced by headlines like one in the *Literary Digest* blaring, "Prison Cells for Trust Sinners."[60] In the second case of jail sentences imposed for violation of the Sherman Antitrust law, Patterson and twenty-six NCR officers were in 1913 convicted felons, appealing one-year prison sentences. Federal Judge Howard Hollister, in passing sentence, had labeled the conduct of the officers of the National Cash Register Company as "despicable," "mean," "petty," and "proceeding from a desire for gain that led them to forget everything else."[61]

The federal suit against the company accused it of achieving control of more than 95 percent of the market for cash registers through unfair competition. John H. Patterson was a ruthless entrepreneur determined to "kill" and "crush" all opposition.[62] Prosecutors at his trial introduced statements in which Patterson had allegedly sworn to "break up any set of men that go into the cash register business."[63]

The National Cash Register Company, according to charges against it, maintained an elaborate network of spies inside rival companies. It used bribery and deceptive sales techniques, such as selling "knockers," cash registers that looked like rival Hallwoods or Americans, but in reality were NCR-made copies that were likely to malfunction. NCR's president hardly appeared to be the model of an ideal businessmen as charges swirled in courtrooms about the exact purposes of the NCR "Competition Department," about the company "graveyard" for its rivals' machines, about company blacklists and secret agents.[64]

In such a climate, Patterson's company desperately needed some good publicity. Welfare work helped provide it. Defenders of the company noted that all the legal evidence proved was that the NCR was a fierce competitor, engaging in tactics that were common throughout the cash register business. Should a federal law compel one company to adopt a higher standard of business ethics than one required by the customs of its trade? Were not NCR officers "men of high personal character" who helped rather than exploited their own workers?[65] Had not John H. Patterson been for twenty years a "pioneer of cooperation in industry," a man who "employed the greatest landscape architect of his time

. . . established gymnasiums, rest-rooms, bathrooms, and every possible comfort for the four thousand people he employed?"[66]

Letters flooded in to the company headquarters. YMCA officials assured Patterson that they firmly believed in the "honesty, integrity, and upright business principles of your company."[67] The Dayton Chamber of Commerce sent a "pledge of faith."[68] Even before Patterson became a national hero as the director of recovery efforts after the massive Dayton flood of 1913, support for his appeal mounted. And indeed, neither Patterson nor any of his company officers ever went to jail. In 1916 the federal government dropped all criminal proceedings against the National Cash Register Company. The company signed a consent decree that forbade it to acquire control or ownership of the business, patents, or plants of competitors without the approval of the U.S. District Court in Cincinnati and the attorney general of the United States. It also promised not to engage in espionage or any of the other unfair business practices with which it had been charged.[69]

In truth, the company got off easily. The government abandoned its right to pursue any of its charges in further prosecution. And NCR officials, in exchange, promised to be good in the future. The company retained its estimated 95 percent monopoly control of the domestic cash register market and its healthy lead in international markets. It surrendered none of its profits. To the extent that the company's reputation for improving conditions for its employees helped secure this settlement, welfare work undoubtedly "paid."

The National Cash Register Company used welfare work, then, in hopes of increasing work force productivity and efficiency and of thwarting carelessness, absenteeism, even worker sabotage. Welfare work also "paid" crucial dividends for the company in favorable publicity.

Finally, welfare work played a role in creating what might be called the corporate culture of NCR. Historians who have analyzed the phenomenon of welfare capitalism have almost always described its programs of employee benefits as created by management for workers, as a tool of management to achieve either greater worker loyalty or productivity or acquiescence to the open shop. To examine the connections between welfare work and progressivism most fully requires a broader definition. At the NCR at least, welfare work did not so clearly divide management and workers. Of course when contemporary analysts used the term *welfare work* in connection with the company they generally meant the washrooms, the showers, the well-lit lunchrooms. Company spokespersons describing the system used the term similarly. But as Stanley Allyn perceptively noted in his autobiography, "Working at NCR was not a job, it was a way of life."[70] Without ever explicitly describing its evolving systems as welfare work for all, the National Cash Register Company sought to tie all employees, blue collar and white collar, low level and upper echelon, together through systems of nonmonetary benefits.

These systems were, certainly through 1922, largely the creation of John H. Patterson himself. Patterson was a larger-than-life figure for his associates and employees. He was a man who prowled the factory in the middle of the night, inspecting desks for telltale evidence of cigar ash or "disorderly minds." He was also a man who declared, "When a man gets indispensable, let's fire him."[71] And executive turnover at the company was phenomenal. But Patterson, contrary to the beliefs of many of his contemporaries, was not a lunatic. Instead, he was one of the first in the United States to create a modern business organization, dependent on standard procedures and set methods rather than on individuals. Such a modern organization could orchestrate the work of tens of thousands of production workers and could keep track of complex national and international sales and distribution networks. Despite the reactions of his often bewildered contemporaries, who thought him crazy for firing such talented men as Thomas Watson, who went on to found IBM, and many others, Patterson was right. Such an organization could not be one in which a few people were "indispensable." Indeed, Patterson set up a large-scale corporation able to run without even him. John H. Patterson frequently made extended trips to Europe. When in the United States, he was often absent from Dayton.

Welfare work, broadly defined, helped Patterson achieve his goal of a business around which employees focused their lives and in which company procedures, not individual preferences, determined decisions. A molder in the foundry had to follow detailed procedures that the company determined. No longer could he, or even his foreman, decide how to make the metal fittings for NCR cash registers. But a company sales agent or comptroller or vice president also had to follow set procedures. Sales speeches came from the company primer. Woe to the comptroller who turned in a financial report that did not follow the NCR "five-key-points" style. The "scientific management" used at the company applied to management as well as to workers. When in 1902 the NCR instituted a time clock system, it decreed that "hereafter, every employee of the company, including the president and all other officers and heads of departments, be assigned a time check and that they be required to lift the same upon entering the building in the morning and at noon."[72]

Workers and their families received nonmonetary benefits aimed at strengthening their tie to the company, and so did managers, sales agents, and their families. Of course if employees were not to suffer from divided loyalties, their families too had to share a commitment to the NCR. For everyone, the company had to become a "way of life." Welfare work, as broadly defined here, helped create those bonds, the social connections of a corporate culture.

Rather than giving a money bonus, Patterson favored sending company officers on trips with their wives. The "New York weekend" became a kind of company tradition. Wives waking up to champagne breakfasts at the Waldorf Astoria were likely to feel kindly toward the company for which their husbands worked. Executives were sometimes treated to a new custom-tailored suit of clothes; their wives sometimes received expensive evening gowns.[73] The all-male NCR sales force competed not for money prizes but for new dining tables, silver services, or china. The company realized that if the prizes in its frequent contests had been merely money, the sums would soon have been spent and forgotten. But the wife of a sales agent who stood a chance of winning not twenty-five dollars she might never see but a new mahogany table would be more likely to support both her husband and the company.[74] Patterson wanted his male employees, who composed the large majority of NCR workers, to be married. He wanted them and their families to feel a part of a larger NCR "family." Most NCR women workers, barred from management and largely confined to low-level jobs, were young "girls" who worked a few years with the company before marriage. Of course, these patterns mirrored employment practices and attitudes found in most progressive era companies. The NCR saw a lifelong affiliation for its former female employees and other women in marriage to NCR workers.

Indeed, company publications happily reported weddings between NCR employees. The ideal NCR woman employee would have graduated from cooking and household management classes. She would retire from her position but remain loyal to the company, continuing to help it in her most important role as a perfect wife and mother. Family enthusiasm and cooperation were crucial to the development of the type of corporate structure Patterson wished to create. As he argued, "Leaving business at the office sounds like a good rule, but it is one that can easily be carried too far because, to my mind, a man who intends to make a success should be collecting ideas and tips, and mapping out programs during every waking hour."[75] Welfare work helped blur the distinctions for both families and employees between their lives within and outside the company.

It also served to help blur the distinctions between white and blue collars. For instance, attendance at the NCR cooking school was mandatory for the wives of all company executives.[76] Of course many of these women had servants. They did not need to learn the most economical ways to make custard or good uses for stale bread. But the cooking school had them kneading bread and testing roasts with the wives and daughters of factory laborers, women whom otherwise they would never have acknowledged socially. The white smocks and sleevelets issued to all women employees helped keep their own clothes neat. But they also, according to Patterson, helped solve the problem of "too much caste." Answering his own question, "Why was it necessary to put white aprons on our girls?" Patterson explained:

> Before this was done the typewriter girls wouldn't speak with the laundry girls. The bindery girls wouldn't speak with the girls in some other departments. Some of them dressed better than others. . . . We abandoned all that by giving them white aprons. They all looked alike. No kind of work around here is any better than any other kind. It is just as honorable for a girl to be in the laundry . . . as it is to be a stenographer. It is just as honorable for a man . . . to have

his face covered with perspiration, as it is for a clerk to sit up
in the office with a white shirt.[77]

This statement epitomizes the multiple purposes of the NCR
Company's welfare work plans. It also in several ways justifies a
definition of the National Cash Register Company as progressive.
Welfare work could, the company hoped, help in its effort to
employ healthy, mentally alert, and contented workers who
would return benefits of greater efficiency and productivity to
their employer. A study of welfare work at the NCR provides a
lens through which to view progressivism's concern with new
techniques to improve productivity. It also illustrates progressivism's effort to exchange gradual reform for the threat of
radical change. John H. Patterson was not the only progressive
concerned about "I.W.W.'s" and "Bolshevization." Moreover,
welfare work provided grand advertisement. The company exploited its publicity potential in dozens of ways. During years
when the advertising industry itself emerged as a genuine big
business, NCR led the way, making its welfare activities a vehicle
for good public relations.[78] Its golf courses, baths, huge company
picnics, and a wealth of other welfare work benefits provided
sophisticated advertisements for the company. They also provided part of an evolving web of connections meant to convince
employees that they all belonged to a large, cooperative company
"family," that they were all members of the same corporate
culture.

Clearly, these uses of welfare work support the idea that the
real revolution during the progressive era was a "managerial
revolution."[79] The small Ohio coal merchant, John H. Patterson,
who saw the value of a new invention that could provide far more
precise control over cash flow and inventory, anticipated and led
the crucial shift during the progressive era from small-scale to
large-scale business organization. His cash register company's
innovations transformed sales and production techniques within
American business. Its management innovations, which featured
the idea of welfare work, were equally influential. The new, large-
scale corporations needed not merely new systems by which to
organize manufacture and distribution, the kind of complicated
systems for which record-keeping machines like the cash register

became essential. They also needed new personnel systems. Executives of new, large-scale corporations that employed thousands at a single factory obviously could no longer actually know most of their workers by name or sight. They had to devise other means by which to convince employees of their concern and interest.

Critics of interpretations of progressivism that have emphasized underlying changes in socioeconomic organization as the key to the progressive era have charged that such views have drained progressivism of its vitality and spirit. They have emphasized that if the progressive era was an "Age of Organization" it was also an "Age of Reform."[80] Such charges have merit. In too many organizational analyses, faceless bureaucrats search for order through statistical innovation or new techniques of mass distribution. Progressivism almost begins to seem an exercise in cost accounting.

Studying the life of John H. Patterson provides a chance to reconcile these different views of progressivism. Patterson was most definitely not a faceless bureaucrat. Rather, he smashed through his own life and that of all others whom he touched. A man with a huge walrus mustache and eyebrows that "growled," Patterson cut a vivid figure. A consummate actor who loved to give speeches to crowds of thousands, Patterson knew how to keep his audience's attention, even if it took stomping on his eyepiece, throwing water pitchers, or dramatically and slowly tearing a ten-dollar bill to pieces. A tireless world traveler, Patteson once returned from a trip to the Middle East determined to recreate the sensation of camel riding. While his contemporaries might have been satisfied with offices that featured leather chairs and ornate woodwork, Patterson had one for a time equipped with an "electrical camel," a machine with all the uncomfortable motion of a real camel. He would mount, throw switches for the desired speed, and be off jolting across imaginary deserts.[81]

Patterson deserved the title bestowed by the early twentieth-century press. He was indeed a "business genius," a man whose vision of economic possibilities outpaced those of most of his contemporaries.[82] He was certainly no saint. Rather, he relished a cutthroat brand of business. Welfare work "paid" if it gave his business one more chance for a competitive edge. Still, the John H. Patterson who scheduled company dances around bonfires when a rival fell to defeat was also the John H. Patterson who justified welfare work not just because it "paid" but also because it was "right."

He was not a hypocrite. Instead, he embodied the seemingly disparate strains of progressive reform. The man who believed in improving the efficiency of the "human machinery" in his factories also believed it his religious and ethical obligation to improve his employees' lives. Until his death in 1901, Frank Patterson acted as his brother's co-owner and partner. He also acted as an opponent of welfare work. In order to persuade his brother to allow him to begin his first welfare programs, which included coffee and a restroom for women employees, John H. Patterson used his own funds. As he told the story: "I had lost one of my carriage horses. It died, and I had planned to get another. I made up my mind that two horses, a coachman, and a maid were not necessary for two small children. It would have a bad influence on them. I concluded that instead of buying a horse, I would convert the money into coffee and soup for the women employees."[83]

Through this and dozens of other actions Patterson practiced his own version of the Social Gospel. A lifelong churchgoer, a vestryman at Christ Episcopal Church in Dayton, then for decades a superintendent of Sunday schools at St. Andrew's Episcopal, Patterson believed that religious people had to be reformers. The churches and their members must be social crusaders. And he argued that churches should "prepare people for earth and Heaven alike."[84]

Although very rich, Patterson was not given to personal ostentation. He was a man for whom "the idea of spending thousands . . . for a string of pearls was unthinkable."[85] Instead, he quite literally gave his money away. He sent hundreds of politicians, teachers, ministers, and employees on tours of Europe and the United States to study new educational, social work, or government experiments. The news of a new kindergarten plan in a German city, for instance, was likely to prompt him to mail steamship tickets to two or three teachers. And a national system of public kindergartens was only one of his many causes.[86]

Not only did he believe that he could improve himself through travel, study, diet, and physical exercise, he insisted that others around him follow suit. After deciding that early morning horseback riding was beneficial, he built a company stable and summoned his officers to daily 5:00 A.M. gallops. When he began to drink a glass of hot distilled water at thirty-minute intervals, trays of hot distilled water became fixtures at company meetings and appeared with what must have seemed terrible regularity at his executives' desks. He banned all smoking and stalked the hallways of offices and shop floors sniffing for offenders. When he discovered calisthenics, the women employees of NCR discovered that he expected them to use their two daily "rest" periods to perform the deep knee bends and arm exercises he had devised. Visitors to the Patterson table learned to expect doses of baked potatoes or toast dipped in vegetable oil, since these foods were "digestible." Luckily for them, Patterson acquaintances and employees were apparently not expected to mimic him when he journeyed to the mountains of Italy to undertake a month-long fast.[87]

The fact that his subordinates rose at dawn and downed startling quantities of hot water meant that they worked for a powerful man with a well-earned reputation for eccentricity. But it also meant that they worked for a man who in many ways typified the progressive reformer: a man firm in his conviction that his actions were moral and right, who held up his values and habits as models to be copied, a man propelled by religious beliefs and boundless optimism, as well as by a desire for order and efficiency. That optimism, and egotism, and genuine fervor for improving humanity were just as much keys to progressivism as was Patterson's search for organizational structures that better suited an industrial society.

Contemporaries called the National Cash Register Company a progressive business. It was. And its welfare programs illustrated much about the nature of progressivism. Stuart Brandes has argued that welfare work was "affected by the progressive milieu, even to the extent of the ambitiousness of its aims, while managing to remain apart from it."[88] A study of welfare work at the NCR, however, challenges that view. Under Patterson's direction, welfare work merged progressivism's search for new systems to thwart radical change and provide "business models" of organization with its search for humane responses to industrialism. And like progressive reform itself, welfare work was only partially successful in achieving its far-reaching goals.

3

Flood Control in the Miami Valley

In January 1913 John H. Patterson would have liked to earn headlines as a "leader in industrial welfare." Instead, newspapers featured stories about the great NCR trust trial. A federal judge found President Patterson and twenty-six other company officers guilty and fined the NCR chief and his executives more than $135,000. Most defendants, in addition, received prison sentences of nine months to one year. Patterson himself was to spend one year in jail and pay a fine of $5,000. Though the sentences and fines were later over-turned on appeals, in early 1913 Dayton's most important company faced an uncertain future. The NCR hardly seemed a model progressive business as reports circulated nationally of its "predatory and unfair methods," its convicted executives, and its teams of spies.[1] No one could have imagined that within three short months John H. Patterson would become a national hero or that newspaper editors in state after state would demand a pardon and his complete exoneration.[2]

Patterson would benefit mightily from a terrible rainstorm, with no recorded equals in volume, breadth, suddenness, rapidity, and length of continuance. Extraordinary conditions of heat and high humidity in the third week of March 1913 created freak storms around the nation. Tornadoes punished Nebraska and Iowa, killing hundreds. Throughout the desert West electrical storms disrupted communication and generated charges so intense that people reported eerie sights; such as glowing wire fences along country roads and sparks flying from animals' ears. Midway through the week the strange atmospheric conditions produced three great cyclonic storms, all of which originated in the far West and swept east. By March 22 much of the Middle West, especially Indiana and Ohio, began to experience an unprecedented downpour. The U.S. Weather Bureau had records of heavier rainfall in smaller localities—cloudbursts releasing great volumes of water over geographic areas rarely exceeding the span of a county and rarely lasting longer than twelve hours. But the Weather Bureau had no records for a monster storm that drenched most of two states and parts of five with two days and two nights of an uninterrupted cloudburst.[3]

Not surprisingly, rivers soon began to overtop their channels throughout the Midwest. One of the hardest-hit regions was the southern Ohio Miami Valley, a hundred-mile-long watershed that received the combined floods of the Miami River and its eastern and western forks, the Mad and the Stillwater rivers, and that extended from the small town of Piqua in the north through Dayton to Hamilton and the Butler County line near Cincinnati in the south. The storm arrived on Easter Day, March 23.

It was to be a holiday remembered by flood survivors as one of "black clouds and mad rain."[4] By Monday flooding had begun in towns and villages north of Dayton. The levees surrounding the Dayton business district withstood the rapidly rising waters of the Mad and Miami rivers through the night Monday, then began to crumble at dawn, Tuesday. By 6:00 A.M. the Mad River levee collapsed. A cascade of water poured into the unused Miami and Erie Canal. At 7:00 A.M., the old canal bed, now swollen with floodwaters, suddenly sent a wall of water over twenty-five feet high rushing into every downtown street with which the canal intersected. All the city's major east and west streets rapidly flooded. Within just five minutes the thousands of Daytonians who had come to watch the rising waters were surrounded.

The deluge came, luckily, at an early hour. Schools and businesses were still closed. Nevertheless, the streets of Dayton echoed with the screams of terrified people trying to outrun the great torrents bursting into almost every street. Within ten minutes, the center of the business district stood under five feet of water. By noon Tuesday, streets not just in the business district but also in much of North Dayton and West Dayton, the city's mansion district, had become roaring rivers over fourteen feet deep, carrying, at great speed, drift that included houses and small buildings.

Villages and towns south of Dayton also flooded. As far south as Hamilton, levees again suddenly burst, and, as in Dayton, low-lying neighborhoods and business districts became scenes of terror, filled with the screams of drowning people and animals, the sounds of shattering glass and wood, the roar of water. But the devastation in the Valley's one large city was worse than that suffered by its neighboring towns and villages. On Wednesday, March 26, gas explosions rocked downtown Dayton. Soon fires raged out of control through the flooded district. People trapped in upper stories and attics made desperate, and not always successful, escapes from burning buildings over rooftops or inched themselves hand-over-hand along dead power lines. Only rain and, by nightfall, sleet and snow, saved the residential neighborhoods to the north and east of the city.

By Wednesday, the flood waters had begun to recede throughout the Valley, leaving in their wake thousands of smashed and charred buildings, ruined business districts, the decomposing bodies of thousands of cattle and horses, more than five hundred human dead, hundreds of millions of dollars of damage to real and personal property, and, everywhere, a coat of foul- smelling, pitch-black mud.

The savage March 1913 storm caused flooding throughout central and southern Ohio, but nowhere was the damage as severe as it was in the one-eighth of the state's territory that composed the Miami Valley. And nowhere in the Miami Valley was the damage quite as severe as it was in Dayton where 361 people died and where over $100 million of property had been damaged beyond repair.[5]

The really extraordinary nature of the death toll in Dayton, however, was not that it was so high but that it was so low. During the first terrible days, before accurate surveys could be made, and when Dayton's sole link with the outside world was through one telegraph wire, rumors circulated that tens of thousands of city residents had perished by fire or water.[6] That several hundred rather than several thousand died was something for which the city's business community, led by John H. Patterson and the NCR, deserved a large measure of credit.

The rescue and rehabilitation efforts in Dayton, as well as the ambitious flood prevention plan that led to the creation of the Miami Conservancy District, provide another example of business-led efforts that some contemporaries labeled progressive.

Were they? To answer that question requires an examination of the nature and consequences of flood relief efforts in Dayton. It also demands an analysis of the early history of the Miami Conservancy District from the passage of the Conservancy Act of Ohio in 1914 to the successful completion of the District's massive earthen reservoir system in 1921.

Even contemporaries hostile to the powerful influence of the business community, such as the local Socialist party, lauded John H. Patterson as the man of the hour during the initial days of the March flood disaster.[7] He himself claimed that he had built his huge factory complex south of town on high ground because he had always known that someday a flood might overwhelm Dayton.

It is more likely that he built far away from the city's late nineteenth-century riverside factory district for two other reasons. Away from the center of town on former farmland, the National Cash Register complex could easily expand and still remain a well-planned campus of buildings with room for gardens and spacious lawns. Moreover, and just as important, the former farmland already belonged to the Pattersons, a pioneer family with extensive southern Ohio land holdings.[8] The model factory would not only be in parkland, but parkland John H. Patterson already owned.

The NCR factory's location gave its owner his chance. While the company's only rival in size and influence, the Barney and Smith Carworks, lay submerged under water and silt, the NCR became the "stricken city's brain, nerves, almost its food and drink."[9]

The fact that the company escaped flood damage did not automatically grant its founder the role he played in flood relief and rehabilitation efforts. But Patterson seized the opportunity. By all accounts, Dayton Mayor Edward Phillips and other elected officials were not in command. In fact, Governor James Cox openly recognized the situation after receiving reports from aides who had made it into Dayton. On March 27 he placed Dayton under martial law, naming Gen. George Wood as commandant and appointing John H. Patterson as head of a "Citizens' Relief Committee."

In truth, General Wood, who traveled through the flood district in NCR rowboats and who ordered all National Guardsmen in the area to report to the company for further instructions, approved of the measures Patterson had begun as early as Tuesday morning, March 25. In all but name, Patterson remained in control of all aspects of flood relief.

In fact, the first few weeks of crisis management after the disaster set a pattern that was followed for years. Voluntary community organization, not reliance on government aid, dominated flood relief and recovery efforts. The Miami Valley business community, led by John H. Patterson, raised millions of dollars, devised new methods and associations to speed the area's reconstruction and recovery efforts, and supported a challenging new plan for permanent flood prevention. Its members repeatedly warned against dependence on outside state and federal monies, and in the enormous work of flood relief and recovery the private sector always dominated. Indeed, to the businessmen progressives who directed these efforts government involvement became a symbol of unnecessary delays and restrictions. In the better world they felt confident they could create, government would play a clearly secondary role to the actions of private associations. It would be their agent, not their arbiter.

Reflecting such beliefs, John H. Patterson took charge of flood relief. Hours after word of the collapse of the levees, and certainly days before the arrival of state or federal officials, the NCR president reorganized his plant as an emergency city headquarters. Without benefit of election, he took over city government. City hall was under water, but Mayor Phillips and his council had not died. Their sheepish letters asking to be notified of decisions or meeting dates are powerful testimony to a highly effective and highly arbitrary transfer of emergency power.[10]

By noon Tuesday, the NCR carpentry shops had become a boatworks. Patterson's carpenters pounded out a flat-bottomed rowboat every five minutes. By Wednesday they had constructed 276 of the ugly but sturdy rescue vehicles. Organized crews of other NCR employees took the boats throughout the flooded district, rescuing people who had been clinging for hours or days to utility poles, trees, or snow-covered rooftops.

Those so rescued joined the thousands of other refugees already at the NCR complex. By Tuesday evening the ten-story brick building used to house the company's managers and clerical workers had been transformed into a giant relief station: a hotel that provided thousands with linens, warm blankets, and cots; a hospital where babies were born and pneumonia cases treated; a newspaper office, which printed the city's *Daily News* until that paper could clear tons of mud from its submerged presses. One floor of the building became a huge dining room, serving hot breakfasts, lunches, and dinners. Waitresses in uniform ushered flood sufferers to tables. In normal times, these waitresses were company secretaries and clerks, accustomed to working in the same rooms but, of course, seated at their machines. Other NCR workers toiled in different parts of the building, sorting and fumigating great piles of clothing, brought to the plant by teams of NCR employees sent to fan through the non-flooded parts of the city to ask for donations. The relief planning even included entertainment. Concerned that the refugees needed something to take their minds off their individual tragedies, Patterson cleared out several offices and installed pianos and musicians. Flood victims could stand around pianos singing hymns or listening to ragtime before going to bed.[11]

By Wednesday night a special relief train filled with medicine and food paid for by the company rolled to the far edges of the flooded area of town. Two others arrived on Thursday and Friday. During the first days of flooding before martial law had been declared and before General Wood's troops arrived, the NCR even assumed certain police powers, incurring no public protest from city law enforcement authorities. The company organized not only rowboat crews but also squads of motorcyclists. The cyclists, company employees as well, patrolled parts of the city not under water, delivering supplies, but also apprehending anyone they suspected might be a potential thief or vandal. Sometimes the company brand of justice was summary. For instance, the Dayton *Journal*, one of the first newspapers to resume publication outside of the NCR grounds, reported that several young women who had been at work taking care of flood refugees at the company were on their way home when "accosted by a Negro with insulting remarks." Hurrying back to NCR grounds, the women reported the incident to the temporary NCR police, three of whom "went in pursuit of the Negro, caught him, taking him to the back of the [NCR] buildings and administered [sic] a sound whipping with a horsewhip."[12]

The dozens of journalists from around the country whom the NCR treated more kindly were suitably impressed by the hubbub of relief activity at the company. The *Outlook*'s star reporter, Arthur Ruhl, commented, "No novelist or playwright trying to picture the drama of modern business ever devised anything more ingeniously dramatic—this heroic use of efficiency. It was almost a sort of throwing down of the gauntlet—So *this* is what you are trying to punish.' "[13]

Army officers sent into the devastated city after the declaration of martial law echoed the praise. Maj. Thomas Rhoads, of the U.S. Army's Medical Corps, appointed by General Wood as the flood district's chief sanitation officer, credited businessmen with the prevention of epidemics of diphtheria and typhoid. The admiring Army doctor saw "the whole system [of relief]" as a manifestation of the "business ability which has been reflected throughout the entire community."[14]

Major Rhoads certainly did not similarly praise the city's politicians. Instead he complained publicly about Dayton's elected officials as he prepared to leave Dayton at the end of April 1913. They certainly, the major charged, deserved no credit for the prevention of an epidemic. Rather, for years they had winked at unsanitary practices. City Hall Democrats had turned the Board of Health into just another patronage post, and unqualified appointees had allowed all kinds of health dangers to persist. For instance, the construction of open privies within city limits continued to be common.[15]

To be fair, Dayton was not the only American city of moderate size, by far, to tolerate such structures. But more than four thousand privies were carried away by the flood, and, naturally the force of the currents dispersed the contents of the then-exposed vaults throughout the flooded areas. Numerous sewer lines burst as well. In a city where thousands were homeless and where certainly many hundreds had endured prolonged exposure to snow and freezing temperatures, the dangers of epidemic were quite real.[16]

Business planning, not luck, ensured that those dangers did not materialize. With the sole exception of Mayor Edward Phillips, appointed as a token gesture to the city's political structure and quickly consigned to an all-but-invisible role, all the members of the Citizens' Relief Committee created by Governor Cox were prominent Dayton businessmen. In addition to its leader Patterson, the committee included John Flotron, president of the John Rouzer Company, one of the country's largest producers of iron frame moulding machinery; Frank T. Huffman, president of the Davis Sewing Machine Company; and Adam Schantz, president of Dayton's largest brewery. Other important business leaders participated in the subcommittees established by the Citizens' Relief Committee to help it with its work.[17]

The Relief Committee did not similarly woo city politicians. In fact, after consultations with chief NCR counsel Ezra Kuhns and conversations with the Ohio attorney general, the Citizens' Relief Committee, acting in tandem with the U.S. Army, essentially arrogated the emergency powers of the Board of Health to control epidemics.[18]

Committee volunteers, along with soldiers, conducted a thorough house-to-house inspection of the entire city, immediately removing anyone with a communicable disease to wards in one of two hospitals on high ground. Groceries, bakeries, restaurants, and schools were only allowed to reopen after passing a rigorous inspection and disinfection. The tent city refugee camp built on donated NCR property included electric lights, sewer lines, showers, and flush toilets. Ten cleaning stations dotted around the flooded regions of the city offered homeowners free lime, chloride of lime, and cresol, along with instructions explaining how to use these chemicals to whitewash basements and disinfect floors, walls, and furniture. The Relief Committee accepted the offer of the Dayton Bicycle Club to remove dead animals.

The members of the Dayton Bicycle Club, the name notwithstanding, were not cyclists. Rather, they belonged to the city's most exclusive business club. Under the leadership of their president, John McGee, Bicycle Club members organized their employees as relief workers, assigning them the grisly but crucial task of removing the bloated and decaying carcasses of some two thousand drowned horses and cattle and more than three thousand smaller animals, mostly dogs, cats, and chickens. The carcasses of many of these animals had to be pried from basements, front parlors, and roofs, where the floodwaters had deposited them.[19]

Once the danger of epidemic had passed, the bodies of the dead had been buried, roads to the outside world reopened, and methods for feeding and clothing refugees devised, the Citizens' Relief Committee did not disband. Instead, by late April 1913, after a formal name change, it became a committee concerned with rehabilitation and planning for the future.

By that date, the national Red Cross, itself a new organization not yet ten years old, had received direct contributions at its Washington office of $1,750,000 to aid flood victims in the Midwest. It earmarked almost two-thirds of that money for the Miami Valley. In addition, Governor Cox designated the Red Cross as administrator of the over $600,000 that local Ohio authorities had received in contributions for southern Ohio flood relief.[20]

John H. Patterson, because of his welfare activities and work with the National Civic Federation, knew either personally or by reputation most of the leaders in the emerging profession of social work. He had already met Edward Devine, director of the New York School of Philanthropy and the special representative sent by the Red Cross to oversee its work in Dayton. Soon Devine, installed in an office at the NCR factory, decided that Red Cross monies spent in Dayton would be channeled through the Citizens' Relief Committee.

With that funding, overwhelmingly raised through private contributions, the committee began its "businesslike" program of rehabilitation. It distributed its own standardized relief application form to prevent duplication of registration and to provide uniform kinds of information about people who wished help. Applicants most often requested help in repairing their houses. Dayton, since the midnineteenth century, had been noted for the very high percentage of its residents who owned their own homes. An estimated two-thirds of Dayton's workers owned or were buying the houses they occupied. Contemporaries attributed this significant percentage of home ownership to Dayton's thrifty German heritage. Fully as important, however, were the relatively high wages earned by the city's metal workers and machinists. Dayton's booming factories, specializing in precision machinery like cash registers, sewing machines, automobile engines, and airplanes, required very skilled laborers. Even in a nonunion town, these workers commanded good wages. But when floodwaters inundated their homes, they could not so easily pack up and move to other neighborhoods or other towns. Moreover Daytonians, like most Americans in 1913, did not as a rule own flood insurance. Virtually no large public buildings, much less private residences, were insured against flood. Small homeowners needed help rebuilding, and the businessmen of the Relief Committee, no doubt eager to retain skilled workers, provided it.[21]

Generally, the rehabilitation help came as aid-in-kind, not as outright cash grants. Teams of laborers traveled around the city helping to return houses to their foundations. Homeowners could redeem vouchers for tools, lumber, plaster, and paint, in cases where their structures could be repaired. When they owned totally demolished property that had to be rebuilt entirely, they received instructions for arranging loans with banks or building societies. Once these homeowners presented evidence of such arrangements, the Relief Committee often helped with initial payments. In each case, these kinds of grants of aid were meant to give the flood sufferer a "good start on his repairs while leaving the burden largely with him."[22]

The program was a success, providing the necessary seed money for reconstruction while avoiding the onus of public charity. A total of 1,082 families received an average grant worth $127 while spending an average of $725 repairing their homes.[23]

A second, and unique, program of rehabilitation organized by the committee sought to help small businesses rebuild and re-stock. Of course the men sitting on the Citizens' Relief Committee were not themselves small businessmen. And small businesses were not only the ones to suffer from the floodwaters. Many large concerns sustained terrible losses. The Barney and Smith Car-works, to name just one, suffered over a million dollars' worth of damage.[24] But the Red Cross and the Relief Committee correctly decided that rehabilitation on the scale needed to save Barney and Smith was impossible. Such companies would have to, as Barney and Smith indeed did, face bankruptcy or receivership proceedings.

But the Relief Committee established a Business Rehabilitation Department to help smaller businesses. By early 1914 more than five hundred such concerns, including drugstores, groceries, barber shops, funeral parlors, and bakeries, had received grants paralleling those given homeowners. They too received a "good start." Tailors bought sewing machines, cement workers molds and mixes, bakers ovens, barbers their chairs and mirrors.[25]

Contemporaries called these 1913–14 flood relief activities the work of progressive business. They were. In fact, in many ways flood relief in Dayton epitomized the mixture of self-interest and humanity that characterized business involvement with progressivism. John H. Patterson could not in his wildest imaginings have planned a better way to repair both his own and his company's national image. The "trust sinner" became the country's hero, its "man of the hour," the person who proved that scientific management and modern organization could save lives.[26]

The Dayton business community shared Patterson's limelight. Known as unyielding opponents of unions, distributors of black-lists, and employers of private police, the members of that community could clearly enjoy a new national image as distributors of food and medical supplies to the needy, as rescuers, as clear-thinking and efficient angels. Moreover, as people with substantial financial investments in the Miami Valley, they had every economic motivation to attempt plans to stave off collapse and begin repairs.

But they were also real heroes, factory owners, bankers, and company presidents who paid their workers for weeks to assist in flood relief. More than seven thousand employees at the NCR alone received their regular company wages for the first two weeks of April 1913 while they cleared debris, shoveled mud, and rebuilt sidewalks. Their labor and that of workers at dozens of other businesses contributed uncounted hours volunteered to relief by their employers. In addition, those same employers donated tens of thousands of dollars' worth of food and emergency medical supplies at a time when such charity earned them no federal or state tax advantages.

The new business systems and methods of organization that firms like the NCR had begun to create in the late nineteenth century successfully underwent a trial by fire and water. On both a large and small scale, the new techniques of "progressive" business helped impose order and ease suffering in the aftermath of a devastating flood. The NCR's national distribution network brought food to hungry refugees days before emergency Army rations began to arrive. The standardized relief and rehabilitation application forms required by the Citizens' Relief Committee did eliminate wasteful duplicated registrations and did create a body of comparable information about applicants that allowed greater degrees of fairness in the distribution of emergency help.

Flood relief in Dayton, then, did reveal businessmen as progressive reformers. Their actions during and immediately after the flood disaster increased their power within the community and improved their reputations beyond it.

Their actions to plan for the future and make not only Dayton but the entire Miami Valley "forever floodproof," provide a far more complex and challenging illustration of the links between business and progressivism.[27] One of the five subcommittees created by John H. Patterson's Citizens' Relief Committee undertook the job of formulating a program of future flood prevention. Immediate flood relief was a task accomplished in a few months. Flood prevention was an effort that preoccupied the entire Valley for almost a decade. Businessmen who built rowboats or distributed coats could scarcely earn much condemnation. Businessmen who led the attempt to create in the Ohio Miami Valley an entirely new system of flood prevention, based on the construction of five huge earthen reservoirs, found themselves in the thick of a bitter fight. They most certainly were not universal heroes. Their proposed system, the Miami Conservancy District, however, was of a piece with flood relief. It was a product of a new sort of business involvement in political and economic affairs, a new sort of business thinking.

But the creation of the Miami Conservancy District was a far more time-consuming task than flood relief had been. The plan proposed a reshaping of the topography of the entire Miami Valley, an engineering feat second only in breadth and difficulty to that undertaken by the construction of the Panama Canal. As an engineering proposition alone, the Miami Conservancy District was complicated. It was a daring departure from all previous American attempts at flood prevention. It required the purchase of thirty thousand acres of farmland and the cooperation of nine counties. It was also a new kind of legal entity, with new kinds of powers of eminent domain. Not surprisingly, discord, debate, and legal challenge rather than quick acceptance greeted business-led attempts to take it from blueprint to reality.

The nature and significance of the Miami Conservancy District as a business-progressives' project may be illustrated by an account of the plan itself, the campaign against it, and finally, after long delay, its actual construction.

Within three weeks of the great March flood, two subcommittees of the Citizens' Relief Committee, the Flood Prevention Committee and the Finance Committee, had already reached two decisions. First, they would waste little time begging either the federal or the state government for financial assistance for flood control. Such assistance, even were it offered, would not arrive quickly and would probably restrict freedom of planning. Second, they should immediately raise a large sum of money to begin flood prevention work.[28]

John H. Patterson officially headed the Flood Prevention Committee, and during the month of May 1913 he participated actively in the whirlwind subscription campaign to raise $2 million for flood prevention. The campaign bore all the earmarks of his acting and advertising genius. A mammoth wooden cash register, thirty feet high and fifteen feet wide, appeared on the courthouse lawn to record totals raised every day. NCR workers fanned out through the city, soliciting donations. Everywhere speakers reminded Daytonians that they should be ashamed to appear in public without the bright strips of ribbon that indicated they had donated to the Two Million Dollar Fund. Patterson put the stereopticon slide and movie equipment so familiar to his own employees to work for the fund-raising campaign. He delightedly organized mass rallies, complete with brass bands, slide shows, and movies. His slide shows interspersed drawings and paintings of Dayton's history with photographs of the recent flood disaster, all flashed on huge screens as trumpets blasted and cymbals crashed in the darkness. After viewing these images and hearing of "the big, individual things" their "stalwart" ancestors had done to triumph over their own crises, after singing rousing old-time songs, following the words on a giant movie screen, after listening to widows recount between heaving sobs stories of their agony as they watched husbands and children lose their grips on windowsills and slip to icy deaths, the audiences were, as Patterson mildly put it, "warmed up." In fact, this master of advertising had them worked up to such an emotional pitch that "you could not have kept money in their pockets."[29] By the end of May 1913, the $2 million had been raised. The flood prevention planning could begin.

After the end of this dramatic fund-raising campaign, Patterson delegated NCR's vice president for engineering and production, Edward A. Deeds, as his representative at flood prevention committee meetings. Very quickly Deeds took control of the committee and remained in charge of the entire effort, from the initial planning stages to the final construction of the Miami Conservancy District. No slouch as a showman in his own right, Deeds was a man who would later bring his audiences to tears as he, "with intense emotion," toured to promote the need for the Conservancy.[30] He was also the sort of man not content to remain in John H. Patterson's shadow. By 1914 Deeds had left NCR, though he was to return in 1931 as the company's chairman and chief executive officer, a position he would hold until his retirement in 1957.[31] But while still a young engineer under Patterson, Deeds had been moonlighting as the business partner of another former NCR engineer, Charles Kettering. Kettering would later become a prominent General Motors executive in charge of research and development, a man whose long list of important inventions included leaded gasoline, nontoxic refrigerants, high-compression engines, and four-wheel brakes. But early in his career, while still in Dayton, he had invented an electric self-starter for automobiles. By 1913 the firm he had formed in partership with Deeds, the Dayton Engineering Laboratories Company, or "Delco," had sold a total of thirty-five thousand of the new starting, lighting, and ignition systems and employed 1,500 workers.[32]

During the years 1913–22, as president of the board of directors of the Miami Conservancy District, Deeds spent countless days testifying in court trials, making speeches, and maneuvering behind scenes as the huge project's most important advocate. During this time, he was also an active president of Delco. In addition, he was the president of the Domestic Engineering Company, a manufacturer of house lighting systems; president of the Smith Gas Engineering Company, which sold clean producer gas for hardening furnaces; and a vice president of the United Motors

Corporation, headquartered in New York City.[33] Moreover, during World War I, Deeds volunteered for military service, and, as a colonel in the Army, acted as chief of aircraft procurement and headed the development of the Liberty aircraft engine.[34]

Despite this stunning variety of business and military commitments, Deeds was, by all accounts, completely involved at every stage of flood prevention planning. He was by no means a token leader.[35] His unofficial chief lieutenants on the commission were two other prominent Dayton businessmen, John Stoddard, president of the Stoddard Motor Car Company, and H.E. Talbott, an engineer and owner of Dayton's largest construction firm. In June 1913, in keeping with good business practice, Deeds felt that the Citizens' Relief Committee, an emergency body appointed by Governor Cox, would be on safer ground for undertaking a long-term project if it incorporated. As the legal successor of the Relief Committee, the Citizens' Relief Commission was a nonprofit corporation, organized under the general corporation laws of the state of Ohio, "to be located in Dayton, and its principal business there transacted."[36] That principal business, of course, was the creation of a comprehensive plan for flood prevention.

Initially, the commission thought only of plans to make Dayton safer from floods: higher levees or deeper river channels. But soon, after inspection trips throughout the Valley, it "commenced to get a view of this thing in a bigger way."[37] By early summer, 1913, the commission had decided to support some kind of flood prevention plan for the entire Miami Valley and issued invitations to neighboring towns to come to its meetings to discuss the possibilities of cooperation. But while they had decided that the flood prevention plan they eventually endorsed must protect the entire Miami Valley, they had little idea what sort of plan would work most effectively. Although both Talbott and Deeds were engineers, neither had experience with flood control engineering. As Deeds put it, "We had enough business experience in large matters to know that we should get assistance."[38]

Their search for assistance led them to hire the Morgan Engineering Company of Memphis, Tennessee, to assess the situation and provide them with a plan for flood control. Their only specification was that the plan encompass the entire Miami Valley. Arthur Morgan, at age thirty-five, headed a flourishing company that had a growing record of success with difficult hydraulic engineering projects around the country. The match between his employers on the Citizens' Relief Commission and Arthur Morgan was a good one, and Morgan remained chief engineer of the Miami Conservancy District project from conception to completion.

Arthur Morgan was in many ways a classic progressive. He eagerly promoted new methods of management as he rose rapidly to national attention. He was barely twenty-four years old when he received his first commission to take charge of a large-scale drainage and dam project. He belonged to the group of scientifically oriented young men who urged engineers to professionalize and impose discipline and standards upon their fellow members. He participated actively in several new state engineering societies. Early he realized that any attempt by engineers to mandate tests and standards would require legislative cooperation. So it was that in 1905, when he was twenty seven, Morgan wrote a draft of a water control code for the state of Minnesota that the state legislature passed in essentially unaltered form.

Arthur Morgan was also a highly moral man, concerned about social problems and issues of justice. He had, before organizing Morgan Engineering in 1910, resigned a job as supervising drainage engineer with the U.S. Department of Agriculture, largely out of disgust with what he condemned as unethical practices of political patronage and favoritism. Further, Morgan had no commitments to any particular version of engineering practice. He had not absorbed the philosophy of any one of the new college departments of engineering beginning to acquire reputations. He was not a graduate of MIT or the University of Wisconsin. Rather, his modest family circumstances prevented him from obtaining a degree at any college.[39] He was a man interested in untried methods, in unconventional techniques, a man who, with the members of the Relief Commission, was willing to "view things in a bigger way."

This collaboration produced the plan for the Miami Conservancy District, a plan designed to endure not just "for the present, but for a thousand years."[40] As an intermediate report submitted by Deeds argued, "It was not local works and encroachments (bridges and embankments) which caused the flood. . . . If we could have been up several miles above the earth and been able to look down on the whole valley, we would then have seen the flood as it really was, a great surging torrent, reaching from hill to hill, a hundred miles in length. Then we would have seen it as it appears to Mr. Morgan, as we too, would see the futility of local improvements to give relief in such emergencies, and we would modify our narrow views with regard to the local causes."[41]

What did this plan that eschewed "narrow views" actually propose? At its core was a radical proposal: flood control in the Miami Valley could be achieved by reshaping the region's topography through the construction of five large dams. Dams had certainly been used throughout American history for irrigation, for navigation, and for power generation. But they had never before been used on any major scale for flood control. Moreover, the dams that Morgan's plan proposed were not the dams most people saw in their minds' eye. In fact, in recognition of that, the plan's advocates insisted, correctly, that what they wanted to build were huge systems of "hills," not dams. Despite their efforts, the name *hills* didn't stick. *Dams* the Morgan constructions remained in the public mind and in court testimony.[42]

Whether called dams or hills, the proposed structures were to function as huge retarding basins—"dry dams" that would only store water during flood times. A system of five of these basins, four built north of Dayton and one south, would hold back river waters, once they had risen to a danger level, releasing them only in such quantities as could be safely carried through the cities and towns of the Miami Valley. Each of the earthen hills creating a basin would cross a portion of the valley of the Miami or that of one of its tributaries, the Mad or the Stillwater River, and would be built in such a way that each would become an integral part of the valley. In each would be constructed tunnels or conduits, through which river and creek water would flow during normal times. As floodwaters poured down the rivers, however, the water would rise in the retarding basins to a point where these conduits would no longer be able to discharge all of it. The surplus water, which could cause destructive floods, would be trapped, and then permitted to come down gradually. So, instead of having the water from a terrible rainstorm pass through a river drainage system in two or three days, the water would be slowed in speed and volume, its journey taking ten, twelve, or fourteen days. The retarding basins would be built to accommodate the floodwaters from a storm 40 percent greater than that of March 1913, which was the largest ever recorded in the history of the Midwest.

While the "dams" themselves were to be earthen, the conduits were to be of very heavy, thick concrete and built upon rock, not earth. The size and number of conduits in each retarding basin would vary, depending upon the amount of water to be impounded, which of course depended on the nature of the watershed or drainage area in each vicinity. In addition to the conduits, a series of rings of concrete piers would be built into each retarding basin to catch any floating debris. It would not take a great deal of water rising in any of the basins to cover the conduits completely. After water had risen to the top of the conduits, each basin would become a quiet lake without any current or suction until its level lowered. Once the proper levels had been reached, the conduits would begin to release water again. They would at all times operate automatically, dependent on forces of gravity and suction. They could neither be opened nor closed wrongly because of human error.

The five basins would have within them approximately thirty thousand acres of land. During normal times, none of that land would be under water. Even during a flood of the magnitude of that in 1913 only some sixteen thousand acres of land would be flooded for a few weeks while the excess waters gradually drained. It would take a storm twice as large as the 1913 storm, the worst ever recorded in American history, to fill the acreage behind the basins. All these tens of thousands of acres would not lie idle, plan advocates assured, waiting for a terrible storm that might never happen. Rather, after houses and outbuildings had been located on high ground, all the acreage could be reused as farmland, conditions of sale or lease to include access by the District in time of flood. Such access would certainly not do permanent damage to the land. Flood damage to farmland came when waters moving at high velocity tore off topsoil or deposited gravel and debris, as they had done to thousands of acres in the Miami Valley in 1913. With its velocity restrained by the retarding basins, any water that might spread out to farmlands behind would actually benefit those lands by leaving behind silt that would improve fertility. So, while they would have to consent to the possible temporary flooding of their lands, farmers as well as urban residents could benefit from the plan for the Miami Conservancy District. City dwellers, living close together, could potentially band together to build very high levees around their business districts, homes, and factories, thus diverting floodwaters onto their neighbors. People in rural areas, however, could not possibly afford to do this. To protect their much more widely scattered lands, farmers would have had to construct similarly high levees along much of the total length of the Miami River. Of course, the expense of such a plan would have been totally prohibitive.

Certainly, its adherents argued, the plan would protect towns and cities in the nine-county Miami Valley. It would protect the city of Dayton, its principal advocate. But it would also protect the majority of people in the Valley who still lived in its rural areas, scattered in tiny villages and on farms.[43] It would, when combined with some levee strengthening and channel improvement around major cities and towns, protect the Miami Valley at a lower initial cost than would other schemes considered, such as plans to straighten the Miami River along an eighty-mile course or dig deep channels along much of its length. Finally, once the retarding basins were finished, they would become a permanent part of the topography, protecting the area with minimal maintenance for hundreds of years to come.[44]

Indeed, this plan, once a reality, was a brilliant success, fulfilling its promise to make the region "forever floodproof." Never again after 1913 did the Miami Valley suffer from a great flood, though many major storms passed through the region, and though floodwaters periodically devastated parts of the same or contiguous watersheds in Pennsylvania, Kentucky, and southeastern Ohio.

It was a plan that illustrated much about the nature of the relationship between business and progressivism. It was a collaboration that reflected the supreme self-confidence and modern organizational skills of business leaders in the Miami Valley, their faith in science and progress, their willingness to take risks for the sake of grand visions. It also reflected business arrogance and disdain for the electoral process.

The Miami Conservancy District's plan was a progressive's plan, bold in its confidence that new, untried mechanical techniques and engineering theories could, in a grand way, solve an age-old problem. Just as important, the plan stimulated bitter controversy. Reaction to it within the Miami Valley divided communities and caused a prolonged debate between opponents and supporters which began in 1914 and did not end until 1918. Transcripts of the legislative battles and court hearings that were the arenas for this debate exposed in ways that an uncontested plan never would have the worldviews and motivations of both sides.

Such a battle did not at first seem likely. In fact, the enabling legislation for the Miami Conservancy District passed quickly. In 1913 few states had water control codes. Almost none had flood control codes. Arthur Morgan realized that the first step in an attempt to accomplish a program of flood control on the order of magnitude he had proposed to the Citizens' Relief Commission would be passage of legislation. And he already had some experience at bill writing. Though without formal legal training, Morgan had previously prepared water control codes for several states: Minnesota, Arkansas, Mississippi. During the summer and early fall of 1913, he drafted a general outline of provisions he felt must be included in the necessary legislation. By October 1913 the Citizens' Relief Commission authorized its attorneys to finish a bill for flood control legislation using Morgan's notes. John McMahon, eighty-two years old and the dean of the Ohio bar, agreed to act as the bill's principal author.

In Ohio, as in most states, drainage and water control laws had emerged in a haphazard fashion, responding to local requirements. Separate legislation governed such actions as ditch building, levee construction, sewer layout, and channel dredging. Often an act had entered the state's law books because the representative from a particular county knew his constituents needed a certain kind of ditch or a certain kind of levee. This system allowed dozens of laws controlling specialized aspects of water control; it also tolerated duplication. Ohio had on its books, for instance, several statutes governing ditch digging alone.

McMahon's draft consolidated this crazy quilt through the creation of a new kind of political entity: a water control or "conservancy" district. Borrowing the name *conservancy* from the Thames River Conservancy project near London, the proposed "conservancy bill" provided that the court of common pleas of any county in the state of Ohio could organize a conservancy—

that is, a flood or drainage control district—when presented with a petition signed by at least five hundred property holders within the limits of the territory proposed to be organized into a district. The "governing body of any public corporation" as well as private individuals holding property in the proposed district could sign as petitioners. When the proposed district encompassed territory from several counties, the court of common pleas of the most populous county would take the lead in organizing a conservancy district. Its judge would head a "conservancy court" composed of one judge from a court of common pleas from each affected county.

Such a conservancy court would appoint a three-person board of directors for the district. At least two of those directors had to be residents of the territory encompassed by the district. Once appointed, the board would authorize the preparation of a plan for the improvements for which the district had been created. When its plan was complete, the board had to submit it at a formal public hearing before a convened conservancy court. At this hearing, any owner of real property within the district had the right to attack any provisions of the plan or offer substitute plans. After considering all evidence, the court would either accept or reject the "official plan" presented by its board. If accepted, this plan would allow the court to declare formally that the district was organized.

The conservancy district thus created would then become a political subdivision of the state of Ohio, with power to sue and be sued, to incur debts, to issue bonds, and to exercise the right of eminent domain. In fact, its powers of eminent domain were unique, a legal innovation later copied by other states enacting flood control measures. Ohio conservancy districts would have "dominant" right of eminent domain, superseding the eminent domain rights of public utilities, cities, and counties. Moreover, the bill severely limited the rights of cities and counties within the district to ask for injunctions through which to delay or halt implementation of the official plan of the district once it had been approved in a formal hearing.[45]

On January 19, 1914, the Representative Victor Vonderheide of Dayton introduced this proposed legislation into the Ohio House of Representatives. Governor James Cox, who had called a special emergency legislative session to consider the proposed measure, urged its passage. The Ohio legislature quickly complied. By February 6 the McMahon draft, named the Conservancy Act of Ohio, but often labeled in the press the Vonderheide Act, was law.[46]

Within days, advertisements appeared in newspapers throughout the Miami Valley stating that petitions for the creation of a "Miami Conservancy District," including land in Montgomery, Warren, Butler, Hamilton, Preble, Greene, Clark, Miami, Shelby, and Logan counties, were available for signature.[47] By the next week, February 18, the Montgomery County Court of Common Pleas received a petition with far more than the required five hundred signatures, and, as the Conservancy Act mandated, it convened a conservancy court composed of common pleas justices from the affected counties.

Those justices, however, did not speedily appoint a board of directors or preside soon over formal hearings to consider an official plan for flood control. Rather, the first conservancy court hearing presaged the next four years' events. It was a madhouse. Thousands jammed into Dayton's Memorial Hall, normally used for large concerts. Among those thousands were hundreds of lawyers, representing cities, counties, power companies, and railroads.

The passage of the Conservancy Act in emergency session caught the act's opponents by surprise, but they soon regrouped. Controversy was to mark all stages of the early history of the Miami Conservancy District save, ironically, the very first stage, the passage of enabling legislation. Not until 1918 were the advocates of the District legally free to begin actual construction. During the years 1914–18, engineers, paid out of the Two Million Dollar Fund raised by the Citizens' Relief Commission, continued to refine Morgan's initial proposals, using the time for research and hydraulics experiments. Not for years, however, would they know whether they would actually build the system. That decision was made in legislative chambers and courtrooms, not engineering laboratories. The opposition to the Miami Conservancy District took two major forms: efforts to repeal or amend the Conservancy Act in the Ohio legislature, and attempts to challenge first the Conservancy Act and then the "dry dam" plan itself through all levels of the state and federal courts.

Throughout 1914 and 1915 challenges to the Conservancy

Act's constitutionality filled the dockets in Ohio courts. And in 1915 two bills, one proposed by Sen. A.R. Garver of Miami County and the other by Sen. Martin Quinlisk of Shelby County, sought to cripple the Conservancy Act through amendment. The bills, usually referred to jointly as the Garver-Quinlisk amendments, sought to forbid dam building of any kind as a flood control measure, to make the directors of any conservancy district elected, not appointed, officials, and to give landowners the right to refuse to sell or lease their land for flood prevention work. Unquestionably the first and third of these proposals would have made the construction of Morgan's plan impossible, but both the Garver and Quinlisk bills went down to defeat.[48]

In 1915, with the legislative challenge in disarray, and after a favorable Ohio Supreme Court ruling declaring all major provisions of the Conservancy Act of Ohio constitutional, the Miami Conservancy Court formally appointed the three men who had been de facto directors of the Miami Conservancy District planning process during its year in limbo in court. It allowed them to propose an official plan.

But that plan, finally presented in open hearings in October and November 1916, continued to generate immense debate. The formal hearings to review it mandated by the Conservancy Act produced a transcript of proceedings in excess of three thousand pages, as opponents and supporters of the retarding basins idea continued to battle. Not until that official plan was finally approved could the District issue bonds to finance construction. And bond funding was crucial. Advocates of the Morgan plan realized that the Two Million Dollar Fund alone could not begin to pay for the kind of massive engineering scheme they had come to support. Not until 1918, when the U.S. Supreme Court refused to overturn the Ohio Supreme Court ruling that the Conservancy Act was indeed constitutional, was there "nothing open for controversy."[49] Not until 1918 could construction begin.

The judicial and legislative debates were parallel ones. In both cases, the leaders of the legislative and court fights were residents of counties north of Dayton, particularly residents of Miami and Shelby counties. In fact, the debate split the hundred-mile-long valley into two neatly divided geographic camps. Most counties, towns, and villages south of Dayton supported the proposed conservancy district. Many north of Dayton, in towns and counties near the sites of the majority of the proposed "dry dams," opposed it. Opponents and supporters discussed the same issues and charges in different forums. Legislative chambers, courtrooms, and editorial columns in newspapers were simply different arenas for the same fierce debate.

An important charge in that debate was that the proposed flood control plan would unfairly benefit Dayton. It was a plan conceived by the clever businessmen in the larger cities of the southern Miami Valley, especially Dayton, to deflect the costs of flood prevention onto their neighbors. It was a plan that would force northern Valley counties to lose tens of thousands of acres of land to the dams, and it would also raise taxes, as the District levied assessments for flood protection on affected lands.

The Conservancy Act, indeed, had only passed so quickly because "[Dayton] money grows on trees" and could easily work its magic on a legislature made up of "representatives with no back bones, and with a great big collar around their necks, and a heavy log chain double riveted to the collars to be hauled and pulled and forced where another Utopian commission-factory Daytonian, Governor Cox, pulls, hauls, and leads them."[50]

It was then, opponents charged, "oppressive class legislation" favoring businessmen over "the rest of us."[51] "The Patterson crowd" could not be allowed this coup.[52]

Interestingly, despite the widespread talk of class interests and oppression by big business, socialists were not quick to join the anticonservancy crusade. The Dayton Socialist party, the strongest in the state and popular enough to garner 35 percent of the vote in 1913 municipal elections, declared itself to be neutral. Its membership, leaders said, was divided, "many Socialists being in favor of it, and many Socialists being against it, as they have a perfect right to be."[53] The Socialists, then, operated on the fringes, rather than in the leadership, of opposition to the Miami Conservancy District. Some, including Dayton Local member and Christian Socialist minister Frederick Strickland, organized a speaking tour to attack the District proposal. But their charges were sensational ones, even given the atmosphere of high emotion surrounding the debate. Strickland, for instance, thundered that "business interests" had conspired to open the gates of the Lewiston Dam, located north of Dayton, so as to further flood damage, making it easier to take over and remake the devastated city.

The charges were unfounded, though widely circulated. They furthered only the socialist reputation for wild-eyed extremism. Well aware of that fact, many Socialists went out of their way to support the plan. The Socialist mayor of the town of Hamilton, Ohio, journeyed to Columbus to lobby for the Conservancy Act. Others decried the press habit of "jumping on the Socialists. . . . Once more we are trotted forth as the heavy villain in the play so that the 'good' citizens will do their duty."[54]

The opposition leaders condemning the plan as "class oppression" and "business tyranny" were not socialists. Rather, they were the "good citizens" Socialist newspapers mocked: lawyers, farmers, and small merchants in towns like Piqua, Troy, and Tipp City. It was farmers' wives who were "aroused to such a pitch that they acted more like tigers than humans."[55]

No evidence was ever uncovered to justify charges that the Lewiston Dam gates had been intentionally opened. The idea that the plan would further the interests of an industrial city like Dayton were harder to deny. Such cities had indeed, through rapid and relatively unregulated growth, encroached on natural watersheds. Certainly any plan that would require dismantling whole residential or factory districts would have been unacceptable to business.

Some of the kinds of financial interest attributed to "Ever Ambitious" Deeds and "his crowd" were unfounded.[56] The dams Morgan had proposed would, in normal times, not be filled with lakes. The big business leaders supporting the plan knew that and did not ever plan to cloak, as opponents charged, a scheme for generating hydroelectric power with the unassailable mantle of flood prevention. Not surprisingly, many people did not truly understand the concept of retarding basins or dry dams, did not understand that only dams constructed as storage basins could be used to generate electricity. Retarding basins, of course, had never been tried before anywhere on a large scale for flood control and drainage purposes.

Still, there was a widespread belief that big businessmen were trying to con the public into paying for dams that would "help them get their fingers on an industry that would produce [for them] many millions of dollars." Some opponents professed detailed knowledge of secret schemes to install as many as twenty-six turbines to generate electricity on the five proposed dams.[57]

In truth, the confusion could not simply be blamed on the pathbreaking nature of Morgan's engineering proposals, or on the difficulty of introducing a name other than *dams* for the structures that would be the key elements of the Miami Conservancy District. Section 24 of the Conservancy Act of Ohio did grant directors of conservancy districts the right to introduce plans for water and flood control that could include hydroelectric power generation.[58] But the Conservancy Act served as enabling legislation not just for the creation of the Miami Conservancy District. It was meant to provide a legal superstructure for other future districts as well.

Clearly many people did not trust business assurances that in the case of the Miami Conservancy District Section 24 would not be used to create electric power plants. In fact, throughout the years of debate, at public meetings as well as in the scientific and popular press, Morgan had repeatedly argued that the creation of artificial lakes through storage dams might be unsafe if such dams were meant to be used for flood control. The entire area had to be available for flooding if necessary. Moreover, he felt, any allowance for hydroelectric power generation might tempt corruption of the basic nature of the Miami Conservancy plans. The Miami Valley was not only to be "flood proof." The plan preventing floods was to be "fool proof," beyond human error. Therefore, it had to rely on conduit systems that worked automatically. But should hydroelectric plants be installed, the temptation would be too strong to install gates in the "dry dams," so that water would continue to accumulate behind them during all seasons.[59]

Both in public and in private the Miami Conservancy District's chief engineer was one of the strongest opponents of any scheme to make profits through the manufacture of electricity. In fact, he condemned profit taking of any sort. At a mass meeting held in Dayton in 1913, he condemned efforts to inflate land values in areas proposed for future District dams and warned, "The success of this plan rests not primarily upon engineers. . . . The fundamental test is the spirit of the people."[60]

Despite these assurances by Morgan and others that the proposed plan would benefit all and generate no unfair profits for any, the spirit of many of the people in counties north of Dayton continued to be one of distrust. In 1915, to support legislative efforts to amend the Conservancy Act, thousands in Troy and Piqua joined in a series of candle-lit parades, carrying banners proclaiming that the Miami Conservancy District was really a "Drown Us First Flood Protection Plan for Dayton."[61]

The business coalition in Dayton that sponsored the Conservancy plan had no wish to drown the citizens of Piqua or Troy first. But they realized that future industrial growth demanded protection from floods. Indeed, as the largest city in the Valley, Dayton had the most to gain from a trustworthy system of flood control that would still permit unlimited growth, as levee systems would not.[62]

Tellingly, Edward A. Deeds admitted in court testimony that not only would a plan based on river channelization and levees be, in the Relief Commission's view, too expensive, it would also stymie future industrial growth in the region, building a "wall around the future development of your cities."[63] The Miami Valley, Deeds argued, was going to grow. With proper leadership, it would be the greatest manufacturing center for high-grade mechanical work west of New England, "and we have got to think of that."[64] As cities and factory districts expanded, levee and channel systems would have to be rebuilt at enormous cost again within a few decades. And of course the lack of adequate flood protection would be a disaster for the cities of the Miami Valley. It would mean the "end of their growth from a business standpoint."[65] Deeds acknowledged that his colleagues in Dayton and Hamilton predicted a drop of some 40 or 50 percent in property values should a cost-efficient plan for flood protection be stalled in the legislature or the courts. The lack of flood protection would be a "worse calamity" for business than had been the great flood of 1913 itself.[66] Supporters of the Conservancy plan, led by urban businessmen, correctly argued that it would protect the entire Miami Valley, farms as well as cities. However, even they implicitly acknowledged the greater stake urban, industrial areas had in flood control. A farmer's crops might be ruined and his land gravel-strewn. But he, or someone else, could plant again the next season. Individual farmers might be ruined, but not entire farming regions. Business, however, would not make the greater investment needed to rebuild factories and large commercial districts without a guarantee of flood protection. Such a lack could be a permanent, rather than a temporary, "calamity."[67]

Opponents attacked what they labeled the inconvenience and unfairness of the District plan; they also charged that the plan was undemocratic and unconstitutional. The Conservancy Act, they said, had been unnecessarily treated as an emergency measure. Under Ohio law, emergency bills could be rushed through the legislature, could receive the signature of the governor, and immediately become law, not subject to the usual routines that allowed ninety days' opportunity to those opposed to the law to study it or file protests. The 1913 flood did not, opponents argued, merit such an emergency process. Flood relief might have merited emergency measures, but flood prevention did not. James Kite, a Miami County landowner, explained the interesting logic of this argument. Such a flood as that of the 1913 had never occurred before in Ohio history, or, for that matter, in American history. The statistical chance of such a terrible rainstorm's occurring again within a few months or years was totally remote. There was, then, no emergency.[68] The Ohio legislature should have allowed more time for deliberation and debate. Instead, Representative Van Deaton from Miami County charged that the Speaker of the Ohio House refused to follow proper procedures, that no "honest and square discussion" of the measure took place, that "they rammed it down our throats."[69]

Opponents claimed, moreover, that such lack of democracy in procedure was nothing when compared with the lack of democracy inherent in the provisions of the Conservancy Act itself. The act created a new political subdivision within the state to be governed by appointed, rather than elected, officials. Those officials, the directors who administered each conservancy district, had considerable authority. They controlled a political entity with power to sue and to be sued, to incur debts, to exercise the rights of assessment and taxation of real property within their district, and, most importantly, the *dominant* right of eminent domain. As an attorney leading the opposition in Shelby County exclaimed, "If there is anything else that they can't do except hang you, I would like to know what it is. Section 15: put that down in your little book. They can do anything—even move the cemeteries and take the bodies of your dead."[70]

relevant to his proposed dry dam project. An opponent who questioned whether records of two hundred years of rainfall patterns provided a sufficient time line must have been crestfallen to hear Morgan agree that the United States had had too brief a history and insufficient records to make complete studies of flood stage and evaporation problems and then summon an aide to bring him records of river flooding on the Danube since the year 1000 and on the River Tiber at Rome since 413 B.C. Opponents were simply unable to ask Morgan technical questions that surprised him. More often, Morgan turned their own questions back on them with instant and impressive command of detail. For instance, when asked if he could give the average flow of water in the Miami River at the mouth of a certain creek, he answered, "Do you want it in cubic feet per second or proportion of amount?"[82]

After several days of such testimony even the presiding judges began to appear overwhelmed. To Morgan's request yet again to enlarge on a technical point, this time a discussion of methods by which to predict storm centers, Judge C.W. Murphy of Butler County replied, "If the rest of the court wishes to bear with you, you may."[83]

Objectors to the Conservancy District plan argued that it was absurd to think that channel improvement would not be possible for the Miami Valley, when it "is possible in every valley in the world and has been the recognized system of flood protection, until Mr. Morgan arrived in the Miami Valley."[84] They predicted that the $23 million price tag attached to the Conservancy plan would balloon to over $177 million.[85]

But the thousands of pages of field survey reports, the hundreds of maps and blueprints, the support of dozens of famous engineers convinced the Conservancy Court to allow the Miami Valley to become the site for a great engineering experiment. They had been overwhelmed by the faith in science and the immense self-confidence of progressive experts.[86]

When the U.S. Supreme Court refused to hear the case in 1918, actual construction finally began. By then, of course, the United States was involved in World War I, and the project had to be approved as an essential one.[87] In some ways, even given the inevitable difficulties of completing such work during wartime, after the monumental debate over the District, its actual con-

In truth, Section 15 did give the district directors significant powers, including an unprecedented legal innovation: a dominant right of eminent domain. What that meant in practice was that these appointed directors could overrule elected city and county officials should disputes occur over acquisitions of property for water control purposes.

Opponents charged that this kind of administrative system was as "undemocratic as the Stamp Act, about which our fathers went to war."[71] They argued, further, that it was unconstitutional. Under the new Ohio Constitution of 1912 only municipalities and counties could exercise the kinds of taxation and assessment powers granted the flood control districts by the Conservancy Act. Besides, any state assessment system that taxed private property for public improvement had to gauge payment levels in direct proportion to potential benefits. Since taxes to be assessed for the construction of the Morgan dams were to be levied on real estate only, they did not balance proportionate benefit fairly and so were unconstitutional. A truly equitable system would assess the benefits of a flood control plan for personal property as well as real estate. J.A. Thomas, a Piqua lawyer, gave an example: "Take, for instance, Rike's store. How much was Rike's building injured? Not much—the counters and things of that kind, but there was probably a hundred thousand dollars worth of goods under water. Now, for the protection of the other hundred thousand dollars, they don't pay a nickel. That is the law."[72]

The Ohio Supreme Court in 1915 disallowed the objectors' arguments about the unconstitutionality of the Conservancy Act, and the U.S. Supreme Court upheld that decision and closed further avenues of legal appeal in 1918. Nevertheless, there was substance to many of the opposition arguments about equity and democracy. Assessments on real estate only did allow prominent urban businessmen, like Dayton's Frederick Rike, who owned the city's largest department store, to benefit from flood protection without paying for equipment and stock as well as buildings and land. If not unconstitutional, it certainly was a flood protection system that favored business. And it was a system that quite deliberately favored appointment rather than election of officials. As Henry Scarlett, city solicitor of Columbus, explained, in a speech opposing the Garver amendment, which would have required Conservancy directors to stand for election, election was not feasible because the "right sort of men cannot be induced to enter a canvass for the positions."[73]

And the "right sort" of men were prominent leaders of the new corporations, people already familiar with the hierarchical business structures, eager to employ experts and the techniques of scientific management. The three directors of the Miami Conservancy District epitomized these characteristics. Edward A. Deeds, to nobody's surprise, became president of the board of directors. Sitting with him were Henry Allen and Gordon Rentschler. Allen, of Troy, was president of the Allen-Wheeler Company, a large milling firm, president of the Tipp Telephone Company, and director of the First Troy National Bank.[74] Rentschler was a large shareholder in the family foundry in Hamilton and a banker. During his years as a director of the Miami Conservancy District, he rose to prominence in national banking circles, becoming, by 1929, one of the country's most influential bankers, as the youngest man ever named president of the National City Bank of New York.[75]

Of these men, only Deeds had an NCR connection. So in a literal sense the posters that appeared throughout several valley counties in 1915 asking, "Do you want Home Rule or NCR Rule in Flood Protection?" were exaggerated.[76] But in important ways flood control under the provisions of the Conservancy Act was "NCR rule," if the phrase meant administration by those confident that their plans, devised by scientific and engineering experts and subject to their own "practical business judgment" were superior to those that might have been created through elections and "home rule."[77] "NCR rule" valued business decision-making models that were not democratic. The emphasis, rather, was on creating a measure that was "water, law, and . . . politician proof."[78]

The Miami Conservancy District was a progressive's plan, if not so simply the noble attempt to rise above petty politics its supporters described. It did favor urban and industrial areas. It did shelter its administrators from direct public scrutiny and control. But, in this case at least, the creators of the District did indeed choose, however arbitrarily, what was in the best long-term public interest.

Opponents' charges that the plan gave unfair advantage to Dayton and was undemocratic had some substance. Their final

major attack, that the plan was unsafe and unduly expensive, proved baseless. This issue most clearly illustrated the District supporters as progressives. Arthur Morgan assembled an advisory group of the nation's most prominent scientists and engineers. These men included university professors, presidents of engineering societies, two generals (each formerly chief of engineers of the U.S. Army), and prominent directing engineers responsible for several of the largest dam and water supply projects in the country.[79] When in 1916 the Miami Conservancy District's directors submitted an official plan for the formal hearing required by provisions of the Conservancy Act, these experts testified that they had already spent two years studying its provisions. The collective judgment of many of the most eminent engineers in the United States that the Morgan dry dams provided an innovative, cost-effective solution to the threat of flooding in the Miami Valley proved hard to rebut.

Opponents certainly tried. In 1915 the county governments of Clark, Shelby, and Miami pooled funds and hired John Hill, a Cincinnati engineer, as their own expert consultant.[80] Hill, like most opponents, proposed a counterplan reliant on river channelization. He was no match, however, for the long line of experts the Conservancy produced who, in day after day of testimony and questioning during the lengthy official hearing, skewered his methods, his mathematical ability, even his honesty.[81]

The victory of the Morgan plan illustrated the influence of the emerging profession of engineering, prominent members of which united to support a controversial, unprecedented plan and to convince a court of assembled common pleas judges with no engineering background to approve it. It illustrated the virtues of business planning and extensive scientific research. The Morgan team, paid through the Two Million Dollar Fund, could engage in elaborate studies, including the most extensive research into rainfall patterns ever attempted in the United States. Morgan even hired engineers fluent in French, German, and Italian to read and translate all relevant European literature on rainfall, earthen dam construction, and other topics.

The plan's mastermind took the stand for five continuous days as an adversary witness during the formal hearings. In these more than forty hours of testimony, Morgan revealed an encyclopedic knowledge of hydraulic engineering detail and theory

struction seemed something of an anticlimax. Opposition did not disappear completely but became disorganized and ineffective, symbolized by the occasional angry editorial or threatening letter sent to Deeds.[88] The construction of the District, not complete until 1921, did not in any way attract the same kind of obsessive community attention as had the initial debate over its acceptability.

In truth, it was no anticlimax. Rather, it was the largest and most complex engineering project conceived anywhere in the world since the building of the Panama Canal. Engineers from many countries came to participate in the project. The reports issued by the Conservancy to explain construction to the engineering profession, known as the *Miami Technical Reports*, had very wide influence. Several volumes became classics in engineering literature.[89]

The actual construction forged links between technology and business and illustrated business support, indeed patronage, of the developing profession of engineering.[90] That union was a progressive one, the building techniques and management practices dictated by Morgan themselves final illustrations of the Miami Conservancy District's existence as a large-scale progressive project that involved business leadership in a central way.

First, engineers and businessmen continued their collaboration during the construction of the Conservancy District. The Conservancy's directors continued to provide "practical business judgment." For instance, engineers realized that in order for the system to work properly, periodic removal of gravel from river channels would be necessary. Rather than have the District itself shoulder the expense of this necessary maintenance, its directors encouraged the establishment of commercial gravel plants in the streams of the Valley, especially at Dayton and Hamilton, where gravel accumulation was a problem. Like Tom Sawyer with his fence, the District in fact established a fee and inspection schedule and made entrepreneurs pay for the right to remove gravel for concrete production. Of course this was the same material that the District otherwise would have had to dredge itself at considerable cost.[91]

Arthur Morgan's promise that the dams would never be used to generate profit through the production of electricity was kept.

The Miami Conservancy directors did not try to run the District as a profit-making company. But, as in the case of gravel removal, they certainly were willing to exercise firm control of expenditures, cutting costs wherever possible by using the kinds of techniques that had made them leaders of the managerial revolution sweeping American business.

The District, a new public sector entity, thus established from the very beginning during construction stages complex and interesting relationships with the private sector. Certainly such relationships illustrated the adoption in the public realm of business models, models to be used for progressive ends: to improve conditions in the Miami Valley, to make its people safe.

Second, and just as important, management techniques used during the years of construction between 1918 and 1921 reflected an acceptance of new "progressive" personnel techniques. Arthur Morgan, like John H. Patterson, wanted to provide good working conditions for his employees and in fact engaged in welfare work practices that paralleled some of those offered during the same time period at the NCR.

Morgan argued that "the design of the organization, and the qualifications of the men who were to become the elements of that design, received the same thorough-going attention as was given to the design of the conduits, the spillways, or the system of hydraulic fill for the various dams."[92] Like Patterson, Morgan was eager to develop a spirit of camaraderie and a sense of family among District employees. And that family was to include workers as well as members of the engineering staff.

To help achieve that, he mandated the establishment of construction camps very different from those common everywhere else in the United States. Large outdoor construction projects were of course by their very nature temporary, and their accompanying construction camps were generally best described as slums. They usually featured tarpaper bunkhouses or shacks without electricity or sanitation, linked by muddy trails, fouled by the odors of overflowing privies.

Morgan, like Patterson, was concerned about more than worker loyalty. He wanted to create conditions that would promote the elevation of character. He was convinced that construction laborers who drifted from job to job spending their money on drink and gambling did so in part because their shabby environments encouraged no better behavior.

In a letter sent in 1918 to recruit C.W. Porter-Shirley as the District's employment supervisor, Morgan outlined his plans for better physical conditions. He wrote that all the dam sites were too far from cities to allow the work crews to live in town. So the District had to be prepared to house and feed its workers. But, rather than the usual shacks, Morgan wanted suitable quarters for "decent, self-respecting men." He wanted to hire men who, in the proper environment, "could be helped in their desire to find themselves socially and economically."[93]

In keeping with that wish, Morgan ordered construction camps able to house from 150 to 300 men built at each of the sites, with facilities strikingly better than were standard at the time. Connected to nearby towns by railway lines, the camps were in fact small permanent villages, with sewer, electricity, and water systems, streets, community halls, small stores, and a schoolhouse. Men with families could rent cottages built in several different styles. The single men who composed the majority of the District's construction crews lived in bunkhouses, furnished with steam heat, lighting, toilets, shower baths, lounges, and janitor service. If they wished to pay slightly higher rent, bunkhouse men could secure private rooms. The rents were competitive, especially in wartime conditions. Cottages rented for an average of sixteen dollars a month. A bunkhouse renter paid fifty cents per week for a shared room, seventy-five cents for a private room. Finally, the District made provisions for free housing at all its camps. Workers who could not afford to pay any rent could live in a large, dormitory-style bunkhouse, with no separate rooms but instead one large sleeping chamber furnished with beds and mattresses.[94]

The District provided schooling for workers' children. In addition, it started free night classes for adult employees at each camp, offering instruction in mathematics, industrial arithmetic, penmanship, mechanical drawing, and English grammar. Foreign workers were encouraged to enroll in a special Americanization program that taught spoken and written English as well as American government. Morgan was personally interested in exposing workers who enrolled in these classes to as many "properly masculine" role models as he could. He specifically hired several male teachers for the adult classes.[95] The subliminal message presented at the Conservancy night schools echoed that promoted by NCR welfare work: social services and education should not be controlled by women.

In fact, there were numerous direct as well as philosophical connections between the camps and the NCR. Camp supervisors asked NCR welfare supervisors for help in starting gardening and recreational programs. As a result, the camps provided tilled and fertilized land for war gardens, where workers could reduce their food costs by growing many of their own vegetables; they also boasted programs that distributed ornamental shrubs and grass seed to plant around the four- or five-room cottages.[96]

Community associations at the camps sponsored dances, bought player pianos, and showed movies "the equal to anything to be found at the theaters in Dayton, with such stars as Fairbanks, Marguerite Clark, Mary Pickford."[97] Through the community associations, workers chose which entertainments and sports to sponsor, which books to buy for the camps' circulating library, what special projects to "boost." This was in keeping with Arthur Morgan's statement that "it would please me very much if the social and living conditions in these camps could be regulated by the men themselves by some sort of self government."[98] The Conservancy *Bulletin* reported that decisions made in the camps were "not imposed by those who had charge of the construction work" but rather were "democratic."[99] But democracy and self-government had their limits. Workers were not allowed to negotiate their wages, and the camps were open shop.

And, as was the case in other business ventures labeled progressive reforms, the model construction camps were meant to pay dividends. As Edward Deeds noted in a letter to Ezra Kuhns, who combined his continued work as the NCR's chief legal counselor with his appointment as secretary-treasurer of the District, "There is no place in this whole job where we can so easily subject ourselves to severe criticism as in spending any extra money in frills at the camps. We cannot afford to be working out any sociology or put anything on any basis other than the coldest business one."[100]

Indeed, reports of the District's board revealed that his fellow directors agreed with Deeds that improvements at the camps had to be justified as a business proposition. In 1922, with all major construction completed, the board reported that throughout the period of inflated wartime wages, the District had never paid as well as many other employers in the vicinity. "As inducements, steady work, good living conditions, and fair treatment were offered. As a result of these inducements a group of loyal men was assembled . . . who stuck with the District even when tempted by extravagant wages elsewhere."[101]

The District also used the promise of good conditions as "inducement" for its employees to work under open shop conditions. After studying the rules of the twenty-eight unions that could claim jurisdiction for some part of the Conservancy work, Morgan then drew up a uniform code and invited officials from the Dayton Building Trades Council to review it. Once they had done so, Morgan argued, these union officials "gladly accepted" his single code as the basis for resolving labor disputes during construction.[102] The code recognized the right of workers to organize in trade unions, but it also clearly stated that "employees shall not use any coercive measures to induce persons to join any labor organization, nor to induce the officers or representatives of the district to deal therewith." In addition, the District did not tolerate what it labeled "jurisdictional distinctions." What that policy meant in practice was that a carpenter might be asked on occasion to dig a ditch, or that an unskilled ditchdigger might be given carpenter's tools and told to drive nails for a morning.[103]

Union officials challenged Morgan's report that they had met at the District and agreed to the principles of open shop. Rather, in a broadside attacking the District published in a union newsletter, they countered, "If the conservancy officials who were present at that conference will refresh their memories they will recall that the statement was made that 'the only open shop is that which is open to scabs.' "[104]

In July 1918, 125 men, mostly carpenters, plumbers, and electricians, struck construction sites at the Huffman, Taylorsville, and Englewood dams. Grant Fink, secretary of the carpenters' union, charged that men were not being paid overtime for weekend work, even though the labor code for the District promised such pay.[105] The Conservancy argued that a few unions, led by the carpenters, had fabricated the charges to try to force a closed shop. The truth of the charges remains unclear, since District pay records did not clearly distinguish overtime. But the victor in the dispute was the Conservancy. The strike, the only one during the years of construction, collapsed when the District replaced the strikers with nonunion labor.[106]

Its opponents charged that in addition to favoring nonunion skilled workers, the District sought to hire foreign workers, unaccustomed to American work traditions and less likely to complain. Conservancy officials replied that they faced situations of severe labor shortage. They argued, furthermore, that skilled workers and laborers from surrounding cities were not eager to travel out to the dams for daily work and were not willing to uproot their families to live in the construction camps.[107]

The truth lay somewhere in between. Indeed during the war itself, when with its necessary industry classification construction work on the Conservancy continued full speed, labor shortages did pose tremendous problems. During the years 1918 and 1919 when work was at its peak, the District needed some 1,800 workers. To secure them during wartime it sent labor agents to scour the country. Not all were successful. One hapless man named Joseph Kugler kept getting into trouble. More than once he sent desperate letters back to his supervisor, C.W. Porter-Shirley. In one, for instance, he reported that he had lined up 215 men willing to work for the District "and of course the foreman of this [sic] men got sor [sic] at me for teking [sic] men away. So they called the police and told police I am an Austrian spy."[108] After bailing Kugler out of jail, Porter-Shirley sent him on to Indianapolis to recruit gangs of Hungarians.

But even after the war ended, bringing postwar recession rather than labor shortages, Conservancy officials continued to hire foreigners, including gangs of Mexican laborers. Dayton's Socialist newspaper ran this headline: "Men Who Import Mexicans While Jobless Dayton Citizens Walk Streets Not Fit To Serve People!"[109] Native-born workers formed a majority in the construction crews at all times between 1918 and 1922, but certainly, in some instances, Conservancy employment agents preferred to "Americanize" foreigners rather than deal with American workers themselves.

With the help of these Mexicans and several thousand other construction workers, Conservancy officials finished the second-largest building project ever attempted in the United States on time. All major work was in place by late 1921. By 1922 Arthur Morgan's dry dam system was officially complete.[110] A comprehensive program of flood control replaced the emergency systems of flood relief in the Miami Valley.

Similar judgments about both efforts can be made. Both effectively solved a crisis: one, flood devastation, immediate and real; the other, the threat of future flooding, potential, but no less serious. Both cases provided illustrations of businessmen as reformers, as progressives. In fact, in interesting ways, both revealed the complex character of progressivism, a movement with virtues and drawbacks.

These business efforts to combat the serious problem of flood inundation brought genuine reform, social changes reflective of progressivism's central faith in science, the decisions of experts, and modern techniques of institutional organization. John Patterson's leadership of disaster relief in Dayton probably saved hundreds of lives, and his methods were widely copied. The Dayton disaster was one of the first in which the fledgling American Red Cross participated. Red Cross officials sent to the city worked in offices donated by the NCR. In effect, they became the company's pupils and used lessons learned during national disasters for decades to come.[111]

The Miami Conservancy District was similarly a success. The District did make the valley region "forever floodproof." In April 1922, only months after the completion of major construction, the system got its first serious test. A spring storm released enough rain to bring the Miami River to its old flood stage of eighteen feet outside Dayton. This time, however, the river rose only to nine feet.[112] In the following decades, the District continued to work well. By 1937, when a huge flood almost the equal of that of 1913 swept over the Ohio River watershed, the people of the Miami Valley had long since accepted their own flood control system as a success. Indeed, few probably even thought about it, since the earthen dry dam works had, as planned, been thickly planted with sod and thoroughly integrated into the landscape. And even during the great storm of 1937, which brought devastation to large sections of the Midwest and Mid-Atlantic states, the Conservancy system was hardly taxed. The Miami River at Hamilton reached its highest stage since 1913. Water, of course, backed up behind the five dry dams but occupied only about 15 percent of available storage space. Severe rainfalls in 1959 and 1963 also left the region unscathed.[113]

Moreover, engineers over the decades concurred with Morgan's initial conclusion that it was his plan, not alternatives, that would be the least costly to build and, by far, the least costly to maintain.[114] Had plans like those proposed by John Hill to straighten and reconstruct the channels of the Miami River actually been tried, the citizens of the Miami Valley would have spent hundreds of millions for systems of flood control that probably would not have worked and would most certainly have limited urban expansion. As it was they spent more than the $23 million first projected by the Conservancy planners, but they didn't spend much more. Largely because of wartime inflation of prices and wages, the project finally ended up costing $34 million.[115]

It was a small price to pay for decades of protection, made possible by the early twentieth-century alliance between new business values and progressive reform. The tenacity and self-confidence of business leaders who were eager to reshape their communities to face the future using ideas and models they felt sure were superior made the Miami Conservancy District a reality. But the creation of the District imposed costs.

The costs were not financial but political. During the great Dayton flood and after, powerful corporate leaders pushed aside local and county officials. They created effective, sometimes brilliant, but usually undemocratic solutions to the problems facing them.

They were solutions crafted not by the faceless institutional bureaucrats of organizational history but by charismatic leaders: businessmen who could bring their audiences to tears. But these businessmen—most important, John H. Patterson and Edward A. Deeds—managed their civic activities as they did their corporations: as heads of hierarchies, as men who did not brook challenge. John H. Patterson really was "almost dictator" of Dayton during the flood.[116] Deeds, another prominent businessman, played a similar authoritarian role.[117]

The Conservancy board Deeds headed had very significant powers, especially during the construction of the district when it taxed or took for public use almost forty thousand acres of land. It even condemned and removed an entire community, the village of Osborn, Ohio, lying ten miles northeast of Dayton. Osborn, with a population of about one thousand people, sat directly in the middle of what would become the overflow lands for the Harshman Dam. Rather than build an additional dam to protect the village, the Conservancy directors wiped it off the map, buying up its lots and retail buildings, moving all its three hundred houses to another site, and saving the District an estimated $1 million in the process.[118] Needless to say, the residents of Osborn were not allowed to vote about their fate. They simply received letters from the District explaining where and when their houses would be moved to the nearby town of Fairfield, newly renamed Fairborn.

And for men with such power, neither Patterson nor Deeds had demonstrated much regard for American law. Deeds was a fellow defendant with Patterson at the NCR trust trials. At the time of the flood both were convicted felons, out of jail on appeal. Charles Evans Hughes, in 1918 a special assistant to Attorney General Thomas Gregory and in charge of the federal investigation of problems with aircraft production, personally recommended that Deeds be court-martialed for alleged profiteering from his service as chief of aircraft procurement during World War I. Neither man spent a day in prison, military or civilian. Appeals courts and a military review board reversed and dropped initial convictions and charges. Nevertheless, their legal problems illustrated the complex characters of these businessmen-reformers.

Edward A. Deeds, John H. Patterson, and the dozens of other business leaders they recruited for the flood control campaign, truly were reformers. They deserved the label progressive. They took risks and committed personal fortunes to grand visions of social improvement. Their correspondence and personal writings reveal men genuinely interested in improving community and nation. And they believed, often exuberantly believed, that such improvement was possible. Nevertheless, many of these men, particularly Deeds and Patterson themselves, fully deserved the label *ruthless*. It was an adjective contemporaries bestowed as often as they used the more flattering term, *reformer*. They illustrated, as settlement house workers did not so easily illustrate, the complicated nature of progressive reform.

For the reverse side of progressive self-confidence was an arrogant willingness to manipulate the lives of others in the conviction that it was either in their own or in the larger public good. Time and again flood relief and flood control efforts revealed that willingness to "improve" and manipulate. In small ways it was revealed in the sanitary codes in effect at the Conservancy construction camps. There men had to soak themselves regulary in vats of cheap, strong cologne, since camp physician, W.M. Smalley, had read that "strong and lasting odors" repelled lice.[119] In large ways it was revealed not just in the obliteration of Osborn, but also in an outburst by Arthur Morgan during a 1913 public meeting called to explain his plans. Exasperated with the large number of belligerent questions from the audience, Morgan burst out, "I wish that there would be a civic standard in Dayton that will permit no man to get in the city's way."[120] He meant, of course, his way. His way was, in truth, a grand plan. Flood relief and flood control in the Miami Valley were wonderful successes. That fact cannot obscure the reality that they were done "for" the people, not, by and large, "with" them.

4

City Manager Government for Dayton

Ray Stannard Baker, famous journalist and political adviser, traveled to Dayton in 1916 to assess Dayton's flood recovery efforts. The great 1913 flood, readers of *World's Work* learned, was the "best thing that ever happened to the Miami Valley." It was, Baker said, borrowing a phrase from one of his principal informants, Edward A. Deeds, a "heat treatment."[1] Steel rails subjected to a period of intense heat during their manufacture were stronger and far less likely to break under sudden strain. The fierce heat of the flood calamity, Deeds suggested, had jarred apart groups and cliques and forged a stronger, more united community in Dayton.

Not content with the creation of permanent flood protection, that united community had insisted on similarly progressive, businesslike efficiency in other areas as well. "The flood enormously increased the responsibility of the city officials, and immediately a new and progressive charter was adopted, providing for an elective commission, which was to employ a trained city manager. They were to get an expert, not a politician, and, like any progressive business concern, pay the adequate salary for an expert."[2]

Clearly Edward A. Deeds had won another disciple. Nevertheless, Ray Stannard Baker's glowing tribute to the "business-minded revolution" in Dayton contained truth. The establishment of a city manager system of local government did indeed provide a very good illustration of the nature of business progressivism. It was, however, a more involved story.

Analyzing two topics helps to prove that complexity. First, a discussion of business progressivism and Dayton municipal politics profits from an investigation of the campaign to achieve city manager government. This almost twenty-year-long campaign was a study in controversy. Its history illustrates the reality, not evident in Baker's account, that the effort to create "business-minded" government in Dayton involved pitched battles between shifting sets of antagonists. Second, such a discussion benefits from a study of the achievements and failures of commission-manager government during its first decade in Dayton. Such an analysis provides additional evidence about the nature of business involvement with this "business-minded" form of government. The commission-manager innovation was a phenomenon both contemporaries and historians have long identified as a classic example of progressive reform. Was it a classic example of business-progressivism?

The campaign to change Dayton's form of local government can be traced to a speech given by John H. Patterson in 1896. In that year, the Dayton Board of Trade invited the National Cash Register president to be the keynote speaker at its annual banquet. Patterson chose as his title "What Dayton, Ohio, Should Do to Become a Model City." Patterson, who by all accounts held his audience's attention for a speech lasting more than two hours, presented a grand vision, constructed from a progressive's faith in science, in education, in human eagerness to improve and progress. His future Dayton was "clothed in green" and ringed by parks and playgrounds. The city's homes and public buildings followed an architectural master plan, so precise that it even recommended the proper harmonious outside paint colors and shrubbery for each neighborhood. A system of free libraries, music conservatories, and art galleries supplemented the free education provided by the revamped city schools. After a program of reorganization these schools now taught students at all age levels manual and business skills in addition to traditional subjects. Stringent new health codes and improved city sanitation, including mandatory regular city "disinfection" of private backyards and cellars, as well as new, scientifically engineered sewer systems and free public baths, greatly decreased disease.

In fifty years, Patterson predicted, such changes would so lessen "the work and worry of life" that crime rates, child labor, poverty, even the demand for medicines would decline. In a thousand years in such a Dayton, "there would be no deaths except from accidents and old age." Though Patterson acknowledged no specific major influence, his perfect city was a utopian construction that probably sprang in part from his fertile imagination, in part from his extensive contacts with the work and ideas of European and American social reformers.

"How," Patterson asked, "shall we get the money to accomplish all these changes?" His answer was simple: "Adopt business methods in city government." To do that, Dayton had to restrict the power of bosses and politicians. It needed a "monitor club, a self-appointed body of men with sufficient ability and integrity to inspire the people with confidence." These men would attend all open city meetings and find out about decisions made during closed ones. They would appear at the meetings of the board of trade and the school board and at all openings of sales of city bonds. They would hold any wrongdoing so discovered up to "public ridicule and contempt" through speeches, public rallies, or advertisements in newspapers. "After five years of service the monitor club will practically cease to exist, for the spirit of reform will be aroused."[3] Patterson's warnings that government needed to be watched by vigilant associations of "self-appointed" citizen volunteers presaged arguments that would dominate the debate over the creation of the Miami Conservancy District: that government was usually a hindrance to, not an ally of, reform.

But Patterson's optimism about the speed with which new associations of reform-minded citizens could correct political abuse was excessive. He needed to play hardball politics, threatening to pull his huge company out of Dayton, even to win creation of the Dayton Chamber of Commerce, a version of his monitor club. Nor did the chamber of commerce win acceptance for its proposals for businesslike government in only five years. And even after its victory in 1913 city manager government in Dayton faced an uncertain future until the elections of 1917.

The campaign to bring city manager government to Dayton and to establish it securely turned on events during four watershed years: 1907, 1912, 1913, and 1917. By 1907 John H. Patterson's speeches to his fellow citizens had lost their euphoric tone. Patterson complained at a mass rally, "When I should have been up in the advertising department or in New York or in Paris devoting my time to my business, I have tried, instead, to do many things which would help the city, but I have been unsuccessful, and my efforts have been ridiculed."[4] This bitter speech was in effect the first volley in an intricate war of nerves between the NCR Company and the city of Dayton.

For years, Patterson's company had feuded with Dayton city government. The city council refused to give any railroad the right to bring lines into Dayton at surface grade. The NCR had since 1899 vigorously opposed the city ordinance that required railroad tracks to be elevated or below street level within city limits, arguing that such city regulations denied it the rail access it had to have. Railroad companies were unwilling to incur the additional expense required to build special tracks. Moreover, NCR officials complained that city regulations prevented them from building private railroad tracks to their shipping facilities, unfairly increasing the company's costs. Patterson himself or one of his officers regularly journeyed to city offices to complain not just about the rail track regulations but also about a variety of other matters. For instance, the company attacked the quality of streetcar service in the city. Inefficient morning and evening schedules made workers late to the plant and prevented their orderly departure at the end of the working day. The city, Patterson argued, should build a bridge over the Miami River at Stewart Street, so that areas directly across the river from his factory complex could become convenient residential neighborhoods for his workers. To his list of grievances the NCR president added lack of support at city hall for his proposals to spend substantially more money on parks, playgrounds, and schools. He could not, Patterson said, attract the kind of skilled labor force the production of cash registers demanded without better recreational opportunities, nor could he hope to count on Dayton schools as places that would properly prepare children for work at the NCR.[5]

Patterson continued his attacks on city government, giving speeches that echoed his 1896 "Model City" talk. He exhorted Daytonians to clean up local political corruption much as they would "drain a swamp."[6] He also sought to shame Dayton by widely broadcasting his complaints. The NCR printed and circulated thousands of copies of the "Model City" speech alone, targeting hundreds of journalists and local officials in other cities for special attention.[7] Despite these efforts, general indifference greeted the NCR president's campaign, and city council members continued openly to deny his huge company's demands.

The confrontation escalated in 1902. By one vote the city council stymied yet another NCR effort to change local railroad crossing ordinances and denied the company's petition to build an elaborate shipping facility including fifteen new loading docks connected to a private company spur track.[8] This refusal aroused Patterson's combative instincts to new heights. He openly raged against his enemies on the council. More important, he initiated a plan that greatly increased the costs of opposition to the NCR.

After several years of private inquiries, John H. Patterson announced that plan in January 1907. It was a bombshell. He had decided to abandon the entire NCR complex and move operations to another city. The NCR president sent a team of key company officers, headed by E.A. Deeds, on a very public tour of the Northeast to determine the company's site choices. Cities throughout the region scrambled to win a chance to become finalists. Officials in Schenectady, Buffalo, and Rochester, New York, greeted the delegation of NCR officials with parades, beauty queens, and effusive promises of plenty of room, good railroad facilities, and low taxes. Buffalo offered the company a hefty cash "relocation" bonus. Even cities that had earlier dismissed the tour as a free advertising scheme publicly backpedaled. The editor of the Cohoes, New York, *Republican* printed his apologies for ever doubting NCR's sincerity, and he promised, "The cash register people need never be lonesome, for their evenings would be one round of pleasure playing 'Five Hundred,' 'Flinch,' 'progressive euchre,' 'Hearts' or at turkey, roast beef or valentine suppers."[9]

As the company entourage swept farther east, Connecticut and Massachusetts vied to join the fray. Newspaper editorialists in dozens of towns and cities promoted the skill of their workers, the healthful qualities of their climates, and the purity of their water supplies. A few candidly spoke not only of the "progress" the NCR could bring their communities, but of the money and jobs as well. The editor of the Bridgeport, Connecticut, *Post* minced no words. "The advantages," he wrote, "are obvious. At present, the company has a weekly payroll of between $60,000 and $70,000."[10]

While Northeastern business leaders feted their visitors from the NCR, their Dayton counterparts panicked. A group of more than 150 well-known Dayton businessmen formed the Businessmen's Boosters Club, a group with one express goal: to retain the National Cash Register Company. These men immediately began to inundate John H. Patterson with letters pleading that he give Dayton one more chance.[11]

In a reply mailed January 17 from New York City to Russell Johnston, president of the Boosters Club, Patterson outlined his conditions. While warning that "it would be almost impossible" for Dayton to retain his plant, he nonetheless mentioned improvements his fellow citizens had to make, if only to attract another large business to fill the empty NCR buildings. The list was a long one and surely familiar to Patterson's home audience: more parks, playgrounds, bridges, rail spurs, and manual training schools. Most important, the Boosters Club must exercise all its influence to change local government, to reform "Dayton's reputation of being the worst governed city of the state." Patterson ended, "All that I have suggested in this letter is for Dayton's benefit, and what will be required to hold the N.C.R. Company will be determined by what other cities offer."[12]

Despite this equivocation, the Boosters Club chose to regard Patterson's letter as a tentative offer of negotiation and set about to meet its stated terms. With the club as catalyst, the Dayton business community coalesced. By February 1907 the Boosters Club had merged with the city's two largest businessmen's organizations, the Commercial Club and the Dayton Board of Trade.[13] The new group, renamed the chamber of commerce, quickly created permanent committees to investigate taxation, street and bridge improvements, parks and playgrounds, schools, and municipal politics. By March a full-scale campaign to force the city to comply with NCR demands was under way. Chamber of commerce members camped out at city hall, lobbying mayor and council; they organized rallies attended by hundreds of businessmen; they deluged the newspapers with letters to the editor. One written by chamber member and local merchant Elias Van Scoyk was typical. Van Scoyk wrote, emphasizing the campaign's theme that better local government was the key to obtaining all other necessary improvements, "Let the city be run on a strictly business plan: not make or create positions for hungry politicians . . . to hold a party in power, no matter what party."[14]

Within months, the pressure had begun to work. The Dayton

City Council, which had for years blocked the company's proposals, agreed to grant the NCR the right to build rail switch tracks and extensive shipping facilities so that it would no longer have to haul goods to public rail depots. It issued one hundred thousand dollars in bonds for public parks.[15] Finally, the chamber of commerce met with the NCR board of directors to assure them of its "complete sympathy" with a written agenda of NCR demands that included the following:

1. Diligence in prodding the Council.
2. Railroads and switch to N.C.R.
3. Bridge at Stewart Street
4. Oakwood village to be incorporated
5. Canal to be abandoned
6. Training schools to be built
7. Better government
8. Republican primaries changed to second week of September
9. Better street car service
10. Universal transfers on all street car lines
11. Parks. Cut weeds on vacant lots.
12. Straighten river and construct levee
13. Dayton to show appreciation by visiting N.C.R. plant frequently
14. The open shop endorsed
15. Cooperation in and endorsement of welfare work[16]

After "full consideration" of offers of tracts of land and cash contributions toward the expenses of moving, the NCR board of directors resolved to accept Dayton's promises of improvement and to remain. Its acceptance, the board noted, was based upon the "pledge of [the] Chamber of Commerce and citizens" to carry out those promises with "due business diligence." Should they fail to do so, the company would of course feel itself at liberty to take up again "this question of removal."[17]

The company, then, appeared to have routed its enemies at city hall, panicking them with the threat of the loss of the community's biggest employer. Was John H. Patterson bluffing? If so, he certainly kept his own counsel. Private documents completely closed to his contemporaries, such as minutes of the NCR board, never even hint that the threat of removal was not a real one. But the NCR in 1907 was very much the creation of one man, and that man was a masterful actor.

But if Patterson was a masterful actor, he was not a magician. Although the drama precipitated by his threat to relocate the NCR Company was a major event in the campaign to change city government, it was not solely responsible for the establishment of city manager government in Dayton. Nineteen oh seven was a watershed year for that effort; 1908 was not. Despite the company's warning that it would reopen its search for a better city should Dayton not quickly fulfill its lengthy list of promises, five more years passed before the campaign for "better government" again accelerated during a watershed year.

During 1912 three signal events made a change to "business-minded" government much more likely. First, the Ohio legislature passed a home rule amendment to the Ohio Constitution. Second, the Dayton Chamber of Commerce appointed a committee headed by Patterson to consider specific ways to rewrite the city charter to take advantage of provisions in the new constitutional amendment for great city autonomy. Finally, bitter rivalries within the Dayton Socialist party, the most important opponent of a change to "business" government, turned its energies temporarily inward.

The passage of a home rule amendment to the Ohio Constitution in September 1912 was not an isolated event. Other state legislatures passed similar measures. All were proclaimed victories for progressive reformers who were seeking ways to change local politics. These reformers argued that state legislatures had interfered excessively in city governments. In fact, they said, American municipal government had not so much failed as it had remained untried. In 1894 a group of influential progressives interested in municipal reform and led by men like Richard Childs, Charles Beard, and Clinton Rogers Woodruff created the National Municipal League. The organization quickly assumed a leadership role, its major annual conference a national meeting ground for self-styled urban reformers, its publications forums for debate.

In 1900 the league called for greater freedom for cities and for home rule as a first step toward municipal reform.[18] The Ohio constitutional amendment, a victory for league supporters, gave

Ohio cities considerable independence. Under its provisions, the state forbade the combination of school administration with other functions of local government and retained some control over local courts and finances, but for the first time in the state's history each Ohio city could exercise all other powers of local government and enforce within its limits public safety, health, fire, and other municipal codes without outside interference, as long as those codes did not conflict with the general laws of Ohio.

The amendment further provided that a city could, either through a request initiated by its city council or by citizen petition, hold a special election to decide whether it wished to adopt a new city charter. Those cities not holding such elections would continue under the existing municipal code of the state and remain governed by councils chosen by wards and mayors elected at large.[19]

But John H. Patterson, who had warred for over two decades with the Dayton City Council and the Democratic party bosses he correctly claimed controlled the body, was not about to lose an opportunity to remove certain council members and exchange mayor-council government for an entirely new chartered form. The Dayton Chamber of Commerce, which had kept its 1907 pledge to lobby for change in local government, had sent representatives to Columbus in support of the home rule amendment. It had, in addition, a signed citizen's petition requesting the right to hold a special city charter election ready to submit to the state legislature within days of the amendment's passage.[20]

Patterson himself had been busy during the summer and autumn of 1912. He had sent representatives around the United States and to Europe to study city government systems and urban reform agencies. The New York Bureau of Municipal Research, staffed with accountants, social workers, engineers, and other experts who were instructed to apply techniques of business management to city problems, particularly impressed Patterson. He decided to imitate John D. Rockefeller and Andrew Carnegie, the New York Bureau's patrons. In October 1912 he founded the Dayton Bureau of Municipal Research.[21]

That bureau, begun with an initial monthly budget of one thousand dollars, wholly paid out of Patterson's personal funds, received a mandate from Patterson "to make unbiased, scientific studies of governmental affairs." In reality, Chester Rightor, an expert in social work management and Patterson's new bureau director, began to collect data useful for a charter reform campaign.[22]

Patterson himself had personal need of such data since, within two weeks of the legislative passage of the home rule amendment, he had accepted an invitation from the chamber of commerce to head a committee of businessmen formed to draft a new model charter for the city of Dayton. The work of this charter reform committee, which was composed of Patterson, E.A. Deeds, Frederick Rike, E.C. Harley, and Leopold Rauh, provided a second major push bringing city manager government to Dayton. Along with Patterson, Deeds, and Rike, E.C. Harley and Leopold Rauh were well-known leaders of the Dayton business community. Harley was a wholesale supplier to grocers; Rauh had interests in construction and banking.

Patterson may have been one of the first to make the connection between business and local government structure when in his widely circulated 1896 "Model City" speech he had declared, "A city is a great business enterprise whose stockholders are the people."[23] But in 1896 one local governmental form dominated the United States. Citizens in a few New England villages still governed themselves through town meetings. Elsewhere, from tiny towns to large cities, mayors, elected in tandem with some form of council, headed municipal governments.[24]

By 1912, however, that near-universal dominance by one municipal system had changed. Citizens in most cities still elected mayors and councils, but at least since 1901 they could study alternatives. In September 1900 a terrible hurricane raged through Galveston, Texas, killing some six thousand people and destroying more than $17 million in property. The once bustling port town of forty thousand lay in ruins. Businessmen who, like their counterparts in Dayton, had been making open efforts to curb the power of ward politicians, saw their chance. Organizing as a "Good Government Club," they successfully proposed the abolition of mayor-council government. Later, Galveston would claim that its replacement, the city commission, was an entirely original creation. In fact, members of the Good Government Club studied some precedents. A commission, for example, had governed Memphis during a yellow fever epidemic in 1878. Nevertheless, the "Galveston Plan" was indeed a major innovation. It mandated government by a small, nonpartisan legislative body, the city commission. Elected at large, commission members severally acted as heads of the city's administrative departments. Not only reformers and politicians but also readers of such national magazines as *Outlook,* the *Nation,* and *McClure's* studied the new system. They heard that Galveston's experiment was a remarkable achievement, a municipal revolution bringing business order and efficiency to city hall.[25]

The commission idea spread very quickly. Within a decade almost three hundred cities, concentrated particularly in the Plains West and Midwest, adopted the system.[26] Had the members of Patterson's committee, therefore, chosen to recommend commission government for Dayton, they could scarcely have been hailed as innovators.

But by 1912 the commission system had a fledgling challenger. Richard Childs, Yale graduate, New York advertising executive, and prominent member of the National Municipal League, had been an early and enthusiastic supporter of the commission experiment. Soon, however, he became disenchanted with what he and other detractors began to call the "straight commission." That body, Childs argued, merged both administrative and deliberative duties. City commissioners were not only policy makers, they also had to be policy executors. That situation posed dangers to principles of separation of powers and provided few checks to potential corruption.

The system was, moreover, not really as efficient as its supporters suggested. True efficiency demanded a single head. Although each commissioner shared responsibility for setting policy and overseeing city government, no one commissioner assumed overall leadership. Instead, as head of a city department, each commissioner exercised control over a particular area of municipal affairs. Not surprisingly, Childs and others argued, city commissioners tended to devote their greatest attention to their own bailiwicks. Rather than making efficient decisions for the city as a whole, in this view, commissioners tended to defend their own interests. A multiheaded administration was, in effect, an administration without a head at all. In addition, true efficiency demanded leadership by an expert in city administration, not leadership by an elected group of amateurs.[27]

Richard Childs did not invent the idea of a city manager as a solution to these problems. The town fathers of the small city of Staunton, Virginia, until 1908 best known as the birthplace of Woodrow Wilson, did. In that year, they hired a general manager, a professional meant to function much as did the general manager of a business corporation.

The Staunton City manager would report to the city council, remaining employed at the council's pleasure, but he alone would supervise administrative detail. Henceforth, the council would exercise policy-making duties only. Richard Childs's innovation was to advocate the revision not of mayor-council government, as had Staunton, but of the new commission system. In 1912 Childs's proposal had just begun to gain national attention. Only one city, Sumter, South Carolina, adopted the new commission-manager form.[28]

John H. Patterson's committee, then, had three models to review: the federal, or mayor-council; the commission; and the virtually untried commission-manager type of municipal government. Not surprisingly, his committee quickly rejected the federal system. It was, of course, the system Patterson had so strongly attacked as the ally of bossism. More interesting was the committee's equally quick rejection of the straight commission system. Of course by an overwhelming margin the cities run by commissions were small, with populations under ten thousand people. Moreover, with its easy access to the publications of the New York Bureau of Municipal Research and the National Municipal League, the committee had plentiful information about the flaws in commission government. But the commission-manager form, universally called by its adherents the city manager plan, was certainly not a system with a proven record for a city of Dayton's size either. Staunton, Virginia, had a city manager but not the city manager plan. Sumter, South Carolina, was a city whose entire population did not greatly exceed in number John H. Patterson's Dayton work force.

Still, Patterson's committee members enthusiastically embraced the city manager plan for their city, at the 1910 decennial census already boasting a population of 116,000 and growing rapidly. In doing so the committee chose a plan that would make Dayton a pioneer, the first American city of significant size to adopt Childs's city manager plan. That plan, to summarize, featured a commission elected on a nonpartisan at-large basis to act as the city's legislative, policy-making body. Commission members were to work part-time for a nominal salary. To coordinate city administration, they would hire a full-time chief administrator. This well-paid city manager would appoint and control all other city employees, while himself serving at the pleasure of the city commission.

Patterson's committee of fellow business leaders quickly accepted the still-infant city manager form as that most directly analogous to the structure of a business, in which the commission acted as a board of directors and, like a board of directors, did not actually run specific departments but rather hired an expert manager to carry on day-to-day operations. Further, the committee, with the blessing of its parent body, the Dayton Chamber of Commerce, prepared an elaborate campaign to promote the plan's victory at the scheduled special city charter election.

Not wishng to emphasize its close business connections, the committee severed its relationship with the chamber of commerce. The five original members invited ten other Dayton businessmen to participate. Each man in this new group of fifteen then chose four others to constitute a "Committee of One Hundred." Such committees, called by the name "One Hundred" even when the actual number of members varied, had become by 1912 an established institution used by reformers in other cities. Dayton's Committee of One Hundred, renamed the Citizens' Committee, chose fifteen of its number to run as candidates for the charter commission, in accordance with the procedures established by the home rule amendment for revision of a city charter. Not surprisingly, John H. Patterson headed the committee's charter commission ticket.[29]

The remaining fourteen candidates on the nonpartisan Citizens' Committee ticket included three lawyers, a dentist, and a union printer. Nevertheless, businessmen still dominated. Each signed a written pledge promising that if elected in the special charter election scheduled for May 1913, he would write a new charter for the city of Dayton that would include two crucial provisions: a commission of five elected at large on a nonpartisan ticket, and a city manager responsible for all city administrative duties.[30]

Once it had chosen its slate of candidates, the Citizens' Committee orchestrated a very well planned "information" campaign promoting the city manager system. Interestingly, the Committee used the mechanisms of the Dayton ward system to help defeat it. It chose a "captain" in each of the city's twelve wards. That person selected a "lieutenant" for each precinct, who in turn chose a leader for every block. This block coordinator enlisted a person for each side of the street who agreed to talk to every single neighbor. By such a system, the Citizens' Committee sought to guarantee that one of its representatives would speak personally with every voter in Dayton and would try to get that voter to sign a card pledging support for city manager government.

The campaign plan was an ingenious one. Rather than crowding into mass rallies to be addressed by prominent men or by employers whom they might not have wished to obey, Dayton voters heard their neighbors describe the virtues of the new governmental form and, should they refuse to sign the asked-for pledge, had to turn down a neighbor, perhaps a friend. No voter opened a door to any campaign worker who lived more than a block away.[31]

The activities of John H. Patterson's Citizens' Committee certainly played a large role in making 1912 a turning-point year in the campaign to change Dayton's government. Its efforts to organize massive door-to-door conversation between neighbors displayed clever use of principles of successful advertising and group psychology. But such efforts, which downplayed spectacular speeches and huge rallies, may have been prompted at least in part by the reality that the Dayton Socialist party was a vocal participant at the few such mass rallies that occurred. But in 1912 that Socialist party, the most important opponent of the city manager system, was unable to devote its full attention to the campaign to change local government in Dayton. At a key moment, bitter internal rivalries temporarily diminished its effectiveness.

It is important to recognize that many Daytonians did not view the Dayton Socialist party as a dangerously radical splinter group, out to destroy capitalism by any means necessary. And in fact it was not. Rather, Dayton Socialists were most often skilled workmen, people with respectable, well-paying jobs as machinists, toolmakers, molders, and the like. In contrast to other Midwestern cities with important Socialist parties, like Cleveland or

Milwaukee, where majorities of members were foreign-born and where German, Russian, and other languages were as likely to be heard as English, the membership of the Dayton local was overwhelmingly native born. Far from agitating for the violent overthrow of capitalism and the establishment of socialism through proletarian dictatorship, Dayton Socialists operated peacefully through the system. As one Dayton party leader, Joseph Sharts, explained in a speech denouncing revolutionary socialism and anarchism, his opponents might represent the left wing of socialism, but he and his Dayton comrades represented the "rest of the fowl."[32] And such a bird, Dayton Socialists argued, could better achieve its objectives from within the flock, participating in the system, urging internal reform. Many nonsocialists listened to such a message and voted for Socialist candidates for the city council. In 1911, for instance, the Socialists polled 27 percent of the vote in city races, a highly admirable showing for a party that listed only around eight hundred card-carrying members.[33]

The fact that the Socialists were distracted in 1912 proved a genuine, if unacknowledged, boon to the Citizens' Committee's efforts. In the summer of 1912 the *Miami Valley Socialist* rang with charges that members of the party's state executive committee had through "treacherous attempts" tried to bind the chapters of the state organization to the "anarchist tactics of the I.W.W."[34] In fact, the Miami Valley newspaper reflected the passions aroused by a power struggle within the Ohio Socialist party between moderates who favored "political action"—that is, participation in existing political systems with the goal of reform from within—and those who demanded more revolutionary tactics for a revolutionary era. The conflicts that raged statewide in 1912 had been simmering in Dayton since at least 1910. The battles between the majority of moderates and a left-wing faction led by Frank Midney, a former teacher recently arrived in Dayton from Chicago, were not always only ideological. Each group sought to expel the other, and meetings more than once turned into melees that ended only with the arrival of the police. In that kind of atmosphere, where words, chairs, and fists flew, Dayton Socialists focused on their own civil war.[35]

The dust finally settled in 1913, when a victorious moderate faction began to try to heal wounds and rekindle a spirit of comradeship among all Dayton Socialists. By that time the Citizens' Committee had enjoyed many months of greater leverage. Indeed the special election charter campaign was in its final stages, with a May election date looming.

That is not to say that individual Socialists did not seek to play a role in the 1912 charter debate. Some did, but they acted generally as individuals. Editors of the party's organ, the *Miami Valley Socialist*, focused on the internal fight. When they did discuss city political issues during 1912, they concentrated their attention on opposition to a bond issue campaign for city waterworks improvements.[36]

In 1907 John H. Patterson had fumed that an "earthquake ought to come and stir up Dayton and make some improvement."[37] In 1913 he got a flood instead. Coming just two months ahead of the scheduled special election, the flood provided an opportunity for Patterson to don the robes of a hero. He, and not the mayor or city council, directed recovery efforts. The Dayton mayor and council sat almost unnoticed while state and national figures, not to mention hundreds of reporters, flocked to see John H. Patterson at his NCR headquarters.

An overwhelming victory for the Citizen's Committee slate of candidates was almost a foregone conclusion. On May 20, 1913, Daytonians approved the selection of a commission to rewrite the city's charter by a six-to-one margin. Only 2,020 people voted against the commission and in favor of retaining the mayor-council system without review.[38] The fifteen men now formally chosen by Dayton voters to scrutinize and change the city's charter worked quickly. Obviously they had long since decided what basic form their recommendations would take. On June 23, 1913, five weeks after their election, the charter commissioners completed a city manager charter. The regrouped Socialists mounted a more effective opposition campaign, but still city voters approved the new charter on August 12, 1913, by a margin of more than two to one.[39]

Interestingly, neither the Democratic nor the Republican party organizations in Dayton provided much public support for the Socialists. There appeared to be truth to the repeated Socialist charges that both the Democratic and Republican parties were in a "desperate pickle" and acceded to the victory of "nonpartisan" government as a way to regain credibility and shut the Socialists out of local power.[40] In fact the stock of both mainstream political parties had fallen during the aftermath of the great flood. Even before March 1913 signs began to appear that Patterson's repeated attacks on corruption and bossism in both political parties in the city, but particularly in the controlling Democratic party, had begun to take a toll. Editorialists, especially those writing for the pro-Republican paper, the *Journal*, stepped up their attacks on "ignorance, graft, and neglect" in city government. By 1910 even the Democratic Dayton *Daily News* had joined Patterson, declaring that it accepted many of his ideas for improving the city, including his idea for a citizens' nonpartisan movement to uproot traditional party ties and change municipal government.[41]

By May 1913 E.W. Hanley, owner of the gasworks for the city, chair of the Democratic Committee, and Patterson's nemesis as the political boss of Dayton, complained, "Relative to bossism let me say that the title of boss as applied to me is a misnomer. . . . It is the natural result of local prejudice and antagonism, and many of my friends on the new good government platform will be carrying the title in a short while, and perhaps with greater emphasis, for the reason that so much of perfection and wonderful progress has been promised."[42]

The new city charter overwhelmingly endorsed by the citizens of Dayton in August 1913 did promise much of "perfection and wonderful progress." Central to the new document were a commission of five members elected at large on a nonpartisan ballot and a city manager appointed by the commission and subject to its dismissal. In one stroke the old ward council system disappeared.

Elections were to be held every two years, the three candidates receiving the greatest vote at the first election being chosen for a four-year term, the rest for two years. The candidate winning the largest number of votes at the election at which the greatest number of commissioners were elected received the title of mayor. The mayor, however, really was only one among other commissioners, since he had no additional power, and his special duties were only ceremonial in nature. All members of the commission, as well as the city manager, could be recalled should 25 percent of registered voters so demand in a signed petition.

In clear contrast with straight commission plans, the Dayton commissioners were to perform purely legislative duties. They were, for instance, responsible for appropriation ordinances and for city regulatory measures, such as codes to govern police conduct or public health. They had the common legislative power to investigate any city department.

The city manager, though ultimately subject to the will of the commission, was the absolute administrative head of city government, the person with the power to appoint and fix salaries for all immediate subordinates, including departmental heads and their deputies. In keeping with John H. Patterson's long-standing insistence on divisions of five in any corporate organizational scheme, there were to be five such departments: a department of law; a department of public service, concerned with street and sewer maintenance, waste disposal, and operation of public utilities; a department of public safety, merging the formerly separate police, fire, and building inspection departments; a department of finance, again combining former city bureaus of accounting, treasury, and purchasing; and finally, a department of public welfare, an entirely new creature in American municipal politics, to supervise city health, parks, playgrounds, charity work, and corrections.

The new city manager, however, did not have absolute power to hire and fire employees in any of these new departments. The 1913 charter also created a civil service board not subject to either the commission or the city manager. City employees relieved of their duties had the right to have charges reviewed by that board. Moreover, the city civil service board was to set guidelines for wages and could change a salary amount should it determine that city employees in different departments did equal work but did not earn equal pay. The city manager had to choose new employees from lists of those who had achieved at least minimum scores on separate civil service tests that the board, with the assistance of outside experts, was to devise for each particular department. Only department heads themselves could avoid the testing procedures.[43]

The Dayton Socialist party lost its fight to defeat this new charter in 1913. That loss, however, did not really mark the end of its campaign. For an additional four years, until 1917, the Socialists continued vigorously to oppose city manager government. Only after the municipal elections of 1917 was the new system secure.

In July 1913 Carl Thompson, secretary of a special committee established by the national Socialist party for the study of commission government in cities, published a lengthy summary of party reaction to the city manager and commission forms. That reaction could be easily condensed into one sentence: All commission and city manager forms lacked the vital element of democracy.[44] The Dayton local echoed that attack and added two other major issues. The city manager innovation was not only undemocratic, its claims of efficiency and economy were open to question. Finally, it was wrong to oppose municipal ownership of city services and utilities.

The Dayton Socialists outlined their reasons for calling the new Dayton charter less democratic than its predecessor in a broadside reprinted by the *Miami Valley Socialist* in 1913. Although the party's stump speakers and specific examples changed during the next four years, the basic issues did not. Four important changes in the city charter, according to the Socialists, made it a "brazen betrayal of working class to business interests."[45]

First, the charter adopted a system of balloting that limited the final election to the ten highest candidates at the primaries. It was, Socialists complained, a popularity contest, an arbitrary elimination that gave unfair advantage to the best-known or best-financed candidates.

Second, the charter abolished the ward system and instituted a nonpartisan election scheme under which all candidates ran, identified by name only, throughout the whole city. Under such a system, poor men could not afford to run, said Socialist opponents. Striking the party name off a ballot would not eliminate, as if by magic, the sins of city misgovernment. Rather, it would deny voters crucial information they needed to make intelligent decisions; voters had a right to know the political views of all candidates. The scheme would make proportional voting, under which minority groups received representation even if they did not win a straight majority, far more difficult to institute. Party affiliations would not disappear. Local politicians and citizens alike would continue to identify with state and national parties. The chance of political favoritism would not die. Voters would, however, on the local level lose their chance to identify Socialists, members of the one party that had a clearly distinct municipal, as well as state and national, program.

Third, the charter placed so-called democratic innovations,

promoted as mechanisms by which people could enjoy even greater control over their governments, out of reach. The initiative and referendum provisions of the Dayton charter were, according to Socialist opponents, made intentionally difficult to use. The initiative required that 10 percent of the voters bring an ordinance before the commission. And, if the commission rejected it, 25 percent of the city's registered voters had to sign petitions within a maximum time period of twenty days to force a referendum.

Fourth, the new charter forbade all officers of the city from soliciting or receiving contributions from any political party. That, Socialists argued, would hinder the efforts of Socialist candidates, who did not have either great personal wealth or the backing of powerful businessmen. Since the Democrats and Republicans in Dayton had largely acquiesced to the ascendance of the supposedly nonpartisan Citizens' Committee, accepting a quiet sort of merger and positioning themselves to receive substantial backing from the business community, the only political candidates genuinely hurt by the new election contribution rules were the Socialists.[46]

City manager government, then, was undemocratic, an attempt to "freeze out" the Socialists. It reduced the political clout of almost everyone outside a charmed circle of powerful businessmen. Moreover, Socialists charged, its promises of efficiency and economy were overblown. The Citizen's Committee's slate of five candidates won the November 1913 election for the actual selection of commissioners mandated by the August charter victory. The Socialist newspaper, labeling the new commissioners the "duly grateful five," analyzed election costs: "We note that the modest sum of $3,352.80 was expended in securing the 11,707 votes averaged by the above five, a cost of only 20¢ a vote, very efficient and economical. If we wished to make an odious comparison we might mention that the socialists spent $386.66 and averaged 6240 votes, a trifle over 6¢ a vote!"[47]

The "fake efficiency" of city manager government became a major issue for Socialists.[48] Rather than efficiency and economy, the major goal of city manager government was service to "Organized Business Interests."[49] In the course of that service, the new government increased the city budget by hundreds of thousands of dollars a year, plunged the city deeper into

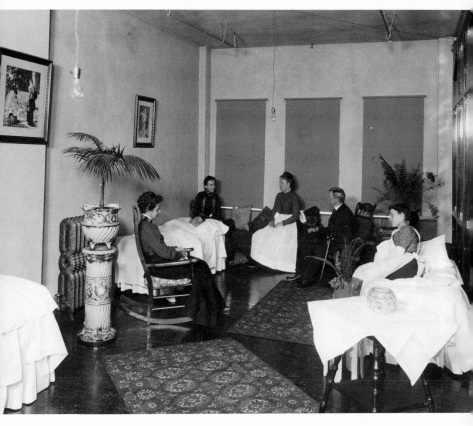

The "girls' rest room" at National Cash Register, 1901. NCR Archives

Above, National Cash Register buildings in the 1890s. The building on the left illustrates the NCR architectural revolution in factory design. *Below,* the NCR factory complex about 1928. NCR Archives

NCR women employees, wearing the uniform white aprons and sleevelets that the company president hoped would abolish class distinctions, perform exercises during a "rest" period. NCR archives

John H. Patterson. Miami
Conservancy District
Archives. *Below,* the NCR
Boys' Gardens in 1890.
NCR Archives

Downtown Dayton in March 1913; rowboats in foreground were built at NCR. *Below,* devastation in the wake of the great flood—Dayton in April 1913. Miami Conservancy District Archives

Flood victims converge on the NCR factory building, transformed into a huge relief station. *Below,* a mammoth cash register records the progress of the Flood Prevention Committee's subscription campaign in May 1913. Miami Conservancy District Archives

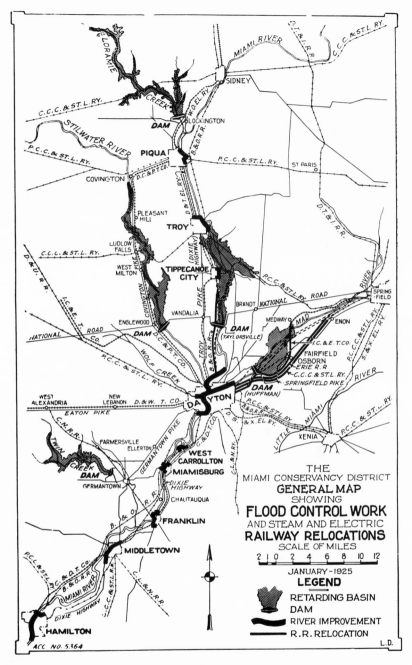

The following labels appear on the map:

LORAMIE CREEK
MIAMI RIVER
D.T.&I.R.R.
C.C.C.&ST.L. RY.
SIDNEY
C.C.C.&ST.L. RY.
STILWATER RIVER
W.O.EL.RY.
DAM
LOCKINGTON
B.&O.R.R.
PIQUA
P.C.C.&ST.L. RY.
COVINGTON
D.C.&P.T.CO.
P.C.C.&ST.L. RY.
ST PARIS
PLEASANT HILL
D.&T.EL.RY.
TROY
(DIXIE HIGHWAY)
LUDLOW FALLS
C.C.L.&ST.L. RY.
D.T.&I.R.R.
WEST MILTON
TIPPECANOE CITY
P.C.C.&ST.L. RY. ROAD
RIVER
SPRING-FIELD
D.&U.R.R.
COVINGTON PIKE
BRANDT NATIONAL
VANDALIA
I.C.&E.T.CO.
NATIONAL ROAD
CO.
ENGLEWOOD
DAM
TROY PIKE
DAM (TAYLORSVILLE)
MEDWAY MAD
ENON
I.C.&E.T.CO.
P.C.C.&ST.L. RY.
S.&X.EL.RY.
P.C.C.&ST.L. RY.
WOLF CREEK
FAIRFIELD
OSBORN
ERIE R.R.
C.C.&ST.L. RY.
SPRINGFIELD PIKE
RIVER
WEST ALEXANDRIA
NEW LEBANON
D.&W.T.CO.
D.C.&P.T.CO.
B.&O.R.R.
DAYTON
DAM (HUFFMAN)
D.S.
EATON PIKE
P.C.C.&ST.L. RY.
B.&O.R.R.
S.&X.EL.RY.
LITTLE MIAMI RIVER
P.C.C.&ST.L. RY.
C.N.R.R.
FARMERSVILLE
ELLERTON
GERMANTOWN PIKE
C.&D.T.CO.
C.L.&N. RY.
XENIA
P.C.C.&ST.L. RY.
TWIN CREEK
DAM
GERMANTOWN
WEST CARROLLTON
MIAMISBURG
DIXIE HIGHWAY
CHAUTAUQUA
R.R.
FRANKLIN
B.&O. R.R.
MIDDLETOWN
P.C.L.&ST.L. RY.
C.&O.T.CO.
B.&O.R.R.
C.C.&ST.L. RY.
C.L.&N.R.R.
MIAMI RIVER
DIXIE HIGHWAY
HAMILTON
ACC NO. 5.364

THE
MIAMI CONSERVANCY DISTRICT
GENERAL MAP
SHOWING
FLOOD CONTROL WORK
AND STEAM AND ELECTRIC
RAILWAY RELOCATIONS
SCALE OF MILES
2 1 0 2 4 6 8 10 12
JANUARY ~ 1925
LEGEND
RETARDING BASIN
DAM
RIVER IMPROVEMENT
R.R. RELOCATION

L.D.

Plan of the Miami Conservancy District, showing location
of the five dams and retarding basins. Miami Conservancy
District Archives

Arthur Morgan, about 1917. Miami
Conservancy District Archives.
Below, A cooking class for the
children of workers building the
Miami Conservancy District, about
1919. Arthur Morgan Papers

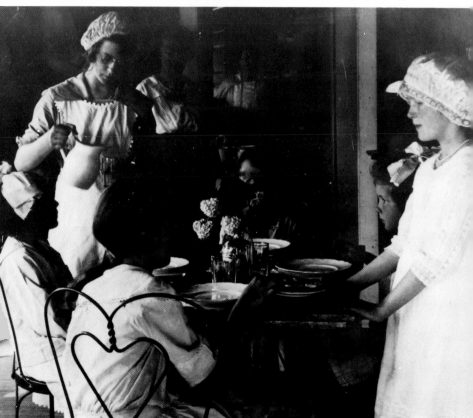

"bondage," at a rate of thousands of dollars a day, and finally saddled Dayton with "such a public debt that our children and our children's children will not be free of the burden."[50]

Socialists argued that true efficiency and economy demanded municipal ownership of city services and utilities. Do not, a Socialist editorial urged voters in 1915, consent to allow the city to borrow more money through bond issues for any purpose. First insist that it take over the profit-producing utilities and services operated in Dayton as city-supervised private franchises: "Take over . . . the gas plant that last year made a net profit of $204,434.80 or the electric light plant that is making about a million dollars a year or the city railway company."[51]

Socialists, thus, continued strenuously to oppose the new city government. Nevertheless, they did not sit on the sidelines. Instead they participated in the election system established by the new charter even as they decried it. Although they could no longer be elected from particular wards as the official candidates of the Socialist party, numerous Socialists did run for seats on the city commission. According to the new charter, of course, they could not campaign as Socialists. Technically they were only independent individuals whose names appeared with all the others on the mandatory nonpartisan ballot. Their participation guaranteed, until decisions made in the aftermath of the municipal elections of 1917 effectively shut off their access to local power, a continued fierce debate about the merits of the city manager innovation.

Even relatively trivial city actions could be subject to Socialist scrutiny, fodder for fiery speeches and the bitter, funny cartoons that enlivened the pages of the *Miami Valley Socialist*. For example, in 1914, when the city commissioners decided to present the citizens of Dayton with a municipal Christmas tree, the Socialist cartoonists had a field day. Drawings of pitiful evergreens adorned with one electric light appeared. This, Socialists crowed, was the city commission's pathetic idea of municipal ownership. And the commissioners themselves, generally drawn in these cartoons as bald buffoons orating from the back of flatbed trucks, could only promise that "when your wife and kids are hungry an' you're blue as blue can be, you'll find a lot of comfort in a municipal Xmas tree."[52]

Clearly many Daytonians listened to these Socialist attacks on city manager government. In the 1915 election to choose two commissioners, Willard Barringer, a Socialist printer, won the second highest number of votes in the unofficial count released immediately on November 5 by the board of elections. Barringer squeaked by the third-place finisher, John Flotron, a prominent Dayton businessman, by 10,872 votes to 10,860 votes. Socialists jubilantly took to the streets, banging a bass drum and assorted pots and pans, celebrating the apparent victory of their first Socialist city commissioner.[53] But when the board of elections completed its final count on November 12, it announced that John Flotron had been elected by two votes over Barringer: 10,875 votes for Flotron to Barringer's 10,873.[54]

The charter commission in 1913 had considered proportional voting systems and rejected them as unnecessarily complex. Had it not done so, the Socialists, who won 24 percent of the vote in 1915, would have gained at least a seat on the commission. But Barringer, officially, was simply just another candidate, another name on the nonpartisan ballot, a candidate who, when all the recounts had been finished, lost by two votes.

The Socialists, nonetheless, were emboldened by the extreme closeness of the vote. They felt, of course, that Barringer's seat had been stolen and began almost immediately to prepare for the next municipal election. In 1915, two years after the adoption of the charter, the terms of two of the first members of the commission expired. In 1917 the terms of the other three members first elected in 1913 expired. In 1917, then, voters could choose a majority in the commission. It was a crucial election for city manager government, one that given the close call in 1915 the Citizen's Committee forces had to win in order to forestall the kind of drastic charter changes the Socialists had proposed.

And it was an election during which Americanism, not the success of the new municipal system, was the most important issue. Of course by the summer of 1917, when campaigning began in earnest, the nation was at war. Three Socialists contended for the three open seats. Dan Farrell, a carpenter and real estate broker, and Charles Geisler, a machine shop foreman, joined Barringer. All three men sought municipal ownership of city services and utilities. All three pictured city manager government as government for the benefit of a business elite. All three asked Daytonians:

What has city government done for YOU?
Are YOUR taxes lower?
Is YOUR rent less?
Is YOUR job any steadier?[55]

By late summer, however, a campaign that began as a spirited debate about the success of commission-manager government turned ugly. The Socialists charged that the Citizen's Committee, having "exhausted facts and figures," tried "to hide their poor administration behind the Stars and Stripes."[56]

Certainly, the Stars and Stripes played a large role in the final months of the campaign, when Socialists stood accused of anti-war slackerism and un-American disloyalty. Socialists fought back, insisting that they too loved their country and had a duty to oppose its wrongheaded foreign policy. They circulated flyers promising a two-hundred-dollar reward to any person who could actually prove that they flew a red flag rather than the American flag at their meetings.[57]

But irony played a larger role in their counterattack. For instance, in a series of pamphlets and newspaper articles, they lampooned the whole 100 percent Americanism crusade. "Here are the facts" began one such satire:

On south Main Street in Dayton stands a Woolworth. A similar store is on E. Third. It may or may not be significant that these stores are painted red. Similar stores, similarly painted red . . . can be found in almost every town in the United States.

Upon the counters in these stores . . . are small books bound in imitation leather. It may or may not be significant that these books are red!

. . . Among these books we have found "Friendship and Other Essays" by Henry Thoreau.

The words "other essays" are a blind.

There is but one other essay.

That other essay is sufficiently revealed by its title: "On the Duty of Civil Disobedience."

We have on what seems reliable authority learned that the real owner of the Woolworth chain is none other than the Standard Oil group.

If this is correct, then the front of this conspiracy is none other than John D. Rockefeller.

Gentlemen of the American Protective League: You have been very active in going after the little fry, in this effort to root out sedition.

We commend you.

But do you dare go after the big fry?[58]

Such efforts, in the end, failed. Barringer, Geisler, and Farrell secured the three highest places in the August primary. Between August and November, the Citizens Committee spent an unprecedented amount, more than fifty thousand dollars, far more than had ever been spent on one election under the old regime. And most of that money went for unabashed red-baiting. The tactic worked. In November, Barringer, Geisler, and Farrell dropped to fourth, fifth, and sixth place. The three incumbent commissioners won reelection. Despite the fact that the Socialists received 43 percent of the total vote, they won no representation at all on the city commission.[59]

The die had been cast. In 1917 the campaign to establish city manager government was finally over, a victory for the Citizen's Committee and its business backers. Socialist candidates continued through the city elections of 1921 to poll respectable percentages of total votes cast. However, they were never able to win, in an at-large citywide election, even one of the two or three highest vote totals in a general election. Thus, they could garner almost half the total votes cast and win not a single commission seat. In such a system of at-large voting without proportional representation, the Socialists were doomed. That was clear, at least to those with the advantage of hindsight, by 1917. Probably not coincidentally, John H. Patterson, who had funneled tens of thousands of dollars of his own money into the Dayton Bureau of Municipal Research, ceased these substantial contributions in 1917. The bureau, whose primary function had been one of promoting the virtues of the new municipal form, found no other patron and soon folded.[60]

After 1917 few new members joined the Dayton Socialist party. By 1923 it had ceased to be a force for significant opposition in Dayton. It faced bankruptcy and sold its downtown Socialist Hall, in a transaction fraught with irony, to the Ku Klux Klan. By

1925 even the *Miami Valley Socialist* had ceased publication. The collapse of the Dayton party was not an isolated phenomenon. Rather, Socialists lost members and influence everywhere in the nation. Bitter internal fights about approaches to Soviet Bolshevism, coming in a time of external political repression, greatly weakened not only the national Socialist party but dozens of state organizations and hundreds of small locals.[61]

The victory of Dayton city manager government was not an isolated phenomenon either. The "Dayton model" proved tremendously influential throughout the nation. It, and not the simple commission innovation contained in the Galveston plan, proved to be the lasting legacy for progressive era municipal government change. By 1915 forty-five cities had chosen the commission-manager system pioneered in Dayton. By 1925 almost three hundred cities and towns had adopted city manager government. And half a century later the city manager form survived. By 1980 more than 2,500 city or town commissions had hired managers. By that time, only a handful of straight commission governments still existed. Even Galveston repealed its commission system in 1960.[62]

The Dayton commission-manager plan, then, had a lasting impact on systems of American municipal government. Was that impact, however, a legacy of business progressivism? A study of the campaign to change and then firmly establish a new form for Dayton city government everywhere shows the controlling hand of a powerful business elite. But a thorough attempt to answer questions about connections between business, progressivism, and commission-manager government demands analysis not just of the campaign itself, but also of the failures and achievements of the new city manager system in Dayton. That system's first decade, 1914-24, provides a useful time frame. By 1924 opponents of the change had met defeat. City manager government in Dayton showed signs of institutional security. A period of major experimentation and change had ended. Those changes, furthermore, the job of the manager itself and the roles played by the new city departments, had existed long enough by 1924 to have a history, long enough to provide evidence for judgments.

There is little question but that hundreds of Dayton business people, always threatened and pushed by John H. Patterson, provided the strong force behind the decades-long effort to change city government in Dayton. They promoted the new municipal government as businesslike and efficient. Was it? What, indeed, did the failures and achievements of commission-manager government illustrate about the nature and legacy of business progressivism?

An examination of the validity of the charges hurled in attack by the Socialist opposition during the years of campaigning provides a focus for judging Dayton's first decade as a city manager municipality. The Socialists charged that the new system was less democratic than the mayor-council form it replaced, not as efficient nor as economical as it claimed, and, finally, not truly innovative. Rather, it opposed major changes, such as municipal ownership, that would bring genuine efficiency and the greatest benefit to the largest number of people. City manager government was not a welcome reform but rather a ruse through which a whole community could be made "subservient" to business. It was "a businessman's government, by businessmen for businessmen, which has never done anything for the workingclass [*sic*] or the common people."[63]

The new city manager system was indeed less democratic, a fact accepted, openly or implicitly, even by some of its admirers. In August 1913 a generally enthusiastic report on the Dayton charter election in the New York *Evening Post* called the approved changes a move toward "cabinet government. . . . In other words commission government has swung around to the point of restoring the office of mayor, but with the difference that he is appointed [by the commission and called city manager] instead of being elected by the voters."[64] The journalist William Renwick called Dayton's first city manager, Henry Waite, an engineer from Cincinnati, an "autocrat" and a "czar."[65] He meant the words as praise.

Although the city commission hired Waite and could fire him at will, both it and the city manager stood subject to provisions for referendum and recall in the city charter. But as the Socialists pointed out, these provisions offered little protection. The charter committee had considered and rejected proportional representation. It had also considered and rejected a requirement that only 10 percent of the city's qualified voters needed to sign petitions in order to initiate a referendum issue or a recall of the manager or a member of the commission. Both proportional representation and a 10 percent signature requirement had been included as recommendations in a majority report of the National Municipal League's Committee on the Commission Form of Government.[66] And the time allowed under the new charter for the collection of signatures, only twenty days, was quite short. The Socialists were also correct in noting that the institution of the nonpartisan ballot weakened the initiative, referendum, and recall. The ballot sought to curb the power of political organizations. But weaker political organizations meant that the people had a harder time using the "direct democracy" weapons of initiative, referendum, and recall because all three required the kind of organized publicity, time, and money most readily provided by healthy political parties.

In truth, the petitioning process often did prove slow and unsatisfactory. In 1914 the Socialists tried to put on the ballot an initiative demanding a municipal electric plant but failed in the face of organized opposition from the Dayton Power and Light Company. Unable to match Dayton Power and Light's budget for pamphlets and other informational materials, and compelled to gather signatures quickly, the Socialists did not succeed in getting one-fourth of the registered voters to sign their petition. In 1915 the United Trades and Labor Council joined with the Socialists to collect signatures on a petition to amend the city charter. Within the twenty-day limit, they collected signatures from the requisite minimum of at least 25 percent of voters eligible to vote in a previous municipal election. Their petition demanded that the 25 percent figure necessary to initiate the referendum process be reduced by charter amendment to 10 percent. The new commission, only installed in office weeks before, instructed the city clerk to examine each signature to determine its authenticity, though such a thorough search had not been mandated by the charter document. At the commission's instruction, several secretaries prepared a card index of the names and addresses of petition signers, to be checked against voter registration information at city hall. After four weeks, the commission announced that a number of the signers were no longer residents of the precincts in which they had last registered to vote and that a number had not signed in ink. Therefore, since it could not consider all signatures valid, and the time in which to collect signatures had elapsed, the Dayton Commission refused to order

a referendum election on the amendment issue.[67] Not surprisingly, given these kinds of barriers, the direct democracy
devices of initiative, referendum, and recall written into the
Dayton charter remained essentially unused.

Of course some contemporary analysts worried that the
Dayton charter was too democratic. Herman James, a professor at
the School of Government at the University of Texas, summarized
the views of other progressives when he scolded Dayton for its
charter provision allowing recall of the city manager. "We have
made a long stride in the right direction when we discard the
fallacy of trying to elect expert administrators by popular vote,"
said James. "Let us not slide back half way or more by allowing
popular vote to determine whether or not such an administrator
shall continue in office."[68]

Unquestionably many progressives went even further than
James. Arthur Morgan of course did not arrive in Dayton until
1913, in the wake of the flood disaster. But he remained in
southern Ohio after the Conservancy dams were completed as
the new president of Antioch College. So during the period
1914-24, Morgan wore several hats—those of engineer, efficiency
expert, educator. In all these roles, he argued frequently that all
levels of government, beginning but not ending with the local,
needed to be even further "professionalized." Morgan argued,
for instance, that for Ohio and Dayton to be true models, the state
too should be considered a public corporation, with all its cities
and counties similarly organized. An elected council of five or ten
men would act as the state's equivalent of a board of directors.
This council would pass laws, determine policies, and appoint all
administrative officers, starting with the governor. These administrative officers certainly need not be state residents, but they
should be, like Morgan himself, expert professionals free to serve
anywhere. As Morgan fantasized, "If the governor of Nevada
should exhibit unusual ability, he might be sought by Colorado."[69]

Nevertheless, the fact remained that Dayton's new commission-manager form was less democratic than the mayor-council
system it replaced. But concern for increasing citizen participation was not a hallmark of business progressivism. John H. Patterson had not taken a poll of his workers before inaugurating
welfare work at the NCR. Edward A. Deeds had not tried to

increase public participation in the decision-making processes of the Miami Conservancy District. Concern with efficiency and economy, not democracy, had characterized these other instances of business-directed progressive reform. It characterized the city manager campaign as well.

But was the innovation more efficient and economical? Did the Socialist challenge, that the new form benefited "the plutes" but did not really bring efficient government to the people, contain truth?[70] An examination of the leadership of the new city government and of the operations of the two new city departments most often identified by supporters as examples of progressive reform can help provide an answer.

Clearly, to use the Socialists' phrase, the "plutes" controlled the commission during Dayton's first decade as a commission-manager city. Citizen's Committee candidates controlled all the seats. And most of those candidates were businessmen. The makeup of the first commission, seated in January 1914, was illustrative. John H. Patterson rejected the Citizen's Committee's pleas to head its ticket, saying he wished to remain a private citizen. So, the successful Committee candidates sitting on the new commission were John R. Flotron, John McGee, George Shroyer, Jesse M. Switzer, and Albert Mendenhall. John Flotron, already well-known within the business community as the head of the Rouzer Company, a producer of iron molds and framing machinery, became a celebrity as a member of the five-person Citizens' Relief Committee that directed flood recovery efforts under John H. Patterson's leadership.[71] McGee headed the wholesale millinery firm of Steeley & Co. As president of the Dayton Bicycle Club, he too emerged as a civic hero during the 1913 flood, the coordinator of the massive job of cleaning city streets and buildings. George Shroyer was a prominent wholesale merchant, and Jesse M. Switzer was office supervisor of the NCR.[72] Only Albert Mendenhall, perpetually damned by the Socialists as the "ever meek and faithful Mendenhall" was not a businessman but rather a printer and union member.[73]

Unlike many other "progressive cities," where businessmen favored a change to commission government but did not run for office, Dayton business leaders themselves dominated the commission.[74] The regular inclusion of Mendenhall on the Citizen's Committee slate did not indicate that a significant alliance between business and labor had been forged. Most officers of the United Trades and Labor Council favored the Socialist arguments. Their pledges of support more often appeared in the *Miami Valley Socialist* than the Dayton *Daily News,* and the union printer they supported for city commissioner was Willard Barringer, not Albert Mendenhall.[75]

Rather, in Dayton commission-manager government between 1914 and 1924 was, quite literally, a "hand-picked" businessmen's government.[76] Did it succeed in leading Dayton to a new era of what it and admirers promised would be "completely businesslike" government?[77] In 1916 the Patterson-funded Dayton Bureau of Research issued a bulletin that argued that "business" government in Dayton should be judged by business standards, by the results achieved by the new city departments, just as "the success of a factory is determined by its product."[78]

Of the five reorganized city departments created by the 1913 charter—the departments of law, public service, safety, welfare, and finance—the latter two, welfare and finance, most clearly were progressive "products." They best reflected efforts by the new business-led government to reform and improve community life in Dayton while at all times emphasizing the principles of economy and efficiency.

In August 1913, while campaigning for the acceptance of the Citizen's Committee charter draft, Fred Rike gave a speech describing "the spirit behind the charter." It was, he said, a "spirit of welfare and social service." Should the new charter be adopted, Dayton could begin to enjoy government based on business models and scientific management principles. But, Rike exhorted, "When anybody tells you that this charter is a rich man's document . . . tell them it is a lie."[79]

The new city Department of Public Welfare exemplified Rike's promise. Previous straight commission governments had been widely criticized for focusing too exclusively on the bottom line of profit and loss.[80] The creators of Dayton's Department of Public Welfare challenged that view. The commission-manager form need not be heartless. Efficient, business-minded government need not neglect either public service or humane concern for the health and welfare of average citizens.

The 1913 charter split the work of the new welfare department into five divisions: a division of health, of correction, of recreation, of parks, and finally of charities and legal aid. Before 1914 the work of the city Health Department had focused on two functions: birth and death registration, and quarantine and fumigation duties during epidemics. The new city Division of Health, much in keeping with the progressives' willingness to expand greatly the government's role in disease prevention and maintenance of public health, vastly expanded the rudimentary duties of its predecessor.

Within ten years, the Division of Health (in contrast to the Board of Health with its five unpaid members under the old regime) employed five physicians and twenty-two city nurses, one food inspector, three meat inspectors, two dairy inspectors, one bakery inspector, six sanitary officers, three chemists, and a staff of seven clerks and secretaries. The physicians worked in new, citywide vaccination programs, answered police and fire calls, and began the "scientific management" of the health of Daytonians, initiating, for example, a system in which area hospitals "scored" newborns by recording such characteristics as weight and responses to loud noises. Under the supervision of the Division of Health physicians, Dayton schoolchildren for the first time received regular testing of their hearing and eyesight. The nurses provided free care for the indigent, concentrating on the care of poor mothers and infants. Health officers began to enforce new city ordinances that demanded more rigorous municipal scrutiny of the meat and milk consumed in the city. Dairies and abattoirs within a thirty-mile radius of Dayton submitted to twice-yearly inspections of their facilities. They also sent samples of their products to the new city laboratory, which in addition to testing foods consumed by the public conducted regular examinations of the city water supply. In the course of a year the staff of health officers made tens of thousands of unannounced visits to meat shops, fruit stores, restaurants, groceries, and bakeries.[81]

Before 1914 Dayton kept its prisoners in a jail constructed in 1840 for not more than seventy-five individuals. Sometimes, however, more than two hundred inmates were crowded into the fetid stone building. When not sleeping two or three men to a bed, prisoners hunched in corridors making mouse- and rattraps to send to a Cincinnati firm that supplied materials and paid Dayton officials forty-five cents a day per prisoner for labor. By 1912 conditions at the city workhouse, always bad, had become intolerable. The building's roof leaked badly and regularly soaked the beds of inmates. The workhouse director even had to admit, when questioned by members of the Dayton City Council, that he did not have enough clothes for his prisoners. Instead, he said, "prisoners have to take to their beds while clothing's washed."[82]

The new Division of Corrections abolished this system. It forbade the heretofore accepted practice of beatings as punishment, allowed prisoners to talk at meals, and set them to work at various kinds of jobs for the city: cleaning streets, cutting weeds, or working in the large new corrections farm on the outskirts of town.

The Division of Corrections purchased 107 acres in 1916 for this farm. The prisoners themselves built its dormitories, sheds, and outbuildings. They grew all their own food and distributed the surplus to the city's poor through the Division of Charities. Completed in 1920, the corrections farm could house 350 inmates comfortably. Proponents of these radical changes in Dayton's corrections policies argued that they represented the best of progressive reform. They were not only more humane, even offering the chance for genuine rehabilitation of criminals, but they also saved money. Costs for feeding prisoners, for example, dropped dramatically after 1914, averaging five rather than seventeen cents per meal by 1916.[83]

City programs for parks and recreation also underwent widespread change. The new heightened interest reflected most directly the transfer of business welfare work practices to the public arena. The crucial role of John H. Patterson in area philanthropy enabled such a rapid transfer. In effect, his NCR gardening, recreation, and parks projects were relabeled as the new city divisions of parks and of recreation. Until his death in 1922, however, Patterson continued, in addition to supplying thousands of dollars of his own money to maintain the programs, to send the city written pledges to make up for deficits incurred in its gardening and recreational programs.

And those park and recreational activities were extensive, including supervised playgrounds, dancing, band concerts, bathing, boating, and city-sponsored baseball leagues. By 1917 all gardening work in the city had been coordinated under city control. The city Parks Division supplied land, seed, and advice to thousands of city gardeners. It created two thousand vacant lot gardens for adults and more than three thousand gardens for boys and girls. In 1918 Patterson gave three hundred acres of parkland and much of the NCR Country Club to the city of Dayton.[84]

Finally, the city's new Welfare Department sought to centralize and redefine public charity work. Its Legal Aid Bureau provided free advice for the indigent. A lawyer paid by the city helped poor people secure wages unjustly withheld, settle room rent disputes with landlords, or reconcile claims of bills owed pawnbrokers. The city, moreover, rented quarters for the Door of Hope, a home for unwed mothers, and built a Municipal Lodging House to provide temporary shelter for homeless men. City officials argued that these municipal actions combined charity with hard-headed business practicality. When the commission approved an ordinance creating the Municipal Lodging House, for example, it also approved an ordinance forbidding vagrancy or begging on the streets of Dayton. Any vagrant wishing sleeping quarters in the new lodging house had first to bathe and then agree to work the next morning for the city to repay the costs of his bed and breakfast. City Manager Waite boasted that the new system not only humanely provided warm quarters for those who truly needed them, but it also reduced vagrancy in Dayton. "Our municipal lodging house," he noted in a letter, "is very poorly patronized . . . the professional vagrant gives Dayton the go-by."[85]

By 1924 the Department of Public Welfare had involved the city in some activities, like city-sponsored vegetable gardens, that previously had concerned private philanthropy only and had revolutionized other, more traditional functions, such as treatment of criminals. The department had 101 salaried employees, excluding the prisoners who worked in the parks and playgrounds throughout the year.[86]

Not all the experiments were completely successful, however. Few people went to the new, city-owned Hills and Dales Community Country Club. The land, part of the large Patterson family holdings south of the city, was certainly too distant to permit walking for most city residents, and the city, unlike NCR before it, did not provide free transportation. The daily admission fee of ten cents, coupled with ten cents carfare each way, probably put the cost of a day's outing at the new city park out of the reach of many working-class families. Patterson had to make good his promise to cover deficits in operating costs, up to four thousand dollars a year, each year until his death.[87]

The city also hired an "elderly" and "increasingly feeble" old woman, a Mother Clark, as matron at the Door of Hope. As a result, the city home for unwed mothers became a Door to Bedlam as the hapless Mother Clark gave away babies for adoption without bothering to do the necessary paperwork, housed women with tuberculosis in rooms with new babies, and persisted in burning coal oil lamps all night in rooms wired for electric lights.[88]

Nor was the Department of Public Welfare untouched by political legerdemain. In December 1917 Dr. A.L. Light, the city's health officer since 1914, resigned. Light, a man not known for his tact, had been a vigorous advocate of major, citywide inoculation and vaccination programs. In October and November of 1917 he had publicly chastised several prominent Daytonians, including Valentine Winters, banker and street railway owner, for lack of cooperation in the vaccination programs among their employees. When rumors surfaced that members of the Citizen's Committee were pressuring Light to resign, fearing a loss of support in some powerful quarters should the crusading and abrasive city health officer remain, a group of nearly eighty of Dayton's leading physicians went to the commission. They brought with them a signed demand that Light not be forced out, arguing that any physician who took the job of city health officer had to be free to enforce health codes and ordinances without pressure. Notwithstanding this evidence of support from his fellow physicians, the commission accepted A.L. Light's "resignation."[89]

The Department of Public Welfare, then, did not enjoy unimpeded success with all its programs, nor was it immune to political pressure in a city that had supposedly wholeheartedly embraced the principle of nonpartisanship. Nevertheless, it existed as a model of what business-led progressive reform could accomplish. City social services were indeed transformed. Daytonians in 1924 had more reason than in 1914 to trust the purity of the foods they ate and the water they drank. Their city treated its criminal and vagrant populations with a combination of humanity and efficiency unknown to the old regime. The poverty-stricken could seek out not only a city-funded bed but also a city-funded lawyer. Even though the bureaus for Sanitation and Legal Aid constantly (and correctly) pleaded that their budgets were inadequate to the tasks assigned them, genuine improvements had been made. And not only the "plutes" benefited.

Obviously the question, But were these services provided in a more efficient and economical manner? was a moot one. Most of them had not been provided at all to the citizens of Dayton before 1914. Proponents of commission-manager government argued that the new divisions operated by the most economical financial practices available. Those practices were those dictated to the Welfare Department and to every other city department by the other progressive centerpiece, the Department of Finance.

That department drastically revised traditional city purchasing and accounting practices to conform with private business practices. Prior to 1914 it had been customary for each department of Dayton city government to purchase its own supplies independently. The new Department of Finance forbade that practice and instituted a central purchasing office, headed by a new city official, the city purchasing agent. That agent had to buy in wholesale quantities for the year's needs. Moreover, only items the quality of which could be determined in the city laboratory through a range of newly devised standardization tests, and items, which by their nature permitted competitive bidding, could be purchased. No item was too insignificant to escape a city specification code. Within a year, specifications existed for almost any kind of supplies or equipment city departments might conceivably require. Those wishing to bid to sell soap, boots, fire hoses, gasoline, water hydrants, or shirts for city farm prisoners, to name only a few of hundreds of items, first had to examine the specification sheets. The emphasis on central stores, competitive bidding, and standardization brought immediate savings. Before 1914 each city office could order its own stationery, and letterhead paper, purchased in lots of one thousand sheets, averaged $16 per thousand. When the city purchasing agent decreed a standardized city letterhead, to be used by all bureaus and departments, the price dropped dramatically. In 1914 the price for city stationery was $2.65 per thousand. The elaborate standards sheets kept by the Department of Finance recorded the savings for lengthy lists of items. For instance, flashlights, bought by the 1913 city government for $2.50 each, cost the 1914 commission-manager government $0.95. Rubber bands, $4.00 per pound in 1913, cost $1.26 per pound in 1914.[90]

The new Finance Department transformed accounting practice as well as purchasing practice. As was common in most American cities, Dayton in 1913 had an accounting system that afforded a check over cash receipts and disbursements only. To the horrified businessmen who ran the commission after 1914 it was barely an accounting system at all. To these advocates of the new management techniques changing American business structure the existing city procedures by which to control monies were, to say the least, lax. There were no cost records for city repairs and construction work. There was no way to make sure that a person who received city pay was actually doing city work. Vouchers for day labor were issued, if they were issued at all, from individual boss's time books. All city workers, not just day laborers, received their pay in cash, though time schedules for payment varied within departments. There was, in fact, no definite city payroll. Property records did not exist.

Under the new system, all accounting was to be done through a central office. And that central office revised the city's accounting system from a cash basis to an accrual basis, with the ability to monitor appropriations, accounts receivable and accounts payable.[91]

Supporters of the charter change in 1913 had predicted that with the advent of such modern business accounting practices the city manager would be able to control expenditures. Like a general manager for a business, he would force the city "corporation" to live within its current income. The years of debt and waste in city government would be only memories.[92]

They in fact were not. Instead, between 1914 and 1924 the bonded debt for the city of Dayton increased significantly. In January 1914 Dayton's general debt was $5,743,380. By 1922 the debt increases had stabilized, but the city's total debt level was much higher: $8,106,480.[93] The city of Dayton had not succeeded under commission-manager government in living within its current income. Rather, city officials had repeatedly campaigned for the passage of bond issues to raise extra municipal revenues. By 1919 the Socialists mocked,

Another little bond issue to be voted into the hands of the
Efficiency and Economy Gang at City Hall! Only $3,153,700.
this time!

They've spent that measly little million they got in 1915;
and they've gaily come back—just like the second story
worker who got away with the spoons and comes back,
encouraged, for the jewelry.[94]

In their defense, city officials and supporters offered several
explanations for the increased city indebtedness. First, they argued, Dayton had had to cope with a staggering increase in
population. Between 1900 and 1920 the city's size had doubled. A
city with 85,333 people in 1900, Dayton had 152,559 residents by
1920 and continued to grow.[95] More than half of those new
residents poured into the city after 1913, drawn first by the high
wages offered by wartime industry after 1917. During World
War I Dayton produced airplanes, tanks, shell fuses, Liberty motors, gun sights, and numerous other war materiel items. Many
skilled workers who came to the city to take war jobs remained as
Dayton turned again in the 1920s to the production of cash
registers, automobiles, and other new "necessities" of the new
era. This great influx of people severely burdened city services,
already strained by the steep rises in costs of goods and services
caused by wartime inflation. Defenders of the city manager system argued that revenues were not commensurate with such a
quick increase in demands. And of course after Prohibition, the
city lost a major source of municipal income, the liquor tax.[96]

Second, supporters blamed state law for making it difficult to
generate sufficient revenues without incurring bonded debt. In
1912 the Ohio legislature had passed the home rule amendment.
But earlier, in 1910, it had passed a taxation measure known
universally as the Smith One Percent Law. That law limited all
taxes levied for state, county, school, township, or city purposes
to fifteen mills, or fifteen dollars on each one thousand dollars of
assessed property values. Moreover, the bill established a maximum tax levy for these five taxing districts of ten mills, or 1
percent, on the dollar for current operating expenses.

The state legislators who passed the Smith Law intended, by
stating maximum tax rates, to place all real property on the tax

lists at 100 percent of its genuine value. But city officials argued that all the ensuing taxing restrictions hampered them unfairly. Without real control over their finances, they lacked an essential ingredient of true home rule. Instead, Ohio municipalities were prisoners of counties, which under the provisions of the Smith Law actually had the power to make adjustments in rates among the state's taxing districts. In reality then, a county budget commission, composed of the county auditor, county treasurer, and county prosecuting attorney, actually fixed tax rates in Ohio. Cities like Dayton protested that they had no voice in their own tax rates. Instead they received only what percentages of maximum taxes were left after state, counties, and schools had had first, second, and third choice.[97]

This revenue allocation system, the creation of a state legislature still controlled by rural representatives, unfairly punished cities. What's more, Dayton commission-manager supporters argued, it did so just when cities such as Dayton faced tremendous burdens. Cities throughout Ohio, but especially in southern Ohio, had been devastated by the great 1913 floods. Unable to generate the necessary operating expenses through taxes, Dayton had no other alternative than bonded debt. Indeed, the most significant of the increases in that debt were taken to finance the flood prevention work of the Miami Conservancy District. And as J.E. Barlow, Dayton city engineer and Henry Waite's successor in 1918 as the city's second city manager, argued, the superstructures of the city had been built in the midnineteenth century and were badly out of date by the early twentieth. The parts of the sewer system that survived the flood, for instance, accommodated a city of 50,000 people, not 150,000. Dayton, then, in the wake of flood devastation, had to rebuild its streets, sewers, and bridges. It had to reconstruct and enlarge its water supply and storage systems. And of course all this work cost money. Many of the bonds issued between 1914 and 1924 financed such construction. The million-dollar 1915 bond issue denounced by the Socialists, for example, funded a new city waterworks plant. And supporters of the commission-manager system argued that it provided a whole range of new services, such as those offered by the Department of Public Welfare.[98]

Finally, defenders of the new municipal government argued that when the new city services, buildings, waterworks, flood protection systems, and other improvements counted as assets, to be subtracted from debt, the total debt increase incurred was really not significant. As Chester Rightor, until 1917 the director of the Dayton Bureau of Research, put it, the question to ask was, "What does the citizen and taxpayer get in return for the taxes he pays?"[99]

An objective observer would have to say that, in terms of issues of economy and efficiency, that return was indeed considerable in Dayton. The Socialists were wrong. The "Economy and Efficiency Gang" they opposed brought genuine, not false, efficiency to city hall. In the face of truly monumental tasks, which included rebuilding a flood-devastated city, helping to finance a huge flood prevention project, and significantly expanding city services—all during years when rising prices and staggering increases in city population added extra burdens—it performed well. During years when the aggregate increase for school, county, and state government in Ohio had been 120 percent, the cost of Dayton city government increased only 28 percent.[100]

The Socialists argued, in their final major objection to commission-manager government, that true efficiency would only come with municipal ownership. But it was an option, they charged, that the new city leaders refused to consider. Here the Socialist charges were accurate ones, but because Dayton did not adopt municipal ownership of transportation services and utilities, questions about the genuine efficiency such a system might have brought to the city remained unanswered.

In the 1896 speech with which he so dramatically launched his crusade to change his city's government, John H. Patterson had argued, "It is a small matter to manage a city, for we have nothing to do but spend money; whereas in a large business we have not only to spend money, but to spend it in such a way as to make money in return, which increases the difficulty tenfold."[101]

Of course their very optimism was a badge of their membership in the progressive effort, but even the enormously self-confident businessmen who took their seats on the new Dayton City Commission soon learned that city government was not a "small matter." Rather, the legacy of their changes, like the legacy of business progressivism itself, was an ambiguous one.

Using the standards by which they most frequently judged themselves, improvements in efficiency and economy, the businessmen reformers who played such a large role in bringing city manager government to Dayton succeeded. They won a chance to try the system during truly wrenching times when the new city leaders had to cope with the aftermath of an enormous flood disaster, with wartime mobilization, with tremendous population increases, and with a Byzantine state taxing system heavily controlled by county officials. They managed, nevertheless, to hold levels of debt increase far below county and state levels, while increasing levels of services to citizens far above county and state levels. Almost every Daytonian reaped a benefit even if he or she did not realize it. At the end of an inaugural decade of commission-manager government, the average city resident had a much better chance of escaping communicable diseases, like tuberculosis, that thrived in conditions of poor sanitation. He or she certainly was not as likely to sicken from eating spoiled meat or tainted milk. Far fewer families lost babies in infancy. In fact the infant mortality rate in Dayton dropped by half between 1914 and 1924, a percentage figure well ahead of improvements achieved by other urban areas.[102]

But "business model" government exacted a price, and that price was a high one. It was a system that was actually, as the Socialists had charged, less democratic. Moreover, it was a system less willing to consider government alternatives, such as municipal ownership, that precluded opportunities for private investment and profit. It was, indeed, government that served more than it challenged the interests of the private business associations that had played such a crucial role in its creation.

Interestingly, a lack of democracy and flexibility was not inherent in the commission-manager form. Rather, these defects could be attributed to business domination in Dayton. In its early studies of the straight commission and commission-manager municipal systems, the National Municipal League had urged inclusion of charter provisions guaranteeing the initiative, referendum, and recall. It had also advocated the use of some kind of proportional voting system. By 1918 that recommendation had become stronger. Prompted by the vigorous lobbying of members like the historian Charles Beard, the secretary of the National Municipal League, Clinton Rogers Woodruff, called proportional representation "essential" if the commission-manager system were to be genuinely democratic. In a keynote speech to the Fifth Annual

Meeting of the City Managers' Association, an organization of which the city of Dayton had been an institutional founder in 1914, Woodruff singled out Dayton for condemnation. "I have no desire," he said, "to under-estimate the importance of . . . business men in a community, but we all realize that a community is made up of other elements as well. The great mass of the community is made up of people who are not identified as business men. . . . [But] in Dayton, the commission [is] made up of a group of men elected by one element in the community, leaving the other element for the time being, at least, unrepresented."[103] Woodruff was not the only prominent critic of Dayton's "unrepresentative" government. C.C. Hoag, secretary of the American Proportional Representation League, worried that Dayton "was dividing itself in two," into a "labor half" and a "commercial half," by so openly refusing representation on its commission to significant groups within its population.[104] City managers of cities like Kalamazoo, Michigan, assured meetings of fellow city managers that the proportional representation plans their commissions had adopted brought fairer representation of disparate groups without a sacrifice of efficiency.[105]

But any scheme of proportional voting would have revived some form of representation of organizations within the commission. In 1911 the Socialists had won Dayton's third and tenth wards, sending two party members to sit on the city council. With almost half the vote in 1917 they would surely have equalled that record and gained one or more seats on the Dayton City Commission. With those seats men like Willard Barringer or Dan Farrell would have pressed for municipal ownership of city transportation and utilities systems.

Here too, municipal ownership was not automatically opposed by city manager systems. In fact, when in January of 1924 Cleveland, a city with more than 800,000 people, became the largest council-manager city in the United States, it operated under a new charter that allowed municipal ownership. But in Dayton, the streetcars, gasworks, and electric light plant remained in private hands, operating under franchise to the city. Even before the adoption of the 1913 charter the Socialists had asked, "Would Dayton pay 85¢ for gas under municipal ownership?" That question remained unanswered a decade later. The Socialists argued that a municipally owned gas plant could offer citizens gas at rates of thirty cents per one thousand cubic feet, rather than eighty-five cents. Had their suggestion been tried and proved right, of course, Dayton government would have saved most city residents significant amounts of money.[106] But experiments with municipal ownership, which would have challenged the Dayton City Commission's franchise arrangements with private business, did not occur, even though the Socialists were not the only ones who declared that true city efficiency demanded that the idea at least be tested.

Numerous, more respectably conservative progressives agreed with Socialist arguments about the efficiency inherent in municipal ownership of transportation and utilities. University professors, mayors, journalists, and even some city managers argued that publicly owned utilities declared no dividends except in lower rates and better services, and cited the lower electric and gas rates enjoyed by citizens in places like Pasadena, California, or Tacoma, Washington, under municipal ownership.[107] But with the exception of its waterworks, already municipal property before 1913, Dayton continued to allow private business to operate its transportation systems and utilities.

In a debate on the merits of municipal ownership held at the Ninth Annual Meeting of the City Manager Association, Delos Wilcox, a journalist and public utility consultant, said that "this business" of franchise granting by cities reminded him of that "celebrated young woman":

> There was a young lady of Niger,
> Who smiled as she rode on the tiger,
> They came back from the ride,
> With the lady inside,
> And the smile on the face of the tiger.[108]

Daytonians did end up inside. But in truth, the stomach of commission-manager government was not all that uncomfortable a place in which to be. As they had before, in the creation of NCR welfare work programs and in the construction of the Miami Conservancy District, the business leaders who crafted city manager government in Dayton during the progressive era had the welfare of average people in mind. They genuinely wanted to improve the lives of their fellow citizens. But city manager government, like these other two projects, illustrated not just the achievements but also the limits of business-led progressive reform. In each case, businessmen-reformers brooked little popular interference with their "grand plans." They constructed barriers, such as the Citizen's Committee majority-take-all nonpartisan election rules, which nullified effective protest. And such rules accentuated the very class conflict progressives presumably dreaded.

But they did not really manage to remove city administration from politics. Henry Waite and his two successors openly campaigned for bond issues and other commission-approved measures between 1914 and 1924. In fact Waite came to believe that such involvement "was not such a bad idea after all." Discussing the 1915 waterworks bond issue, he claimed that he had to involve himself: "The commissioners threw up their hands and said that I was the one to sell the policy."[109]

Waite's experience was not unique. Edwin Fort, city manager for Niagara Falls, New York, argued that "the ordinary business man, the highest type of citizen we have, the man who is fundamentally the best fitted [to serve on city commissions]—is a busy man. Nine out of ten times he is not willing to spend his nights and days in continually campaigning before the public on one subject or another . . . He would prefer to see the burden of selling the proposed plan . . . thrown on the city manager."[110]

So the business progressives' commission-manager system in Dayton, in common with manager systems elsewhere, did not succeed entirely in sheltering the city manager and other municipal executives from political participation. What it did shelter, to a greater degree than had existed before 1913, was the structure of municipal government itself from popular control. And perhaps as a form of response, percentages of registered voters participating in municipal elections dropped.[111]

Here too the problem was not unique to Dayton. Evidence of declining public interest in municipal elections under commission and commission-manager systems was a common topic for debate at meetings of the National Municipal League and the City Manager's Association. A.R. Hatton, field director of the National Municipal League, summarized the general reaction of his colleagues at such conventions when in 1921 he said, "I have quit worrying about getting every voter out . . . I don't see, for my

part, why we should consider it so tremendously important to get
a person to come to the polls and vote if he merely casts an
unintelligent ballot after he gets there."[112]

It was an attitude that the businessmen-reformers who brought
city-manager government to Dayton shared. It was an attitude
that sometimes warped the institutions that were their progressive legacy.

5

Educational Engineering

The legacy left by the long fight in Dayton to establish "business-like" city manager government was an important one. Indeed, the eventual victory of the Citizen's Committee affected not just governmental institutions. In interesting ways, changes at the schoolhouse even more than changes at city hall illuminated the complicated nature of business involvement with the progressive movement.

John H. Patterson often liked to say that "business is only a form of teaching. You teach people to desire your product. You teach workmen how to make the right product. . . . You teach others to cooperate with you."[1] A concern with the proper education of its employees permeated the NCR's innovations in welfare work. The businessmen who directed the Miami Conservancy and the city manager campaigns frequently portrayed themselves as teachers. The people of the Miami Valley often emerged in their explanations of their activities as students, sometimes unruly students, but, willingly or not, students in the progressive businessman's "classroom." If they would only learn their lessons correctly, they would come to see what benefits they would derive from NCR's new factory system, from Deeds's Conservancy District, from Patterson's innovations in municipal government.[2] And the techniques used to build support for these new ideas were those of the teacher: slide shows, lectures, pamphlets and newsletters, "experts" sent into neighborhoods to inform and reassure.

The question, What impact did business progressives have on the schools themselves? is, then, a logical one. Few areas in the country experienced such intense experimentation—at both public and private schools, and at the grade school, high school, and college level—with what even contemporaries called progressive education.

An analysis of the history of the private Moraine Park School, of changes in the Dayton public schools between 1908 and 1929, and of the "revolution" at Antioch College in the 1920s provides diverse examples of educational institutions being profoundly influenced and often changed by the region's self-described progressive business community. Such an analysis provides another vehicle for examining the nature of business progressivism. And like welfare work, or scientific engineering, or commission-manager local government, the phenomenon of progressive education has stirred scholarly controversies that can benefit from an in-depth examination of its history in one region.

Few historians would challenge the statement that American society became increasingly concerned with education, especially public education, in the late nineteenth and early twentieth centuries. In Massachusetts and Connecticut public school systems were founded by prominent schoolmen like Horace Mann and Henry Bernard before the Civil War, but most states did not establish adequate school systems until the mid- to late nineteenth century. By the 1870s, however, drives to provide universal primary public education rapidly gained momentum. At the time of the First World War most American communities had established "common" school systems that provided at least some form of education free to their children.

By the turn of the century, as the country's industrial economy matured, literacy became a basic requirement for more and more jobs. Moreover, as millions of new immigrants flooded into the country, American towns and cities could no longer assume that their residents shared a common religion or a common language. Schools thus were a necessity, institutions with the responsibility of teaching not only skills necessary for economic survival but values basic to the American way of life. Particularly in urban areas, they assumed functions once performed by families, churches, and masters training apprentices. By 1918 every state had passed compulsory education laws. Eight out of ten children between the ages of six and fifteen were in school. A new, very important American institution had emerged.[3]

But this quick growth of American public education was not trouble free. By the turn of the century, both specialized journals and popular magazines bristled with articles challenging the quality of American education. Too many schools, critics charged, were physically unsafe, overcrowded, and unsanitary. Students crammed into these inadequate structures spent their days memorizing outdated information, to be shouted back on command from their teachers. Too often they studied "classical" subjects like rhetoric or Greek, rather than subjects that would prepare them to contribute to society and lead a useful life.[4] Moreover, school systems were wasteful and inefficient, headed by "narrow-minded pedants."[5]

In this climate of criticism, the Progressive Education Association organized formally in 1919.[6] The phenomenon that contemporaries called progressive education, however, preceded the establishment of the association. John Dewey's famous Laboratory School at the University of Chicago, established in 1896, was by then over twenty years old. Dozens of other small, private, experimental progressive schools dotted the country. The emphasis in these schools was on "child-centered education": curriculums that allowed children to develop at their own pace, motivated by their interests rather than by fear of punishment for breaking rigid rules. Teachers were to be guides and friends, not taskmasters.[7]

Some large public school systems also made changes contemporaries described as progressive. Led by Gary, Indiana, numerous cities approved a series of innovations, generally called the platoon or Gary plan, that attempted to make schools less costly to operate, yet more responsive to the needs of different student populations. Divided into "platoons," students marched between gyms, playgrounds, and classrooms, ensuring continuous, efficient use of the school plant during the day. New programs, such as Saturday schools, night schools, and vocational schools kept that plant busy at practically all other times, while expanding traditional grammar and high school curriculums.[8]

Given this variety, contemporaries, not surprisingly, differed in their judgments about the worth and even the definition of progressive education. Was progressive education a wonderful effort to make education more humane, a movement that stood for "the right of every individual to the highest physical, mental, spiritual and social development of which he is capable?"[9] Was it instead a silly effort by dreamy radicals to give students, from grammar school to university levels, "too much freedom?"[10] Or was this movement that emphasized the need to connect school and society something else altogether? Were the supporters of curriculums that provided students with useful skills and prepared them to cope with the problems of everyday life actually the leaders of the "exploiting class?"[11] Were they really most interested in saving tax dollars and preparing future workers for their places in the new industrial order? Adherents of this view, such as journalist Upton Sinclair, argued that powerful business interests supported school "reforms" because they wanted malleable "goslings" who would "goose-step" to their foreordained tasks in factories and offices. And the goslings had to be trained at the lowest possible cost.[12] Scott Nearing, a radical economist, charged in 1917 that such changes were possible because, in city after city, businessmen had packed the school boards.[13]

Scholars have as yet neither resolved these conflicting interpretations of progressive education nor raised significantly new questions not first debated by contemporaries. However, their interest in progressivism's impact on educational institutions has lagged far behind their investigations of progressivism's roles in shaping other institutions. Lawrence Cremin's Bancroft Prize-winning *The Transformation of the School* pioneered scholarly study of the subject. Cremin's work, still the most widely read interpretation of progressive education, echoed the optimism of the organizations and individuals whose activities he chronicled. Progressive education reflected the most "noble" impulses within progressivism. Its adherents, though guilty sometimes of naiveté, truly did try to use the schools to expand democracy and opportunity in society.[14]

But as Cremin rediscovered the publications of the Progressive Education Association or the Laboratory School, other historians and economists rediscovered the work of critics like Nearing and Sinclair. Like their mentors, they attacked a positive vision of progressive education and discovered a conspiracy. They too saw early twentieth-century educational change as masterminded by a business elite eager to fit people into the industrial system. As one of these scholars, historian Joel Spring, summarized, "The socialized classroom taught one how to act in a corporation but not as a free man."[15]

Recently a few historians of education have emphasized the "paradox" of progressive education, arguing that the progressive education movement, like progressivism itself, often paired unlikely allies: settlement house workers and U.S. Steel in Gary, Indiana, for example.[16] Still, Michael Katz's charge that "historians have done astoundingly little research . . . on relations between [progressive] reform efforts in education and in other places" remains overwhelmingly valid.[17] Moreover, even those scholars who have identified the business community as the driving force behind organizational changes they decry have not taken that community into bright light. It has remained in its accustomed position: a powerful but vaguely described entity. John Dewey, William Wirt, Nicholas Murray Butler, and a host of other progressive educators emerge in the scholarly literature as clearly drawn, complex individuals. Businessmen and the business community never do. But any attempt to grasp the complicated nature of progressive education must acknowledge business influence and bring business leaders out of the shadows.

Any researcher using the archives of the Moraine Park School should soon come to see businessmen not as shadowy powers but as flesh and blood people speaking up at parents' night meetings. The Moraine Park School, the most elaborate attempt to create a Dewey-style progressive laboratory school in Ohio, received in addition to business funding the charge to educate businessmen's sons and daughters. During its ten-year lifetime, from 1917 to 1927, its roster of students was a who's who of the progeny of the Miami Valley's business elite.

As he explained late in life in a letter written to his granddaughter, Arthur Morgan felt he was "not equipped to be a good father." His work with the Conservancy, his constant sense that any fault with the work might result "in a hundred thousand people drowned," left him almost no time to spend with his young sons and daughter. In a telling phrase illustrating once again the emphasis members of the Valley's business progressive community put on "manly" reform, Morgan wrote that he wanted a school that would be a "substitute father."[18] So he created the Moraine Park School. Morgan, whose compelling ability to persuade had already received ample public demonstration during the prolonged Conservancy campaign, enlisted the aid of several powerful business leaders whom he had met through his Conservancy work.

Chief among these men were Edward A. Deeds and Charles Kettering, both older than Morgan, men in their forties who had already become very wealthy from their Delco Company ventures.[19] Kettering, who began his career as a schoolteacher, shared Morgan's deep interest in education and quickly consented to become the school's chief financial angel, a role he played until his duties as a vice president of General Motors took him to Detroit in 1925. Kettering offered the use of a greenhouse on his estate in suburban Moraine, Ohio, on the southern outskirts of Dayton, saying he would "rather raise kids than cucumbers."[20]

Kettering's greenhouse was a huge, rambling building that the inventor had used previously for his numerous photosynthesis experiments. Kettering not only donated the building but also hired carpenters who in late 1916 went to work laying flooring, making partitions, and installing movable screens and windows. Soon a light-flooded schoolhouse emerged. It had every necessity and most luxuries: a gymnasium, project rooms, study halls and assembly rooms, "reading porches," an elaborate science laboratory, a photographic darkroom, and a library.[21]

Arthur Morgan, meanwhile, took more than a month's time away from his other duties to traverse the country from Seattle to New York City between December 1916 and January 1917 to interview candidates for teaching and headmastership positions at the planned school. The notes he jotted for himself during or immediately after each interview reveal many of the prejudices common to the era's white male elite. Morgan, for instance, worried that Arthur Sides, a principal at a Connecticut high school, looked "a little like a Jew." When the man, unsolicited, told him that he was Irish, Morgan allowed in his notes, "He has the appearance of an Oscar Straus type of Jew—not the ordinary kind."[22] The fact that a young woman graduate of Columbia Teachers College was a Roman Catholic bothered him, though he eventually rationalized that her "common sense" and "wholesomeness" outweighed her religious beliefs.[23] None of the planners for the Moraine Park School had any thoughts of allowing it to be integrated. Nevertheless, Morgan noted as he summarized his impressions of one candidate for the headmaster's post that although the man was very bright, "his ideas of negro capacity are exaggerated."[24]

For a man like Morgan to have been free of such prejudices would have been unusual, rather than the obverse. What separated him from others, what made Morgan a progressive, was his obsession for remaking and improving social institutions and his certainty that his new school could be a wonderful example of successful "educational engineering."[25] "The problem of modern education," as he put it, was an engineering problem. The needs and minds of children and young adults could be studied scientifically, just as he and his fellow experts had come into the Miami Valley and studied its hills and river channels in order to devise a system of flood control. And just as the Miami Conservancy project was an engineering experiment that abandoned conventional notions, so too should schools eschew traditions and conventions.

In Frank Slutz, Morgan found a headmaster who shared his faith in logic, in science, in the need to remake schools as small communities able to prepare students for life, not just by imparting knowledge and teaching skills, but by strengthening health and character as well. Slutz, the thirty-four-year-old superintendent of schools in Pueblo, Colorado, was, Morgan thought, a man of "keen mind . . . sound morally . . . with advanced ideas in education."[26]

Morgan hired Slutz personally. He then solicited the help of the Moraine Park school board and hired the three other teachers who made up the new school's first faculty. Two, Laura Gillmore and Bertha Stone, had prior experience with progressive experimental schools, most notably, for Stone, New York City's Lincoln School. The third, Arthur Hauck, principal of a high school in Idaho, was later to serve for many years as president of the University of Maine. In 1917, 46 children enrolled to study with this new faculty. The school remained small. At its height in 1923-24 it still had only eight teachers and 132 students.[27]

The key to progressive education, according to Frank Slutz, was to integrate schooling and life. "Education," he wrote, "is in part but not in all secured through books; the printed page is a tool . . . but not a fetish."[28] The Moraine Park School was to be a community, with the students assuming responsible roles as its citizens, roles that would help prepare them for life. Throughout the school's history a board of prominent businessmen supported this goal. The Moraine Park school board, in fact, included Dayton's most famous inventors and self-made business successes. In addition to Deeds, Kettering, and Rike, all of whom had worked with Arthur Morgan on the Conservancy, Orville Wright, coinventor of the airplane, and William Chryst, an electrical engineer and collaborator with Deeds and Kettering at Delco, served as board members.[29]

As was proper in an idealized progressive community, a commission style of government prevailed. Not surprisingly, since so many of their fathers had played pivotal roles in the creation of the new Dayton commission-manager charter, the children of the Moraine Park School formed a student government parallel to that of their city. They elected commissioners who appointed a Moraine Park student "community manager." And that manager presided over departments of Public Safety, Welfare, Recreation, Law, and Finance.[30]

Slutz's intention that students participate fully in all aspects of running the school was largely successful. For instance, student members of the Law Department, not teachers, policed the building. Anyone "arrested" for running in the halls, for instance, went before a student judge and court who often sentenced offenders to extra dusting or window washing.[31]

Even the dozen or so children under age eleven in the Beginners' Group at the school were to take the initiative, choosing activities for their play periods and books and stories they wished to read or have read to them. Student interest generated classroom activities. For instance, during the 1920-21 school year several of the little boys in Beginners had become fascinated with trains. After the entire group of children voted to study trains, their teacher helped them devise a series of projects that not only taught them about trains but also simultaneously about math, writing, science, and other subjects. The children wrote letters to railroad companies, asking for promotional brochures with pictures of trains. They took field trips to the Dayton depot and toured the roundhouse and engine yards. They drew blueprints of engines and created wooden models of trains. They wrote poems about trains. They took railway timetables and used them as the basis for solving numerous arithmetic problems as they planned imaginary train trips around the country.[32]

The older teenagers, ranging in age from twelve to nineteen, in the Senior Division had even more responsibility as citizens of the Moraine Park community. An important part of the school's creed was the belief that "a real community is kept alive by its business interest, and to be like a large community, therefore, it is necessary that Moraine Park School should have its business interests."[33] Each Senior Division student had as his or her project a small business. Individually or in groups they got ideas for their businesses and applied to the Moraine Park Commission for a franchise. During the 1919-20 school year, several boys, perhaps more attuned to the real business world than their teachers and parents would have wished, applied for franchises for a whole host of conceivable student businesses, then sat back as their get-rich-quick scheme of forcing other students to buy their franchises thrived. Once the student commission outlawed this practice, however, all students had to run actual businesses, and, contrary to the rules of the real world, could only sell those that had made a profit.[34]

And the businesses were real, using real money. Students acquired their initial start-up capital through loans from parents or from the student-run Moraine Bank, which, once started, made its own money in the traditional way, by charging interest. Dozens of businesses prospered. Some catered to the school community only. The Moraine Lunch Company, for instance, sold sandwiches to students. Students with the franchise for the *Moraine Critic* ran the school newspaper. Other businesses actually worked in the larger community. The Alpabaco, short for the Allied Paper Baling Company, bought paper from students, baled it, and sold it to Dayton paper mills for shredding. Two students in the Camera Company made large profits contracting themselves out as commercial photographers to area businesses.[35]

Of course some businesses, as in real life, failed. But patterns of failure and success did not always follow patterns in real life. The owners of the lunch stand were richer by far than the hapless students who tried to form a law firm, only to discover that their fellows preferred to argue their own cases to the Law Department. The students who formed the Moraine Stock Exchange to deal in capital stocks for all the incorporated projects at the school also found themselves with a losing business proposition. The exchange, admitted its partners, "has a fine board, beautiful stock certificates, but no patronage."[36]

Although the student businesses were central to Moraine Park's teaching methods, the businessmen who created the school were not interested in simply creating another generation of business tycoons. They were sincere in their efforts to emphasize character, ethics, and healthy living. Students not only regularly exercised their bodies, they had opportunity, as the founders intended, to exercise their values. The elaborate reports sent to parents by teachers at the school commented on the child's language and math skills but also detailed his or her physical and ethical development. Slutz and his colleagues scrutinized the results of the extensive physical exams regularly given students. They also made regular efforts to evaluate their charges' ethical development. The reports they sent home to parents included judgments about student progress in such areas as "trustworthiness," "fairness of mind," and "honesty," as well as assessments of student abilities in such traditional subjects as English, French, or mathematics.[37] The Moraine Park School headmaster said that he hoped parents would be just as concerned if a child's report showed a deficiency in honesty as in algebra.[38]

By all accounts the school succeeded. Charles Kettering called it "the only school that I know of that you have to lock the doors to keep the kids out." The school had, he joked, "taken my kid and taught him to lie more than anything I can think of. That kid tells me more fool things and reasons as to why he must go down to that school than you can imagine. I told him the other day, 'What's the use of telling me all that stuff. I know where you are going.' "[39]

Kettering's son Eugene was not the only student who liked the Moraine Park School. The dozens of student-written newspapers, pamphlets, and printed bulletins that survive from the school reveal a relish for learning and a genuine sense of fun.[40] A majority of the school's graduates went on to college or normal-school training, and most seemed to adjust to more traditional forms of education.[41]

Of course they were a select group. Although the school's board of directors established a sliding tuition scale based on parental income, virtually all Moraine Park School students were the children of affluent businessmen and professionals.[42] Given these children's home circumstances, some of the school's constant efforts to prepare them "for life" assumed an element of play-acting. Little nine-year-old Martha Chryst dutifully reported in a school bulletin her success at school cooking classes, her victories with escalloped potatoes, chocolate honey cake, and creamed eggs in bread cubes. She then admitted somewhat wistfully that "cooking has not done me much good, for we have a cook."[43]

Furthermore, the school's obeisance to student originality sometimes led to excess. There is no hint that Arthur Morgan sought to pull his audience's leg when in an after-dinner speech he told the following anecdote to illustrate the virtues of Moraine Park's emphasis on creative thinking. One of the boys at the school had "found a mistake which had been running through Shakespearean editions for over a hundred years": "I believe he was reading 'As You Like It' that part where a description is being given of the summer home in Arden. And the poet said, '. . . sermons in stones, and books in the running brooks.' This young man was originally minded, and he read it over carefully again. And finally he found what was wrong, and he suggested it being changed to read, 'sermons in books and stones in the running brooks.' "[44]

But most students had time enough in later life to learn the received wisdom on the use of metaphor. The businessmen sponsors of Moraine Park were clearly not interested in educating their own children to be corporate automatons. Rather, they created an ideal of an independent-minded citizen who saw business as central to society but who also demanded that business be conducted in socially responsible ways.

Of course ideal circumstances made teaching easier. Students at Moraine Park worked in an airy greenhouse, filled with color and comfortable wicker child-sized furniture. By 1923 the school's patrons had added a swimming pool, playing fields, and hiking trails to the original gymnasium, so that all conceivable equipment for organized recreation existed. And the school always remained small, with a hand-picked staff of dedicated, enthusiastic teachers.

In retrospect, some of Moraine Park's efforts at "society serving" seemed patronizing. Students "adopted" poor Dayton families and French children orphaned after World War I, making sure that they had enough food and clothing. Each year students crafted special handmade Christmas presents for the poor. But without these kinds of activities the Moraine students would have remained in their comfortable neighborhoods. The fact that some of these privileged children spent leisure time reading to patients in charity wards at hospitals or knitting for "their" orphans did not guarantee that they would become reformers as adults. Their schooling was but one of many influences in their lives. Nonetheless, a significant number of Moraine graduates who returned to or remained in the Miami Valley did gain names for themselves as community activists. Challenging stereotypes of the idle second generation of the self-made rich, members of the Kettering family led a variety of community improvement campaigns in Dayton in the 1970s and 1980s. After reaching adulthood, Ernest Morgan lived in Yellow Springs, Ohio, for many years, always active in numerous social and political crusades. He and many of his classmates have led the kinds of interesting, socially responsible, lives the Moraine Park School envisioned as an ideal.[45]

But if the school represented much that was praiseworthy, if it in a sense embodied a vision of business roles in society shared by members of the reform-minded Dayton business community, why did it close by 1927? In a letter written to a Harvard student in 1947 Morgan argued that the Dayton schools "had greatly improved" so that businessmen saw less need for a private school.[46]

In truth, in 1927 the Dayton public school system was entering a period of crisis and cutbacks. Its great era of dramatically quick progressive innovation came between 1908 and 1916 under the superintendence of Edwin Brown. The Moraine Park School did not even open its doors until 1917.

The Dayton schools in the early twentieth century were not fighting progressive education. They were embracing it. But even an innovative public school system could not provide children with the kind of teacher–student ratio available at Moraine Park. It could not provide the green rolling lawns of a private suburban estate for a school campus. It could not provide the lavish equipment and lovely building.

Despite their plan for tuition based on income and their talk of a school open to all, the sponsors of Moraine Park did not recruit seriously outside of their own circles. Since the school was in an exclusive suburb, parents or their servants generally delivered the children by car. Obviously only the well-to-do could have coped with the transportation dilemma alone. By the late 1920s Ernest Morgan, Sue Rike, Eugene Kettering, Adam Schantz, Jr., Charles Deeds, and the other children of Dayton's business elite had grown into teenagers and young adults, ready to leave home for college, finishing school, or, in a few cases, first jobs. Even more important, after 1925 Charles Kettering no longer lived in Dayton. Though he kept his Moraine mansion and returned to Dayton often, Kettering spent the next several decades as a key executive at General Motors in Detroit. No other businessman emerged to take his role as patron for an experimental school. The next generation of Miami Valley businessmen, certainly after 1929, faced the crushing problems of the Depression. In that climate none summoned the time or money to try to create another attempt at a perfect community in which children could learn. Perhaps, after 1929, none could summon the optimism that perfect communities, even tiny perfect communities, were possible.

The progressive education experiment at the grammar and high school level that affected the greatest number of children and lasted the longest took place not at the elite Moraine Park School, but inside the Dayton public system.

At the turn of the century, the Dayton public schools reflected patterns common to growing city systems throughout the Midwest and East. The city had one public high school, but public support for it was not great. A high school, even if free, was still a place where the favored few who could afford so to delay their entrance into the labor market prolonged their education. Between 1870 and 1890 the attendance at the high school varied from 250 to 300 students, this during years when the city's population itself boomed, increasing from some 55,000 people to more than 81,000, and when, by 1890, there were more than

12,000 young people between the ages of fifteen and nineteen available to form a pool of potential high school students.[47] The high school emphasized a traditional curriculum of Latin, German, Greek, philosophy, history, algebra, and rhetoric. It was tauntingly known as the "Girls' School," since the overwhelming majority of its pupils were young women preparing to be schoolteachers. In 1880, for instance, the high school enrolled 87 boys and 151 girls. Most children who attended a public school at all went to one of a dozen district grammar schools, where they left their fixed desks only to stand and recite.[48]

By the time the great crash ended an era, a whirlwind had swept through the system. In the late nineteenth century, students at the high school had only one choice: a course of study heavily reliant on classical subjects. By 1927 they had seven alternatives and could enroll in either a "General, Commercial, College Preparatory, College Preparatory in Engineering, Cooperative Industrial, Cooperative Retail, or a Cooperative Commercial" course of study.[49] High school education had become varied, divided into strikingly different tracks, with a huge new vocational high school added to six other high schools and junior high schools. To supplement the district schools, which had expanded greatly in number, a system of free public kindergartens emerged after 1921. Moreover, the school system—which at the turn of the century, had been very simple, consisting of twelve to fifteen elementary schools and one high school—had twenty years later become a complex urban bureaucracy, with seven high schools, twenty-seven elementary schools, twenty-four manual arts centers, twenty-seven domestic science centers, twenty-eight kindergartens, a public school for the deaf, six night schools, which admitted adults as well as working teenagers, and thirty-three "special schools," which included schools for juvenile delinquents, handicapped, gifted, and retarded children. The Dayton population had grown enormously, more than doubling to almost 190,000 by the end of the twenties, but the growth of its student population far outstripped population growth alone. In 1880 fewer than 300 Dayton young people attended high school. By 1913 almost 1,944 did, and by 1927, 3,680 did. Similar though slightly less spectacular increases occurred in the elementary schools.[50]

As it had for the Moraine Park School, the Dayton business

community again played a pivotal role in promoting these changes. Were businessmen, when they intervened in the public schools, playing different roles from ones they had played as concerned parents, shaping the educations of their own children? Did they wish their own children to develop creativity, while manipulating the futures of other children? Did they want those other children, their potential employees, to become, as Upton Sinclair had charged, "goslings" ready to "goose-step" to their assigned places in the industrial order?

This scenario, so heavily emphasized in recent scholarship, did not emerge in Dayton. That is not to say that progressive businessmen were unconcerned with training an adequate work force or with forcing businesslike management methods on school systems. But to outline a conspiracy in which progressive education in the public schools was "a tragedy in American education" engineered by businessmen, overstates the case.[51] Such an interpretation simultaneously exaggerates the influence of the progressive business community and understates its concern for a just as well as an orderly society.

That business community alone did not transform the Dayton public schools, though its role was an important one. As early as 1885, the city's superintendent of schools, J.J. Burns, anticipated the criticisms that would in the next two decades shake the city's school system. Burns, a former administrator at the Cincinnati Normal School, delivered a long and stinging philippic, rather than the usual dry recitation of attendance figures and teachers' salaries in his 1885 personal report to the Dayton Board of Education. "Simple cram is not instruction," he blasted. "Teaching is something more than drill." He went on: "It is a very sad thing to see a boy who has loved to read about men and countries fed upon facts and dates as a mode of fattening for examinations . . . and effectually cured of his curiosity."[52]

Burns went on to criticize a hiring system that made it impossible for him to fire incompetent teachers and strongly implied that incompetence in teaching was rife. The picture he drew of Dayton public classrooms was one in which, with a few exceptions, "noisy" teachers shouted repetitive drill at benumbed children. The teachers themselves received ratings based on their charges' scores on tests, so, predictably, the answers to examination questions composed a heavy percentage of drill work, and neither teachers nor students looked much beyond the next examination. Burns concluded his unusually lengthy report with the admission that he realized such a report, especially one delivered by a brand-new superintendent, might not be as "altogether agreeable . . . as pleasing rhetoric about a utopian state of affairs."[53]

It was not. By 1887 Burns was gone. Teacher complaints about the harsh nature of his leadership, combined with their misgivings about the nature of the changes he advocated, convinced a bare majority on the school board to fire him. But the issues he raised did not lie buried in the records of the board of education. John H. Patterson would not let them. Not surprisingly, since the skills blended, Patterson the master actor was also Patterson the master teacher. The National Cash Register president was a man with a passionate interest in education and firm ideas about methods by which it could be improved both in his hometown and in the nation.

Patterson and most adherents of progressive education shared the same key ideas: that the walls between school and society had to be removed, and that words and books were not the only useful educational tools. Acting upon these beliefs, Patterson in 1891 endowed the city with a school in which practical skills and subjects were to be taught. Among the teachers hired for the largely male staff at the new school was Edwin Brown, a Dayton native and the first man to graduate from the normal school the city had established to train teachers thirty years before in 1869. In Brown, Patterson found a disciple and ally, the man to engineer major change in the Dayton public schools.

Between 1891 and 1908 the Patterson School flourished. Still privately funded by Patterson himself, the school's range of classes expanded, including, among others, classes in mechanical drawing, machining, carpentry, applied chemistry, and millinery. In addition, again completely funded by Patterson, the Dayton schools adopted the boy-gardens programs first promoted for the children in the neighborhoods surrounding the NCR. Each year after 1896, in the spring and during summer recess, hundreds of Dayton schoolchildren worked tilled portions of school yards and vacant lots. The NCR Company supplied them with seeds and tools. It also sponsored an elaborate bonus-prize system to sustain enthusiasm and provide tangible rewards to youngsters who grew the best tomato or the largest pumpkin. Finally, the company helped the schoolchildren market the extra produce their families did not need.[54]

As much as it welcomed his substantial donations of money and equipment, the Dayton school board, like the city council, did not view Patterson's wishes as commands. The fight for "progressive education" paralleled the fight for "progressive" municipal government. Both were lengthy, and both featured John H. Patterson and his company in a leading role. After J.J. Burns lost his job, the position of superintendent of schools rested uneasily on the shoulders of four different men between 1887 and 1907. Two of these administrators, W.N. Hailmann and John Carr, lasted only two years.

The superintendency was a revolving door in part because the school board itself was in conflict, split about the direction public education should take. Its numbers ranging from ten to fifteen members, the Dayton Board of Education included ministers, lawyers, a dentist, farmers, and former teachers, as well as businessmen. Full transcripts of its meetings for the years 1899-08 no longer exist, but scattered evidence, including information appearing in its *Annual Reports*, indicates conflict, both support for and concerted opposition to change. As Superintendent W.J. White remarked in 1899, "The timidity of the teacher accustomed to the former methods" could pose a real barrier.[55]

Edwin Brown, who in his years of teaching at the Patterson School had come to know John H. Patterson personally, and who believed the NCR president to be a "gentleman . . . whose every influence is for the good of all our institutions," clearly belonged to the faction that wanted change.[56] In 1908 a bitterly split school board elected Brown as the system's new superintendent. Teachers and their adherents on the boards seem to have been his most vocal enemies. Only thirty-seven years old when he became superintendent of schools in 1908, Edwin Brown was dead only eight years later, killed by a heart attack.[57] But during his relatively brief tenure "this man with a big vision" had managed to revolutionize the Dayton school curriculum.[58] That vision was one he shared with John H. Patterson: to broaden the curriculum and increase the functions of the schools for a larger public constituency, even one including adults. Remarkably, within a few years, he achieved much of it.

Brown introduced an elaborate program of night schools attended yearly by an average of three thousand students, mostly young boys who had to work during the days and recent immigrants seeking occupational skills and a place to study English. The manual training programs of the system assumed a much larger importance. Stivers Manual Training High School, able to accommodate two thousand students, opened. Dozens of Miami Valley industries participated in the cooperative and continuation schools, where each year about a hundred boys worked part-time at factories and attended school during the day from four to ten hours a week on factory time to supplement night school training. The new superintendent founded an extensive summer school program and a network of special purpose schools, such as the School for Backward Children and schools for deaf and crippled children. About the only identifiable group left to languish was a tiny population of black children, during these decades composing only 4 or 5 percent of children in most age groups in the city. Of course other small minorities of children, like the physically handicapped, received concentrated attention. Their race and not their numbers explained the slighting of black children. Their segregated school received little attention from Edwin Brown or any other administrator.[59]

Ironically, given his own obesity, Brown constantly preached the progressive education dictum that education should nourish the whole person, body as well as mind. Under his leadership, the Dayton schools acquired a national reputation as innovators in the use of playgrounds. The superintendent equipped school yards with swings, slides, baseball diamonds, and other amenities and mandated that they stay open not just during school hours but at night and on weekends too.

"Open Air School Rooms" made their appearance, where temperatures were never over fifty-eight degrees unless it was warmer out of doors. Charts kept of student weight gain and general physical condition in these rooms convinced Brown that they were more healthful. By 1914 such classrooms were common, though not universal, throughout a school system that also introduced medical and dental inspection and provided free dental care for elementary school pupils whose parents could not afford it.

Also in keeping with progressive education's faith in logic and science, Brown inaugurated an elaborate program of intelligence and "efficiency" testing for public school students. Even kinder-garteners were not spared. They may have thought they were only playing with crayons, but their teachers were, no doubt, watching them carefully in order to be able to answer question 2-H on a five-page form. An ability to handle a crayon with "easy, light movements" indicated according to this "child-measure-ment" form, "development of power of initiative." A whole host of activities were to be categorized. Tests asked for judgments about everything from children's abilities to hop rapidly to their interest in planting seeds.[60]

As Dayton public school pupils matured, the pace of testing only increased. By the time they reached high school, they had become veterans of repeated batteries of intelligence and aptitude tests. Because of these tests, most had received ratings of A, B, or C by the time they reached ninth grade. A students were excellent achievers, B students, average, C students, below average. Teachers were to expect more of A students, to allow C students extra time. The classifications were not kept secret. Administrators perhaps protested too much when they offered repeated assurances that there was no stigma attached by either students or teachers to the system, that instead all worked happily within the limits of their abilities.[61]

Assurances that school buildings could honestly be called city "social centers" rang more true. In 1912, in advance of most school systems in the state, the Dayton Board of Education adopted a resolution agreeing to a plan to make the buildings in the city system available to the general public, both during and after school hours. Public groups could meet in school buildings, provided they had applied two days in advance to the board of education. No political or religious discussions were to be held, and school janitors were to be compensated for their extra work. And, as Brown planned, the schools did become "social centers" for the community. In most neighborhoods, school buildings stayed brightly lit at night, as numerous groups showed films, hosted lectures, and held debates.[62]

After Edwin Brown's sudden death, Frank Miller, a Dartmouth graduate, acted as superintendent of schools. Miller neither expanded nor dismantled Brown's structure. His interim leadership ended in 1921 when he chose to enter state government as an adviser to the governor's office on educational matters. To replace him, the board of education hired Paul Stetson, a man already nationally known in education circles for administrative innovation.[63] Stetson, whose reputation as an efficiency expert preceded him, came to Dayton from a superintendency at Muskegan, Michigan. By late 1929, when he left Dayton for a yet larger superintendency at Indianapolis, Stetson had completed the educational revolution begun by Brown.

Since Stetson taught at the University of Chicago during summer breaks and served frequently as a leading consultant on national school surveys, the Dayton system received wide publicity as a "model." Journalists and educators from around the country visited often.[64] Stetson's superintendency, like Brown's, contained the key elements of progressive education: a search for efficiency; a faith in science; a commitment to expansion of education to include vocational, physical, and health subjects, as well as academic subjects; and, finally, plans to open the schools to the community.

His drive to create a more efficient school system led Stetson to campaign successfully for a major reorganization of school administration. Prior to 1921 there had been few middle managers between school principals and the school superintendent. Principals generally reported directly to the superintendent and retained considerable authority.

By 1928 a new, more complex hierarchy existed. Over the course of several years the board of education had approved its new superintendent's suggestions and divided the system into departments. Rather than a circle of dozens of relatively autonomous schools reporting to a superintendent, a pyramid emerged. The system now included departments of primary education, upper elementary education, visiting teachers, secondary schools, athletics and physical education, publications, and business management.

Nowhere was the concern for efficiency so clearly manifested as in the new Department of Business Management. No longer were principals of separate schools able to contract individually for janitors or hire cooks for their lunchrooms. Rather, the system's new business manager, John Graham, was the authority to whom they sent their requests. Graham's office centralized janitorial and cafeteria services for the system, and coordinated all purchasing, all building construction, all building maintenance and repairs, and all transportation.[65]

The advent in 1923 of the platoon system, made famous by the Gary, Indiana, schools, marked another effort to use both school personnel and equipment with maximum efficiency.[66] Dayton school administrators tried five platoon schools in 1923 and steadily expanded the number in following years, until almost half of all elementary schools used the system. No doubt the platoon school, which promised to eliminate the maintenance of unused space, as different groups, or platoons, of students worked alternately at academic and nonacademic subjects so that all building areas were always in use, would have found an interested advocate in Paul Stetson under even normal circumstances. But during the twenties, when the population of Dayton doubled, the population in the schools more than tripled. Even given voter approval of bond issues to finance the construction of new school buildings, the system could not keep up with demand. Classes were literally held in hallways and on front steps in fair weather. The platoon system provided not just a promise of maximum efficiency, a promise that no classroom would sit idle for forty minutes while students ate lunch or played outside; it provided a solution to a desperately real problem of overcrowding in a system growing with dramatic rapidity.

Building on Brown's legacy, Superintendent Stetson also emphasized health and physical education, expanding the medical inspection system and programs of testing students regularly to determine mental and physical development. Stetson enjoyed a large construction budget, the pleasant inheritance of a $3 million bond issue for school construction passed by municipal voters in 1920, to which he added other monies granted by voters in 1923, 1924, and 1926. In his first two years as superintendent alone, Stetson presided over the construction of a new junior-senior high school and four new elementary schools. In all these buildings, architects hired by the school board had strict instructions to pay attention to ventilation, "healthful" heating systems, and sports and recreation facilities. All the new schools featured landscaping, playgrounds, gymnasiums, and running tracks. The new high school boasted the rare luxury of a natatorium, with enclosed year-round swimming pools.[67]

Vocational and nontraditional education, as well as physical education, received emphasis. The programs begun in the 1890s at the Patterson school and incorporated into the school system by Edwin Brown after 1908 reached maturity. In the school year 1926-27 the night schools peaked, with an enrollment of about five thousand teenagers and adults, who studied everything from Shakespeare to automobile repair. The cooperative high school system enrolled hundreds of young people. Most were boys, though girls could study cooperatively in secretarial and retail selling programs. These students worked in pairs, each one working one week at a shared outside job and attending classes full-time the second week.

Naturally enough, given its birth under NCR Company sponsorship, the cooperative high school had first emphasized the metal trades, helping boys to combine work as apprentice machinists, pattern makers, or tool and die makers, with schooling. By the late twenties, the cooperative high school had expanded in many directions. Students held part-time jobs in many occupations and trades. Popular programs included co-op training in retail selling, carpentry, bricklaying, and plumbing. In all cases, advisory committees of business owners and master tradesmen played important roles in setting policies for the programs, known within the framework of the cooperative high school as "extension schools." By 1928 scores of stores and factories participated. They not only provided the co-op jobs. Many also sponsored scholarships to enable young employees to become part-time students. Several provided classroom and office space.[68]

Such an expansion of the schools into the community would have pleased Edwin Brown, the first to open up school buildings for general public use. Paul Stetson continued that emphasis. The new departments of Visiting Teachers and of Publications helped promote that goal. As Elizabeth Kennedy, director of the Publications Department, admitted to a visiting journalist, her department might "better be named the Bureau of Public Relations." And indeed the Dayton school system did pioneer in the field of educational public relations, distributing dozens of pamphlets and newsletters, each year sending all parents of children enrolled in the system nine monthly issues of its magazine, *School Progress*. Stetson expected Kennedy, moreover, to be his "official public fixer." She had the "delicate" task of negotiating with newspaper reporters and editors to try to get them to portray the schools in a favorable light. She was to be the system's representative for a lengthy list of civic events, showing the public that the schools cared about everything from Thrift Week to the Municipal Dog Show.[69]

The activities of the visiting teachers supplemented Elizabeth Kennedy's near-constant forays out into the community. These individuals were to visit the homes of children who were having trouble in school. An expanded version of the traditional truant officer, the visiting teacher was to attempt to counsel parents and relatives. If she found them uncooperative, she was to call in the police or, in cases of suspected child abuse, the new city Welfare Department.[70]

This new structure faced a crisis by the end of the decade. In 1927, for the first time, voters rejected an appeal for additional money. They turned down a one mill levy by a small margin, 13,230 for and 14,656 against. The system, which peaked in 1927-28 with a total of 165 schools and 1,188 teachers on the payroll, began to cut back. By 1929 the departments of Publications and Visiting Teachers were gone. Most of the summer schools closed. The night schools and special schools curtailed many courses of study. The system offered fewer physical education, art, and music classes.[71] And teachers lost their jobs, as Stetson mandated increases in minimum class sizes at all levels— to an average of forty students per class in elementary schools, an average of thirty-five in junior high, and thirty in senior high classes. Beginning in 1928, the financial crunch forced administrators to issue dismissal notices to at least ninety teachers a year.[72] Stetson himself left.

By the time the Depression hit in full force in 1929, the heady optimism of the early twenties had already faded. And the hard years that followed the crash were not ones that allowed the dream of creating a perfect progressive public school system to revive. Contemporaries blamed overconfidence for the failure of the school bond issue in 1927. Dr. H.B. Millhoff, president of the board of education, plausibly blamed the "light vote."[73] Indeed, a very small number of voters set into motion a chain of events that led to over a decade of severely reduced budgets at the schools. After years when the voters had approved bond issues by comfortable margins, school administrators had become lulled into expectations of automatic victory. They had spent almost no time campaigning for the bond issue, neglecting to note that among other issues on the ballot were two road levies that had been vociferously opposed by a neighborhood organization. Turnout in November 1927 was light. The few who voted probably were motivated to voice their opposition to the routes the proposed roads would take. The road levies met overwhelming defeat. Voters probably allowed their negative mood to cause them to check the "no" box for the school levy as well. Chastened school officials vowed to bring the issue back to voters. But by the fall of 1929 voters caught in the first month's panic after the great crash were in no mood to approve extra spending for schools, roads, or anything else. But the public never delivered any clear repudiation of the changes in the Dayton school system engineered by Superintendents Brown and Stetson. The 1927 election was a case of overconfident school administrators' not bothering to woo voters. By 1929 time had run out. For the next decade, hard times, not anger at educational change, fueled public unwillingness to continue to spend so lavishly on the schools.

In fact, an examination of progressive education in the Dayton public schools does not reveal the simple patterns of business conspiracy or business venality outlined by contemporary radical critics and still in favor among numbers of scholars of education. Clearly the business community was a major force behind the revolution that swept through the Dayton schools in the early twentieth century. Paralleling a national pattern pointed out by Scott Nearing, businessmen did, between 1906 and 1928, gain an increasing number of seats on the city's board of education. They had a majority by the early 1920s. And the men they chose as superintendents were deeply committed to the goal of creating a more businesslike school system. Indeed, they were men who thought of themselves as businessmen. When C.J. Schmidt, clerk of the board of education delivered a eulogy for Edwin Brown in 1916, he emphasized that the superintendent was "more than an educator, he was a businessman in every sense of the word."[74] Paul Stetson's national reputation as an efficiency expert certainly did not hurt his chances in 1921 with that same board of education. The term *businesslike* appeared with near-omnipresence in the reports and publications of the school system during these years.

Increasing business influence in education, then, undoubtedly formed part of the central matrix of progressive education in Dayton. But that influence did not necessarily pit businessmen against a wary public. In fact, the educational changes were largely popular. There were perpetual waiting lists for classes in practical subjects like bricklaying and automotive repair at the night schools.[75]

The cooperative high school programs were intensely competitive, accepting only about a quarter of the students who applied. Clearly the educational system was class- and income-bound. The businessmen on the Dayton School Board were not promoting identical opportunity for all. They did not provide the children of their workers with the same kind of chances they provided their own children at schools like Moraine Park. Nevertheless, it would be a mistake to see efforts like cooperative or vocational education as selfish attempts by business to create a better-trained and compliant work force. Such an interpretation unnecessarily demeans the intelligence of that potential work force. In Dayton at least, those future employees embraced the opportunities opened by the schooling provided. Was a worker who wished to make more money with skills learned at a vocational high school simply an unwitting tool in a business conspiracy?

The chance to advance was not illusory. An amazingly high percentage of cooperative high school students during the twenties did get good jobs or further education past high school. Helped by a program of factory scholarships, some 30 percent went to specialized trade schools or colleges. Colleges graduates attended included Cornell, Cincinnati, Ohio State, Purdue, and the University of Pennsylvania. And a significant number became colleagues of their former businessmen sponsors. Many became leading NCR salesmen.[76] While it was certainly to the business community's advantage to support an educational system that produced graduates with skills and attitudes that helped them fit into the American corporate system, it was also to the advantage of those graduates. The fact that school enrollment increases far outpaced population increases in Dayton during the first two decades of the twentieth century was testimony to a more complex reality.

Of course, sometimes the efforts to achieve maximum efficiency and perfectly coordinated schedules begged for satire. Between 1914 and 1916, gongs sounded during the day in all Dayton elementary schools at 9:15, 10:50, 1:50, and 3:15. Boys rushed over to open all the windows and doors in the classrooms, and all children rose to stand for exactly three minutes of "light calisthenics," after which doors and windows were closed, and routine activities resumed.[77]

But at least some teachers and administrators injected a little necessary skepticism as they examined the results from all the new tests and schedules. Superintendent Frank Miller, for instance, in his report to the board for the school year 1916-17, supported intelligence testing and vocational placement programs inherited from his predecessor but issued a caveat. The tests were not foolproof, he warned, "and a great deal of mischief can be done by that type of adviser who assumes that he can gauge the abilities of a pupil well enough to determine for what definite calling this pupil is specially fitted."[78]

The opposition to the new system did not come from the general public. As was the case in other cities, it came from teachers. In small and large ways administrator-imposed rules invaded their classrooms. Not only were they to stop everything to engage in three minutes of exercise at 10:50 A.M., they were also to use administration-approved lesson plans and administration-approved tests. They found their days interrupted by a whole host of administration-planned activities, from dental inspections to mandatory schoolwide participation in Thrift Week rallies. Moreover, neither of the two important administrators during this period paid enough attention to good relations with their teaching staffs. Many teachers considered Edwin Brown, for instance, "oppressive."[79] Even some of Brown's supporters agreed that he "preferred to hurt feelings rather than resort to evasion."[80] Whether public school teaching had ever allowed teachers significant control of their classrooms is, however, an open question. Nineteenth-century common schools featured a great deal of rote memorization from approved texts. They also featured poorly educated teachers and powerful school principals. Teachers who disliked Brown or Stetson may have been responding to the arrogance these men so often displayed. In a genuine sense, though, they may never really have had much autonomy to lose. Of course they had pride to lose. As administrators formed their own professional societies during the period, so did teachers. Although Dayton teachers did not form a cohesive union, like the Chicago Teachers Federation, they were aware of the existence of it and like organizations in other cities. They were aware that as administrators gained power and prestige, their own status, at the best, remained static.

Stetson and Brown, who realized that the Dayton public had to be wooed and who even, under Stetson, created a public relations office, did not soothe and cultivate their own teaching staffs sufficiently. More important, by the end of the 1920s, teaching conditions had indeed deteriorated, as administrators, facing budget cuts, increased class sizes and teacher workloads.

Indeed, the attitudes of the teaching staff formed the clearest difference between the elite Moraine Park School and the Dayton public schools. Every one of the Moraine teachers seemed to burst with enthusiasm about the program at the experimental school. Of course, comparisons between a handpicked staff of half a dozen highly trained teachers working under ideal conditions and a very large and diverse public school staff that reached more than a thousand by the midtwenties would be necessarily strained. But the similarities, rather than the differences, between the Moraine Park School and the revamped Dayton public school system, seem significant.

In large part, both were creations of the same reform-minded business community. Both sought to connect school and society, to promote the idea that the schools should prepare for life by participating in life. Both emphasized physical, health, and vocational education. Both subjected their students to frequent intelligence and aptitude testing. Finally, both failed to survive intact. The Moraine Park School closed its doors altogether. The Dayton system retrenched. Both depended on an economic climate of growth and prosperity. That climate, crucial to an understanding not just of progressive education but of the larger progressive movement as well, nourished heady optimism among business leaders. It stimulated their belief that "school progress" was just one of many kinds of progress possible.

Interestingly, the Miami Valley became nationally known for experiments in "school progress" at the elementary and secondary level and in addition for an attempt, selectively, to transpose progressive education's central tenets to the college level. The prime movers in this effort, Arthur Morgan and Charles Ketter-ing, were already familiar figures to area educators when in 1919 Morgan accepted the presidency of Antioch College in Yellow Springs, Ohio.

Antioch College was in 1919 a school with an illustrious past and a gloomy future. Founded in 1853 with prominent educator Horace Mann as president, the college had a tradition of experi-mentation. It was one of only a handful of nineteenth-century colleges that admitted blacks and women for coeducational study.

Its nineteenth-century history was to be more troubled than idyllic, however. Even during Mann's presidency, battles over religious issues divided the faculty. The Christian Church, a fundamentalist Protestant sect that provided funds for the col-lege, quickly denounced some of Mann's Unitarian nonsectarian views. Financial problems and disputes about curriculum and goals continued to plague the college for decades. It even closed its doors in 1881 and 1882 for lack of money. By 1913 the college seemed doomed. The graduating class that year numbered only ten students. Faculty members received only irregular pay. In 1917 Simeon Fess, who had been working without salary for several years as president and who was away most of the time anyway as a U.S. congressman from Ohio, resigned.[81]

The trustees, a dispirited group of elderly men, many of them ministers, tried and failed to sell the college to the YMCA. In 1919 Arthur Morgan accepted their invitation to join the board. Within months he had agreed to become president of the floundering college, provided that he be given wide latitude to remake it.

Morgan's wife Lucy remembered his telling her that Antioch "looks dead enough to do anything I want with it."[82] He was right. Morgan's later claims that he was surprised to have been named to the board were probably disingenuous.[83] He was a man with a national reputation in progressive education circles and was, in fact, elected first president of the new Progressive Educa-tion Association in 1921. By creating the Moraine Park School he had acquired a number of allies among prominent educators, chief among them the former president of Harvard University, Charles Eliot. And he, like Eliot, was an important figure in the Unitarian Church, an institution that since the days of Horace Mann had had an emotional and financial interest in Antioch.[84]

Morgan, whose schemes for the Conservancy District had

begun to reach fruition by 1919, was ready for another major challenge, ready to engineer another grand plan. The Antioch board's offer of the college presidency offered the District chief engineer his chance. That the trustees accepted the conditions he imposed illustrated their desperation. Morgan received the right to demand the resignations not only of the Antioch faculty, but also of the trustees who had just appointed him head of the college.

With that kind of power, and within the context of his new leadership of an old college that had for many decades tolerated significant experimentation, Morgan could begin to try to implement his vision of a college that would "see education whole."[85] Such a vision would require a radical transformation of the curriculum. For too long, Morgan argued, the leaders of liberal arts colleges had been like "the natives of Tierra Del Fuego . . . short and squatty with large protruding stomachs, who . . . think of short, potbellied persons as the ultimate expression of physical beauty." American educational institutions, said Morgan, like the Tierra del Fuegans, needed new ideals, new standards for comparison, but they "could not expect strange ships to appear on the horizon, bringing new revelations of perfection."[86]

Indeed they would have no need to wait for prophets or strange ships if they would only use the scientific method to determine educational policy. The scientific attitude, Morgan concluded, "with its rigorous methods, its iconoclastic analysis . . . will do for ordinary intelligent men what only the brilliant originality of genius would otherwise accomplish. If we can, through the atmosphere of the college, transmit this spirit to our students, our work will not have been lost."[87]

For Morgan the scientific method applied to education constituted the progressive education ideal: development of the whole person by means of a curriculum that provided a broadly based liberal arts education in which independent study, vocational education, and an emphasis on health and proper physical development played large roles.

The new Antioch plan provided a core of interdisciplinary survey courses to be taken by all students. These courses included a substantial introduction to English composition and to literature. The mandatory four-year survey of "social science" integrated the study of world history, economics, and the development of law in society. All students were to spend two years studying a survey of psychology and of the history of philosophy. Required core courses in the sciences included one-year reviews of physics, chemistry, biology, and "earth sciences," defined to include introductions to the study of geology and astronomy. In addition, they were to take courses in "college aims" and ethics.[88] Beyond this common curriculum, students were expected to choose areas of concentration. By their junior or senior years, they were to be engaged in "autonomous courses," projects in which consultations with professors took place only when students realized they needed further guidance. Such a plan, whereby the upperclass student "must dig out for himself as much as he is able, then go to the professor for help," contained the promise that students would discover "unsuspected powers" within themselves, that they would learn to think creatively rather than simply to take orders.[89]

But Antioch students were to develop not merely through required courses and autonomous study. They were to balance classes at Antioch with work at outside paid jobs. In a scheme labeled the Cooperative Plan, students would study at Antioch for five weeks, then work full-time at a job for the next five weeks. The outside employment was to be an "apprenticeship with real life."[90] Given the time such paid employment would involve, an undergraduate education at Antioch would generally take six years to finish.

During these six years, finally, the college would seek to prepare the student intellectually and vocationally, but also physically and ethically to begin adult life as a responsible and productive citizen. Since a human being had to maintain good health in order to perform most efficiently, the college would require that each student participate in regular physical activity. And students should know not only how to exercise, but also how to sleep, eat, and maintain correct posture.[91]

The college would certainly seek to encourage the development of character in its students. As Morgan warned in a letter to prospective students, the new Antioch would not "be a place to teach clever men and women to make better livings than their neighbors, or simply to have intellectual tastes."[92] If the college failed to develop graduates who shaped lives noted for their integrity and social purpose, the Antioch dream would not have been fulfilled.

It would not be fulfilled if education continued to be "feminized" either. For central to the Antioch idea was the "introduction of a masculine element." By that Arthur Morgan did not mean the literal presence or absence of women. He supported and continued Antioch's long coeducational tradition, although during the twenties men students greatly outnumbered women. Morgan even hired women instructors. Antioch, however, he said, had to be an "Almus Pater," a place that deemphasized the traditional college's efforts to play the "woman's role" of "sheltering" students. In 1929 Morgan still scornfully remembered a visit he had made decades earlier to a "great Eastern university." His impressions of "filmy curtains and fragile bric-a-brac" and male faculty members serving tea remained vivid. That unnamed college was "feminine," even though it had an all-male faculty and did not admit women students. Antioch, with female undergraduates in residence, was still to show "the sterner stuff of real living."[93]

Although women enrolled and taught at Antioch, they played secondary roles. Once again attitudes displayed toward women by Miami Valley business progressives emerged. The world was a rough and dangerous place. Hardheaded, practical men could improve it. But they had better be careful that excessive feminine influence did not mute the "sternness" they would need to accomplish their objectives.

Arthur Morgan needed money, of course, if he was to turn his vision of a new Antioch into reality. Not surprisingly, he turned to the business community of which he was a member. When in 1916 he had sought supporters for the Moraine Park School, he had solicited funds from "manufacturers and merchants who realized . . . the imperfections of our school system." His hope that "they will give our efforts very substantial financial support" was fulfilled.[94] In 1920 as he planned an even more ambitious experimental educational venture, he turned to many of the same people. Most important, he approached Charles Kettering, who accepted a seat on the transformed Antioch College Board of Trustees and showered the college with more than $300,000 in gifts and loans.

With Kettering playing a familiar role as chief financial angel for his educational plans, Morgan constructed a new board of trustees dramatically different from the previous one. In 1919 quarreling ministers from several local Protestant denominations had dominated the Antioch board. By 1921 the new board had become a national showcase for progressive business. A majority of board members were prominent businessmen sympathetic to Morgan's ideas about social and educational reform. Gordon Rentschler, the Hamilton, Ohio, owner of ship engine production factories and foundries, was a man who as a director of the Miami Conservancy District already knew Arthur Morgan well. Other trustees included John Haswell, owner of a group of steel plants and president of Dayton Malleable Iron Company, Will Mayo, Henry Ford's chief engineer, George Verity, president of the American Rolling Mills, and Henry Dennison, president of Dennison Manufacturing. Along with these important corporation leaders were several bank presidents, three Wall Street lawyers, two influential publishers, Edwin Gay of the *New York Evening Post* and Ellery Sedgwick of the *Atlantic Monthly*, and Frank Slutz, who after the closing of the Moraine Park School in the late twenties resigned his trustee's seat to join the Antioch faculty. Most of these men served as Antioch trustees for the entirety of the 1920s. The few replacements necessitated by resignation or death did not significantly change the board's character. The trustees who oversaw the Antioch revolution were powerful businessmen, but Morgan took pains to characterize them as "idealists and dreamers, somewhat after the Edison type, and moneymaking is secondary with them."[95]

The money they brought to the Antioch experiment, however, was certainly not secondary. Between 1921 and 1933 Charles Kettering alone contributed more than $500,000 to Antioch. Other trustees and their associates also gave generously. Samuel Fels, president of the Philadelphia-based Fels Company and an heir to the Fels-Naphtha Soap fortune, donated over $177,000. Allen Balch, president of the Southern California Gas Company, gave stock and cash contributions to the college worth in excess of $160,000. These kinds of major donations by board members and their friends totaled more than $2 million for the decade.[96]

These men and their organization gave such sums in an era when significant tax advantages for individual and corporate giving to educational institutions did not yet exist. Federal income tax provisions allowed certain kinds of individual charitable deductions after 1917, but deductions for contributions to schools were rarely accepted. Indeed it was not until 1913 that a constitutional amendment made it possible for the federal government to tax income at all. Corporations had to wait until 1935 to receive permission to deduct charitable contributions. States generally taxed inheritance bequests to organizations much more heavily than they taxed bequests to blood relatives.[97] So a search for tax advantage cannot have played any significant role in the trustees' financial support.

Rather, excitement about a college that would "train proprietors" fueled such generosity. William Mayo of Ford said that although his company had "no trouble" finding machine shop hands, it had a "such a hard time" hiring good foremen and superintendents.[98] As Charles Kettering argued, "Our colleges have only been dealing with the theory of life and the theories of the professions they teach." Such a practice was a "glaring weakness." Too many college graduates had no exposure to the realities of the business world and were unsuited to enter it.[99] They did not have the abilities of initiative, coordination, and management necessary to a business career. Many in the business community had high hopes that the Antioch experiment could produce the administrators they needed. George Roberts, vice president of New York's National City Bank, thought executives had to be "all-round men." Antioch, with its motto of "seeing education whole," could train such men, for "the process of seeing things in all their relationships is the peculiar function of the executive."[100]

Kettering and other major patrons hoped to create at Antioch an institution that would produce a graduating class of several hundred such potential administrators a year. But they had a larger aim as well. They wanted to produce a national model for advanced higher education. As Kettering explained, he was certainly willing to "spend time, money, and sleepless nights . . . to make a model of a machine" but only if that machine "were duplicated in the millions or thousands."[101]

In keeping with that aim of creating a national model of a better machine for higher education, the college recruited widely both for its new student body and for its faculty. The first group of students matriculated at the new Antioch in the fall of 1921. In contrast to nineteenth-century classes, which were overwhelmingly made up of local Ohioans, the new Antioch freshman class had members from more than twenty-nine states and seven foreign countries. More came from the East Coast than from Ohio. As the board had become national in its representation, so had the student body. That first year 203 students arrived. By 1924, the sex ratios and numbers of the combined Antioch classes had reached what Morgan considered an ideal: some 600 students, about two-thirds of them male. The college used that number as a benchmark in recruitment and admission. During the 1927–28 school year, student enrollment rose to high point of 706. But the college, throughout the decade, remained intentionally small.[102]

The fact that Antioch students, through the cooperative program, could be at least partially self-supporting meant that the costs to students and their families were substantially lower than they were at other small, private liberal arts colleges in the twenties. The college estimated that students during the first two years of their course would probably need about three hundred dollars a year. They could earn the money to pay the remainder of their room, board, and tuition costs. Upperclass students could expect to support themselves entirely with better-paying part-time jobs.[103]

But interestingly, Morgan and other college officials constantly downplayed the chance for self-support the college offered for students of modest means. The most important object of the cooperative work-study regime at Antioch was not self-support but "training for proprietorship." And such training provided opportunities for students to test their occupational interests in the real world, to develop self-discipline, a sense of responsibility, and initiative.[104]

In fact the well-known Unitarian minister Charles Francis Potter, who had quit his pulpit at New York's West Side Unitarian Church in 1925 to accept a position as executive secretary of the college, asserted that "far from being a university for the poor, many children of the rich are already matriculated; and it is urged that the Antioch experience of self-help in the real world is for them especially useful."[105] Ida Clarke, one of the great number of journalists who came to Antioch over the course of the decade, chose to follow a day in the life of several students for her story, published in a January 1924 issue of the *Pictorial Review*. One of the students she interviewed was a "high-bred" young woman named Wilma Compton, whose work-study job during her first year at Antioch had been as a clerk in a department store. Compton at first was bored with her job. But a turning point came, she told Clarke, when she went to the post office at Christmas to find that for her present her mother had mailed her a fur coat. "Suddenly the thought popped into my mind that I would have to work three years at my present job to save up enough money to buy that coat!"[106]

Not all students had families wealthy enough to send them that kind of extravagant Christmas present, but in truth Wilma Compton was more typical of the Antioch students of the 1920s than would have been a younger Arthur Morgan, struggling to find ways to educate himself without family funds or backing. Morgan saw education as a key to democratic progress. At both the Moraine Park School and Antioch he had, with programs of sliding tuition scales based on income and cooperative work-study, tried to ensure that these experiments in progressive education would be open to all, at least to all whites. Instead, he had created two schools for the middle and upper classes. In fact, the new board of trustees broke with the school's tradition of recruiting talented blacks as scholarship students. Without making it a formal policy the new Antioch was a whites-only college. And its own enrollment records revealed that fewer than 6 percent of its students were the children of unskilled workers. The vast majority had fathers who were business executives or professional men. These enrollment patterns linked Antioch with elite colleges like Harvard or Dartmouth rather than with the growing state universities and junior colleges, where far higher percentages of students came from families where the father was a farmer, factory worker, or laborer.[107] And through the early 1930s, many students seemingly copied their parents' examples. First among career choices for male graduates was business. Despite their untraditional training, a majority of Antioch women graduates married and left or never sought employment.

In 1932 Antioch Dean Algo Henderson produced an extensive internal study for the use of the college of 332 of the total number of 520 men and women who had graduated from the college since its reorganization in 1921. Henderson excluded from his report Antioch graduates who were still studying as graduate or law students at some other institution, as well as women graduates who had married rather than seek employment, so his report naturally emphasized the fate of male students. Henderson and his assistants interviewed these 332 former students at length, asking them to judge the value of their Antioch education, to chart job choices, to assess the worth of the Antioch revolution after several hundred of its products had entered the real world of full-time employment.

The first graduates from the years 1926 and 1927 had worked at jobs near Yellow Springs. During the first year of the program, all but 1 of the 113 cooperative employers were from Ohio. Most students traveled the fifteen-mile distance to Dayton by trolley line to work at the NCR and 50 other factories and stores. But by 1930 a majority of Antioch students left the state to take co-op jobs in places as far away as Chicago, Boston, and New York. By decade's end, almost 1,000 companies scattered over the country had participated in the Antioch experiment.[108]

A small minority of responding graduates were disappointed with their Antioch educations. Glenn Argetsinger, for instance, "got an overdose of factory experience at the possible sacrifice of experience needed in meeting people . . . above that general plane."[109] But most of the students who answered Henderson's questionnaire thought that their direct exposure to real world jobs had been of benefit. Generally they reported that the co-op work made vocational adjustment after graduation easier. Many noted that they had been able to eliminate as well as choose possible careers through a process of trial and error. Mildred Hawhurst, for instance, who eventually became a librarian, decided after jobs at several elementary schools that "I would never succeed as a teacher." The co-op work had not, then, directly prepared her for her future career, but it had forced her to make "a realistic estimate of my abilities."[110]

Although some of the many businesses providing jobs offered only the kinds of work that left Glenn Argetsinger unhappy, a majority treated their pairs of Antioch employees as junior executive trainees. As of 1930 fully half of Antioch graduates found employment with companies for which they had worked as co-op students. An average 40 percent of its first five graduating classes entered business careers, with engineering careers running second, and teaching third.[111]

Business involvement with Antioch, moreover, extended beyond significant financial contributions and widespread participation in the cooperative plan. By 1923 Antioch had further tightened its ties to business with the creation of the Antioch Industrial Service. Through this department, Antioch offered the skills of its faculty members and administrators as consultants. Many of the thirty-five to forty persons who composed the Antioch faculty during the decade combined their Antioch teaching duties with work as consultants and industrial researchers.[112]

In 1925, for instance, the Ohio Association of Lumber Dealers subsidized Antioch's establishment of a "Department of Research in Lumber Retailing." Antioch professors who taught regular students biology, chemistry, engineering, and accounting set up two- and four-week intensive courses intended for people in the lumber business. They offered seminars in such subjects as building materials, estimating, blueprint reading, and accounting. In 1926 lumber dealers from Pennsylvania, Indiana, Illinois, New York, West Virginia, and Ohio paid a seventy-five-dollar fee and came to Yellow Springs to attend the courses. The involvement went beyond the seminar arrangement.[113] In 1926 the college undertook a major study of wood waste in American industry, seeking ways to use the short lengths usually wasted by the lumber industry.[114]

By the end of the decade the industrial research activities of Antioch professors had been formalized with the creation of the Antioch Industrial Research Institute. As a college report published in 1931 explained, "The cooperative plan has served to keep the college in intimate relation to the world of practical affairs. . . . It was inevitable that this community of interests should gradually be extended to include a definite program of industrial research."[115] Many college professors worked part-time on institute projects, which, with a few exceptions, enjoyed the financial patronage of major corporations. By 1930 the institute had supplemented the work of part-time Antioch professors by hiring full-time chemists, metallurgists, and engineers with no teaching or other duties at the college. Bethlehem Mines sponsored institute investigations into better methods of iron ore extraction. General Electric granted funds for experiments on photoelectric cells. Other companies patronized experiments attempting to perfect a vacuum still meant to simplify the separation of chemicals in solution.[116]

Within a decade, then, the small college had attracted a national network of corporate patrons. That network existed in part because of the publicity Antioch received. Charles Kettering had said that he was interested in making Antioch a model. The bonanza of good press treatment the college received spread the word far beyond Ohio. Throughout the decade journalists from business and general interest publications descended on the sleepy village of Yellow Springs. Most left impressed. Arthur Morgan was the "lean, keen worker whom some of us . . . consider the flower of American culture."[117] He was a man whose life "should be written and placed in the hands of every young American."[118] In 1926 the editor of the *Los Angeles Times* bubbled that he "could have been knocked over with a feather" when Morgan appeared in his office. As the editor recounted the meeting, "As soon as we could get our breath, we spoke up and said if only Thomas Edison, Henry Ford, and John D. Rockefeller were to walk into this little room we would have the unique thrill of sitting in the presence of the four greatest living Americans."[119] Journal after journal echoed the conclusion George Marvin of the *Outlook* reached: the Antioch plan "replies to the challenge that modern life hurls at education."[120]

Any avid reader of the popular magazines of the period would probably have heard of Antioch and would probably have concluded that the college faced a bright future. The truth was much less simple. Even before the 1929 crash sent the economy reeling, greatly reducing the number of work-study jobs employers could offer and considerably dimming the prospects for Antioch graduates, the college faced a crisis.

That crisis was both intellectual and financial. It involved a bitter debate between Antioch professors and their president over goals, directions, and achievements at their experimental institution. It also involved looming money problems posed by the growing disenchantment of the college's most important individual benefactor, Charles Kettering. It was a crisis that illustrated the complex nature of business progressives' involvement with early twentieth-century educational reform.

Arthur Morgan had played a direct role in the creation of his new Antioch faculty. He interviewed and personally chose almost all of them, again traveling around the country, as he had done during the winter of 1916 when searching for a headmaster for the Moraine Park School. The faculty then was, like the college plan itself, Morgan's personal creation. Morgan offered better-than-average pay and the chance to participate in a novel experiment.[121] Moreover, the new Antioch president placed far more emphasis on actual work experience, character, and "sound judgment" than on academic degrees.[122] A majority of the faculty, for instance, had only bachelor's degrees, during a decade when normal schools became teachers' colleges, when teachers' colleges became state universities, and other elite private schools increasingly demanded graduate degrees of their faculties.[123] The faculty included people who offered, instead of Ph.D.s, knowledge gained in established careers as architects, engineers, chemists, advertising executives, and government bureaucrats.[124]

Despite his typically intense involvement in the hiring of this group of people, Morgan and his faculty were often at odds.[125] In early 1931, while traveling in Europe, Morgan mailed his faculty a lengthy critique, more than eighty typed pages, outlining in passionate detail where and how he felt the great Antioch adventure of the 1920s had failed. This attack, quickly copied and widely distributed, became known as the "Letter from Portugal."[126] Along with the equally lengthy faculty responses it inspired, it provides a detailed evaluation, from differing perspectives, of the Antioch experiment. It exists, in fact, as a vivid contemporary critique of progressive education.

Other conflicts had preceded the elaborate cross-Atlantic written debate provoked by Morgan's stinging criticisms. In 1920 Morgan had searched the country for a group of people able to combine teaching skills, creativity, and practical experience. He had succeeded in gathering at Yellow Springs an interesting faculty of independent-minded men and women. But Morgan intended that they share his values and his vision of a college that was a miniature version of an ideal society, one that combined study, practical work, and proper emphasis on physical exercise and ethics.

As early as 1921, minutes of faculty meetings showed Arthur Morgan taking the podium to scold his faculty for insufficient cooperation with each other. Within weeks of the start of the first term after reorganization, Morgan openly talked of his disappointment that professors did not visit each other's classes enough, did not seem enough interested in what each of their colleagues was doing, did not seem to plan to learn each other's methods.[127] By 1925 a faculty meeting erupted in angry charges and countercharges when the Antioch president "called attention to the fact that some faculty advisers seem to think that students who had any intellectual interests should go elsewhere, telling them that Antioch is not the place for them."[128] By 1926 Morgan had called a special faculty meeting to discuss the college's financial situation. The generosity of trustees alone could not keep the college afloat, he said. He was on the road constantly searching for additional money. In fact, he felt that he had become a mere "financial agent." When he could free himself from that onerous role he saw an Antioch that was "growing to be less and less the Antioch I had hoped for." He had dreamed that the college would be "a Great Adventure, faculty and students traveling together, and risking together." Instead, students seem more eager to take than give; faculty members were not sufficiently committed to "bringing life to a higher level."[129]

So, the "Letter from Portugal" was not the bombshell some scholars of Antioch history have alleged it to be.[130] Rather, it was the final draft in a series of charges the president had been considering for years. Interestingly, Morgan's concerns reflected the anguish of a successful progressive businessman whose priorities clearly challenged common historical interpretations of the roles played by businessmen in the progressive era.

Morgan was a man who, in his continuing engineering career, was intent on mastering all aspects of scientific management, both of materials and labor. He was not a scholar who supported such new business methods abstractly. He was an insider, a businessman himself, who supported them concretely at Morgan Engineering Company. As a consequence he had amassed both national fame and considerable personal wealth by the time he became president of Antioch.

But the Letter from Portugal did not assert that the Antioch experiment had failed to prepare students adequately for vocations or that it did not give them a broad enough exposure to the sciences and the liberal arts. Rather, it was the pain-filled lament of a dreamer who had begun to doubt that perfect communities could exist on earth. Antioch at the end of the decade was not the Antioch Morgan had hoped to create because it had not succeeded "in achieving a great pattern of life."[131] Its students were interested in putting on risqué commencement plays. Its faculty spent too many evenings playing bridge. Frequently, Morgan lamented, Antioch upperclassmen "leave us with cold, deliberate selfishness, with no warmth of social hope, with no high plan . . . for their lives."[132]

The faculty response to this extraordinary letter was immediate. Numerous committees met to draft long memos, filled with analyses of the Letter from Portugal. Faculty members scheduled open forums and evening meetings with students. Some professors sent their own private replies back across the Atlantic Ocean to Arthur Morgan.

Antioch College's first decade after reorganization, then, ended not with jubilation. It ended instead with soul searching and bitter public accusations of failure. The anguished letters, memoranda, and transcripts of meetings that left a voluminous record of student and faculty responses to Morgan's charges reveal that troubled reflection was not limited to the college's absent president.

Some professors accused Arthur Morgan of acting too much like a "dictator." He expected the faculty, they charged, to be "puppets dancing as the president pulls the strings."[133] One even wrote, "Is Mr. Morgan a sick man, who is not responsible for what he says?"[134]

Others, less angry, thoughtfully assessed their participation in the Antioch experiment. Some argued that it had, in fact, achieved much. But to become the ideal community Morgan wanted, Antioch students and faculty would have had to be driven idealists, exactly in the Morgan mold. And all were not. As a faculty report on the autonomous course plan distributed for discussion at faculty meetings in 1928 had already acknowledged, Antioch students were, on average, ordinary human beings who often procrastinated. Many students, on their own to choose subject matter and course direction, delayed serious work and made only "last minute attempts to cover the subjects."[135] Others bit off more than they could chew, selecting projects that were too demanding and ending up burdened with "too much pressure and a feeling that the faculty was unjust in its demands."[136] Economist William Leiserson said he was not the only Antioch professor who found his upperclass students "not advanced enough" to do so much independent work. Leiserson freely admitted that he had started lecturing and setting up formal meetings with students who had chosen him as an autonomous course adviser.[137]

Lucy Morgan was Arthur Morgan's wife. But when she rose to defend her absent husband at an open forum called to discuss the Letter from Portugal, she made it clear she wanted to be heard in her other role as a chemist, a teacher of "domestic science" and a fellow member of the Antioch faculty. Firm in her defense of Arthur Morgan's vision, she nonetheless admitted that many students lacked the self-direction necessary to carry it out. Rather than "climbing stairs on their own," some students "wanted to sit in the shade and have petting parties." Then, Lucy Morgan argued, "faculty members get concerned and hunt up various ropes and try to haul the laggards part way up—and they find that to do so it is easier to have the ones to be pulled go in compact groups."[138]

That was unacceptable. Arthur Morgan's stern dream had no room for petting parties, for student laggards, for faculty wives who objected that the Antioch plan made too many demands and disrupted family life.[139] But, as Dean Henderson sadly acknowledged, a faculty and student body of crusaders did not exist. Too many students, Henderson charged, "laid greater stress on monetary return" than on social reform.[140]

Ironically, prominent business patrons such as Kettering had begun, by the end of the decade, to worry that the college faculty and students were too radical rather than too mercenary. At the beginning of the decade, Morgan had argued that the Antioch plan would "spoil many a radical, because he comes to have respect for those long, hard processes, that long, hard road that the human race has traveled to find its present status."[141]

But Kettering and others were not so sure. At the end of its first decade, Antioch's honeymoon with business patronage had begun to sour. Hints appeared of the controversies that would loom large in the 1930s and 1940s. During those decades many business leaders, charging that the college tolerated Communism and other radical doctrines, resigned from the board. Trustee Russell

Steward summarized their feelings when he angrily charged that "Antioch has been supported mainly by employers and money . . . from business and as such owes them an obligation . . . but the college has not evidenced good faith with the people from whom they accepted money in large amounts." By the midforties Charles Kettering himself would repudiate Antioch. In a bitter letter making final his break with the college he doubted that "there is anything worth while at Yellow Springs. I think Antioch today is just another liberal arts college that has played with the radicals to get the attention of the public."[142]

Though the changes Kettering so decried really took place in the thirties, there were a few free spirits at Antioch during the 1920s, some of whom probably saw themselves as radicals. Professor William Leiserson, for instance, frequently lectured to socialist groups and attacked company unions and company paternalism. "Now," he would say, "is the time to take over these social programs again. Employers are binding wage earners to them by these various devices. . . . The working people of this country have fallen for that stuff."[143] Student Mather Eliot denounced an Antioch that was just another "finishing school for American businessmen."[144] Nevertheless, such students and professors, while often dramatic presences on campus, were members of a minority. In truth Algo Henderson's version of an Antioch where most students were eager to join the system and get ahead was the more accurate one. Still, Antioch's tradition of encouraging creativity and independent thought provided forums for the views of all. Some of the business leaders on the board were not at all convinced that the college was a "finishing school" for businessmen. By late 1928 meetings of the Antioch board were no longer love feasts for the college that sought to train proprietors; they instead rang with questions about teachers and courses.[145]

Arthur Morgan had never wanted to create a compliant educational adjunct to business. In fact, he may have turned down a huge corporate donation in order to maintain independence. In 1926 the *Outlook* reported that John Patterson had offered to finance Antioch, if it would leave rural Yellow Springs, reestablish itself on NCR grounds in Dayton, and rechristen itself the National Cash Register College. The magazine said, "Similarly tempted Trinity, in North Carolina, sold its birthright for a forty

million dollar mess of potage . . . cheerfully scrapping [its] name
. . . to enshrine the reputation of a cigarette millionaire." But, the
Outlook continued, Antioch was not Duke University, not interested in simply "fabricating" human products to meet current
industrial standards.[146]

Antioch may not have been interested in total business domination, but both college officials and business patrons agreed that
the creation of proprietors was a key goal. Their definitions,
however, sometimes differed. In 1921, for instance, Arthur Morgan and Charles Kettering sat on the same podium and shared
keynote speaking honors at a fund-raising dinner for Antioch.
Was each really listening closely to what the other said? Morgan
argued that "I would prefer not to have our young men trained at
Antioch become part of great organizations like the Pennsylvania
Railroad or the United States Steel Corporation."[147] Rather, he
wanted them to take the intellectual and practical skills gained at
Antioch to go out to start hundreds of new small businesses. His
proprietors wanted to be their own bosses. Morgan envisioned
them as socially responsible people who produced necessary
goods and services in a climate of fairness to their workers. In
fact, the new Antioch president worried that big businesses had
the ability to produce conditions "which menace our entire social
structure. . . . Let the village blacksmith mistreat his apprentice
boys if he will, and it has no effect on the world in general, but
take a great corporation employing half a million men, and let
them put economic pressure on their men, and the situation is a
direct attack on our entire country."[148]

Morgan sat down, and Charles Kettering rose. Kettering also
began his speech praising "proprietorship." He wanted to help
with the creation of a college that would train proprietors. But
then Kettering continued, "For the large number of foremen in
our various industries play a big part in the relations existing
between capital and labor. In fact I believe they control the situation, because they represent the management, and the policies of
the management to the men at the machines. So I believe that one
of our jobs at Antioch will be to fit these type of men for their jobs,
for it is a real job of proprietorship."[149] Indeed the time had
passed "when men are to be handled with the molder's hammer,
by having the policies of the company . . . pounded into them."

But the Antioch experiment would be proved "worth-while" if it created in the persons of its graduates "a better method of doing" the necessary work of passing the policies of the organization "down the line."[150] The audience politely applauded two strikingly different versions of proprietorship and Antioch's mission.

Scholarly interpretations of progressive education have been strikingly different as well, agreeing only that progressive educators were moderates. Lawrence Cremin, for instance, argued they were "fundamentally moderates," willing to "take time."[151] Michael Katz disagreed strongly with most of Cremin's sympathetic analysis but still concluded that the progressive education movement "sought reforms profoundly congruent with the conservative commercial ethos at the heart of American life."[152] Focusing on educational systems and leaders, these and most other scholars have viewed business only in a peripheral way, as a powerful force for regimentation that progressive educators either rebelled against or succumbed to.

A closer examination of progressive education in the Miami Valley suggests a more complex role for business. First, it suggests that the interpretative choices posed by scholars of progressive education have been too narrowly conceived. The student of progressive education has been limited to two general interpretations. One viewed the progressive classroom as an attempt to create an ideal community, opposed to business conformity and dedicated to the individual development of each student. The second saw that classroom as a factory, committed to aping business standards and values and interested in producing willing human cogs for the industrial machine. Only by continuing to see business as a faceless abstraction, however, can researchers allow such a dichotomy to persist.

In fact, businessmen in the Miami Valley were central to the progressive education revolution that changed public and private schooling. They wholeheartedly supported the introduction of business values in the schools and the imposition of business methods of management. They favored practical education and vocational education. But many also were committed to creating schools that encouraged morality and social responsibility and provided varied educational programs to suit individual needs.

There were important parallels between schools like the Moraine Park School and Antioch College, where businessmen sent their own children, and the Dayton public system.

The work-study programs of the Dayton public schools actually provided a better model for Arthur Morgan's Antioch co-op program than did the system at the University of Cincinnati Engineering School, which both contemporaries and later scholars have labeled Morgan's inspiration. Morgan, who chaired the Dayton Public Schools Building Project during the 1920s and who was an outspoken ally of Edwin Brown, clearly had an intimate acquaintance with the system.[153] The similarities among the three institutions here studied suggest that business progressives were interested in something more than shaping education to prepare students for their foreordained roles in the most cost-efficient manner possible.

Indeed, these progressive businessmen were idealists, interested in creating better communities, within schools and in the larger world. They were convinced, as they had been convinced of the value of welfare work, or of the Conservancy, or of city manager government, that their vision of a better community was the correct one. Progressive education in the Miami Valley was not dominated by a democratic impulse. Paul Stetson succeeded in shrinking the size of the Dayton School Board to five members.[154] Arthur Morgan deserved the epithets hurled at him in one faculty memorandum. He was "arbitrary, impatient, and dogmatic."[155] As he himself admitted in a letter, he was perfectly willing to "compel students into freedom" if need be.[156] It has been too easy, though, for historians to focus on this arrogance. In doing so, they have not seen clearly enough the passion that linked businessmen-reformers with ministers, social workers, or teachers like John Dewey. They have looked at the cost-accounting manuals and mandates about maximum efficiency in use of school property. They have neglected, however, to look carefully at the other side of business involvement with progressive education, a side revealed in the letters and correspondence of such men as Arthur Morgan.

Morgan, for instance, argued that "the critical issue in civilization was not "technical progress . . . but the enobling of human purposes, and the arousing of aspirations to that end." The Morgan who warned in that same letter that "only a burning and sustained passion will be effective" in seeking such a social goal was not so diametrically opposed to progressive figures like Washington Gladden as historians have often concluded.[157]

Finally, this closer look at business involvement with progressive education in the Miami Valley illustrates that even the reform-minded business community was not united entirely in its vision of what education should and could accomplish. Clearly Charles Kettering and Arthur Morgan were talking past each other at the same testimonial dinner. But at least a few, such as Morgan, the most important businessman-educator of the era for the region, stretched the limits of the adjective *moderate*, so universally applied to progressive education.

Far from seeking only reforms that would buttress the existing system, Morgan was a man in search of "a better economic order and a new religion."[158] That new religion took as its most important creed a commitment to the raising of human society to a higher plane. That Morgan brooked no dissent and spared no patience for any alternative vision exemplified the dilemma of the progressive business reformers here studied. As they devised benefit programs for employees, new flood control plans, city manager local government, or new systems of education, they were men who wanted to compel their fellow citizens into freedom. And they possessed, at least until the onset of the Great Depression, unbridled optimism that they could indeed reshape human nature. They also possessed the managerial skills and ruthless temperaments helpful to them as they imposed their grand plans and defeated entrenched interests opposed to change. But as they discovered by the end of the decade of the 1920s, they could not so easily control the process of change itself.

6

Conclusion

Changing is the one adjective that best describes the United States during the decades between 1890 and 1930. Scarcely anything about the country's life and culture remained unaffected. The reform phenomenon known to contemporaries and historians alike as progressivism was both engine and product of this maelstrom of change.

Recognition of the nature and importance of business involvement is central to an understanding of progressivism, in the same way that recognition of the nature and importance of business change is central to an understanding of the dramatic organizational changes sweeping the United States during the progressive era. If progressives are defined as persons seeking to make a better society, not just for themselves but for all citizens, then a community of reform-minded businessmen in southern Ohio earned the label. They were not only important progressives; they were the most important progressives in the region. Under their tutelage their communities drastically reshaped institutions like municipal government and education. They created others, like structures for regional flood control and corporate personnel relations, from whole cloth.

Robert Wiebe has argued that "progressive businessmen singularly lacked a grand social vision."[1] But the efforts of progressive businessmen here chronicled challenge that conclusion. Indeed, they did have grand plans, plans propelled by a vision. Given the right mechanisms, they believed they could create social institutions that would be models for the nation. Dayton, Ohio, could be a "model city."[2] Its public schools could "extend their influence" by showing citizens and school administrators alike how children should be taught.[3] The "eyes of hundreds of thousands of people" would rest on the region and find solutions to the problems a rapidly urbanizing and industrializing country faced.[4]

It was not a vision motivated solely by practical self-interest. Clearly the businessmen who created the programs this study has described were not selfless individuals. They wanted a well-ordered, efficient community that respected private property and private enterprise. Such a type of community would likely encourage stability and promote their own profits.

But historians who have repeatedly emphasized the role played by self-interest as a motivation for businessmen's involvement with progressivism have unnecessarily downplayed the roles also played by religious conviction and moral fervor. Arthur Morgan once impatiently chastised people with "one-track minds" who assumed that any strong interest excluded its opposite. "Tell such a person that you are interested in science," Morgan complained, "and he will say, 'Oh, but religion is so much more important.' "[5]

Historians would do well to heed his warning. The businessmen reformers of the Miami Valley were nobody's sentimental fools. But to have them simply represent "the hard side of progressivism" implies that business had nothing in common with a "soft" side of reform.[6] And that overstates the case. In fact, social worker and businessman, missionary and corporate tycoon were not separated into such easily identifiable sides.

Prominent businessmen-reformers like John H. Patterson, Arthur Morgan, and Edward A. Deeds were also well-known churchmen, active proponents of variations of Protestant Social Gospel doctrine. Such kinds of membership were, of course, not unusual for community leaders. In and of themselves they signified little. But unless great numbers of their public statements are to be discounted, these businessmen coupled a fervor for morality with one for efficiency. Scholars should not impose a double standard on documents, reading Washington Gladden and finding a hunger for a better, more ethical society but reading John H. Patterson and finding only clever words meant to disguise a hunger for ever more profit.

The morality these businessmen advocated differed from that

of other progressives only in the heavy influence placed on the need for a strong masculine influence in reform efforts. Without it, too much sentimentality could reign. Men as well as women had a duty to be concerned about educating children, feeding the poor, providing safe food and water. If women alone led such efforts citizens would only be "mothered." But they needed to be "fathered" as well. As Arthur Morgan argued, "The father . . . knows that the storm can make its contribution as well as the fireside, that only rigorous living can develop stamina, that a morality which has never faced stress is not yet secure."[7]

Mrs. Milan Ayres, secretary of the Progressive Education Association, found when she journeyed to Dayton for a national meeting of the organization in 1921 a place "permeated with spirituality."[8] But it was not, as she said, like the "emotion" she found back home in the East. Her male allies there, she said, were "largely of the mother-type." Ayres hastened to add that she did not mean that they were effeminate. They were, however, more willing to work with and be led by women, who were "struggling" for better education and social justice.[9] Mrs. Ayres thought that the unwillingness of Dayton businessmen to work with women as equals might have harmed their causes, but she softened her criticism with well-worn rhetoric about feminine wiles and manly virtues: "In Mr. Kettering's speech last night didn't you get the feeling that there were some things the hard-headed men can do?"[10]

Mrs. Ayres thought it was extraordinary that not a single trustee for the Moraine Park School was a woman. In the context of national and state progressive movements in which women played key roles, it was. In the Ohio Miami Valley, so influenced by a progressive business community concerned with "masculine morality" women played secondary roles, even though women in other parts of the state were very influential reform leaders.[11] And men held jobs often held in these other areas by women. Men overwhelmingly dominated the new boards for public and private schools for which businessmen were patrons.[12] Males filled the new city posts of welfare director and health inspector. If anything, women, in subordinate posts, emerged as opponents of at least one major progressive reform in the area. Many female teachers in the Dayton public schools apparently hated superintendents Brown and Stetson and their unhappiness, if not their names, found its way into school board records. Other women, also in subordinate posts, reinforced stereotypes about female incompetence. Pity the wayward un- wed mother condemned to a black comedy of disorder at the Door of Hope. But of course women teachers protesting against Edwin Brown's new curriculum or, worse yet, the Door of Hope's Moth- er Clark, burning oil lamps in a new building wired for electricity, just confirmed many Valley business progressives in their em- phasis on "masculine" reform and their belief that women should be in the home.

If these kinds of leadership differences were common in areas dominated by a reform-oriented business community, they de- serve a great deal further scrutiny by scholars. Roles assigned women might be one of many elements dividing business pro- gressivism from other reformist variations. At the very least, the events here analyzed in the Ohio Miami Valley suggest that historians should stop dividing progressivism into "hard" and "soft" sides—a side concerned with morality and a side con- cerned with manipulating the system for self-interest, a side for moral reformers and a side for businessmen. They would be better advised to investigate the kinds of distinctions different groups of progressives may have made in their moral codes, in their choices of leaders, and in the priorities they placed on a range of goals and programs. What were the common links? How important were any differences? Was the pattern seen in Ohio's Miami Valley unique?

If indeed, as seems plausible, businessmen in the Miami Valley shared traits with their counterparts elsewhere, the American business community was not peopled by the same nerveless bureaucrats who appear as characters in the works of some histo- rians whose main purpose has been to depict the emergence of a new organizational society in the late nineteenth and early twen- tieth centuries.

Historians such as Samuel Hays, Louis Galambos, and Robert Wiebe have made signal contributions to an understanding not just of progressivism but also of business interaction with pro- gressivism. They are undoubtedly right that businessmen and business models played a major role as people came together in the decades spanning the Spanish-American War and the Great Depression to remake American society. Businessmen and their creation, the business corporation, indeed helped to shape a new national society that was more urban, better connected geographically, and more dependent on technical information and specialized vocations.[13]

But any student of the progressive era should remember that it was a period in which society was in rapid transition. Progressivism was a movement of response to transition, itself perpetually in transition. No one group, certainly not the businessmen who shaped reform in the Ohio Miami Valley, realized the outlines of change with the kind of steely-eyed clarity that in retrospect they have won from organizational historians.

Men like John H. Patterson, Edward Deeds, Charles Kettering, and Arthur Morgan helped to shape modern corporate structures. But they were part of a process in progress, not defenders of a system in place, not even themselves sure of or in agreement about final outcomes. Progressive era businessmen, these men suggest, were not yet men in gray flannel suits. Instead they were members of the last whole generation of business leaders who could be called both charismatic men and corporate men. They were men who sobbed on speaking platforms, not anonymous bureaucrats with some well-understood blueprint for the new organizational society. They too were confused and divided, at times even among themselves. And important to remember was the fact that in the Miami Valley only a minority of businessmen deserved the label *progressive*. Far more businesses in Dayton allied with John Kirby than with John Patterson. But this minority, at least in the Miami Valley, exercised an influence out of all proportion to its numbers. Perhaps in numerous other regions business communities echoed this pattern.

Unlike the members of the Dayton Employers Association, united by fear, progressive businessmen were united by optimism. The Employers Association dreaded unionization and sought to crush it. It wanted to stop change. Businessmen who deserved the title *progressive* often welcomed change, confident that they and society would benefit. Although all the prominent members of the progressive business community here studied were members of Protestant churches, their real religion was science. They shared an optimism stirred by a boundless faith in the positive promises of science and the scientific method.

If society could only become propelled by logic, its every aspect could improve. Human beings could even engineer their own improvement. Some business progressives, like Arthur Morgan, carried a faith in scientific method into a vigorous advocacy of eugenics. In a 1927 Antioch College newsletter, for instance, Morgan indulged a "New Year Fantasy." "Have you heard," he wrote, "how the Martians achieved their remarkable level of health, vigor, endurance, beauty, intelligence, and character?" It was through the development of a "point system." Under such a point system, Martians were rated on every important personal quality, with the completed ratings placed in public records halls. Hearing, sight, condition of nerves, glands, muscles, and many other physical traits were weighted and recorded. Alertness, stability, "sanity," and dozens of other mental and moral traits were appraised. Copies of the appraisal in hand, "Martianesses" decided which Martians to marry. The system, run by the Martian Rating Society, was entirely voluntary, but when Martians learned that "to be unrated was to lose standing" nearly all joined up.[14]

No doubt to Arthur Morgan's regret the Ohio Miami Valley never became "Mars." But Morgan's fable illustrated a central truth behind the optimism spurring business progressivism. It was a faith in process, in the ability of a few to engineer better systems for the benefit of all. But it was certainly not a faith in the people. In fact there was a profoundly antidemocratic streak in business progressivism. The appointed—often self-appointed— group of experts in a local community was the ideal agent to stimulate action. Interestingly, at a time when their own corporations were becoming very large, when they were learning to develop national and international marketing strategies, these businessmen still looked to communities and voluntary associations, not state or federal government, for solutions when crises arose. After the great 1913 flood, for instance, the Dayton City Council quickly petitioned federal authorities. "The federal government," a council resolution read, "should at once appropriate a sufficient amount of money to place the city of Dayton beyond the liability of another disaster such as that through which we have just passed."[15] On a vote of fifteen ayes and zero nayes, the council sent the resolution to the district's U.S. congressman, with instructions that he should plead for sufficient funds to cut a new channel for the Miami River.[16] The business-sponsored Citizens' Flood Relief Committee was not interested in such an approach. Morgan later explained that one of the group's first jobs "was to get the people to see that waiting for federal relief would be long drawn out and possibly futile in the end, and that the way for them to get results was to help themselves."[17] It was a point of view that had to be "developed quickly" so that "no one would have to start off on futile trips to Washington and dissipate his energies through seeking federal aid."[18]

Popular opinion had indeed to be "developed." It certainly did not have to be followed. A unanimous vote by their elected representatives on the Dayton City Council meant simply that once again the people were wrong. Their general wariness of federal intervention reflected Miami Valley business progressives' more central lack of faith in electoral government at all levels. And that lack of faith in popular judgment, that lack of trust in democracy provides a key to understanding the successes and failures of business progressivism in the Ohio Miami Valley.

Of the four "grand plans" here described, the Miami Conservancy District was the greatest success, an engineering breakthrough that did make the region floodproof at a fraction of the cost of conventional methods. Moreover, the dam system, when complete, blended into the southwestern Ohio landcape, providing thousands of acres of public park land for the region's citizens to enjoy, as well as thousands of acres of enriched farmland.

Of course, the Conservancy District was in a literal sense an engineering problem. Much of the initial public resistance to the plan was actually based on popular ignorance of its use of new, very sophisticated concepts in hydraulics engineering. Morgan and Deeds were right. The farmers in the Valley's northern counties who marched in the streets shouting that they would be drowned were wrong. The experts knew what they were doing. The fact that many average citizens feared the new scientific ideas did not keep the Conservancy planners from pushing ahead, to the entire region's eventual benefit.

Engineering dams proved easier than engineering human beings. Business progressives rightly believed in the science of hydraulics engineering, but they also believed that, with the discovery of proper methods, there could be a science of educational engineering, governmental engineering, personnel engineering. They sought to discover logical rules for promoting maximum productivity and amity between employers and employees.

In their search for the structures and techniques that would perfectly engineer the work accomplished by schools, at city hall, or on the factory floor, Miami Valley business progressives emphasized literacy and creativity. They wanted children in schools to have more options and opportunities geared to their inclinations and skills. They encouraged their employees to spend time, even sometimes paid time on the job, reading and learning. They wanted a municipal government that was businesslike and efficient. But they also wanted a municipal information center that shared knowledge with the citizenry about health issues, the economy, and a host of other topics. In essence, these reformers wanted to create in the Miami Valley a model series of communities. They hoped to create towns and cities where responsible, highly literate citizens used logic and creativity to attack their problems.

They expected a great deal of the very people for whom they often expressed barely disguised disdain. Ironically, the reforms they engineered reduced the chances for a better-educated citizenry to participate freely in shaping the region's workplaces, schools, or forms of government. And as a result they were never truly popular. Not being firmly rooted but rather heavily dependent on the patronage of an elite dominated by businessmen, progressive education, city manager government, and welfare work were all innovations more than usually subject to economic cycles. They were quick to decline when hard times hit. They were certainly not able to fulfill their promise of bringing perfection to a corner of the United States.

But the promise of perfection had seemed real. It was that promise that propelled businessmen-reformers like John H. Patterson to seek to remake the Miami Valley. For some, like Patterson, no detail was too small. For instance, during the summer of 1914, in an act clearly illustrating both the generosity and arrogance of business-progressivism, the National Cash Register president personally supervised the repainting of houses he saw along his route to work. Deciding that the structures were too "dingy," Patterson sent an agent to the owners of the homes he had to pass to announce that he would provide paint and workmen, free of charge. "A week or two later," an admiring reporter noted, "there was not a house in a stretch of more than two miles that needed painting."[19]

Neighborhood beautification was, of course, only the beginning of Patterson's plans. It was, however, a relatively simple matter to persuade homeowners, many of whom were NCR workers and in no position to challenge their boss, to accept a free coat of house paint. It proved more difficult to create a harmonious and vastly improved society. By the late 1920s the mood of enthusiasm for what had seemed boundless possibilities had begun to evaporate. Even the Dayton *Daily News,* owned by Governor James Cox's family and a supporter of the enthusiastic visions of business reformers, faltered. A 1927 editorial warned, "Much ignorance, incompetency, and general foolishness stands [*sic*] between us and the land of our dreams. . . . The only way is to muddle along as best we can, making mistakes and learning sense by hard knocks. This precludes socialist utopias, and it precludes making ourselves sheep under some Mr. Mellon Shepherd capable of immediately delivering the goods."[20]

The grand plans left important legacies, providing models, as their creators intended, not just for southern Ohio, but for the nation. None of the institutions changed during the progressive era returned to its nineteenth-century form. But with the exception of the Miami Conservancy District, the grand plans certainly did not "immediately deliver the goods." They were not the grand successes their businessmen creators had wanted. In fact some of these men ended the era filled with anguish, haunted by a feeling that they had failed. And indeed their ideas had not managed to reengineer society for steady progress toward a better world. The institutional changes wrought by business progressivism actually struck a significant blow to one potential mechanism for social improvement, popular electoral participation. In the stern light of historical hindsight, the grand plans were too often simply grandiose, naively ambitious, based on an imperfect understanding of human nature, burdened with a disdain for democracy, and dependent on prosperity to survive intact. Nevertheless, that judgment must be tempered with admiration for the faith and fervor pushing a group of committed businessmen-reformers who, armed with incredible optimism and a heady faith in the scientific method, tried to remake and improve their communities. In purpose, if not achievement, the grand plans really were grand.

Notes

1. Business and Progressivism

1. Population statistics from: John Andriot, ed., *Population Abstract of the United States* (McLean, Va., 1980). Detailed discussion of sources for information about industrialization in nineteenth-century Dayton and the Miami Valley can be found in chap. 2, note 1.

2. Quoted in Michael Weber, *Social Mobility in Nineteenth Century America: Myth and Reality* (St. Charles, Mo., 1975), 4-5.

3. For analyses of the nineteenth-century American economy, see Simon Kuznets, *Economic Growth and Structure* (New York, 1965); Harold Vatter, *The Drive to Industrial Maturity: The U.S. Economy, 1860-1914* (Westport, Conn., 1975); Seymour Harris, ed., *American Economic History* (New York, 1961); Alan Trachtenberg, *The Incorporation of America: Culture and Society in the Gilded Age* (New York, 1982).

4. For discussions of the "organizational synthesis," see Alfred Chandler and Richard Tedlow, eds., *The Coming of Managerial Capitalism: A Casebook on the History of American Economic Institutions* (Homewood, Ill., 1985); Louis Galambos, "Technology, Political Economy, and Professionalization: Central Themes of the Organizational Synthesis," *Business History Review* 57 (1983): 471-93; Robert Cuff, "American Historians and the 'Organizational Factor,'" *Canadian Review of American Studies* 4 (Spring 1973): 19-31; Robert Berkhofer, "The Organizational Interpretation of American History: A New Synthesis," *Prospects* 4 (1979): 611-29.

5. For discussions of this anxious mood in late nineteenth-century America, see Otis Graham, *The Great Campaigns: Reform and War in America, 1900-1928* (Englewood Cliffs, N.J., 1971), part 1; John Chambers, *The Tyranny of Change: America in the Progressive Era, 1900-1917* (New York, 1980); Lewis Gould, ed., *The Progressive Era* (Syracuse, N.Y., 1974); R. Jackson Wilson, *In Quest of Community: Social Philosophy in the United States, 1860-1920* (New York, 1968).

6. Peter Filene, "An Obituary for the 'Progressive Movement,'" *American Quarterly* 22 (1970): 20-34.

7. Frank Stewart, *A Half Century of Municipal Reform: The History of the National Municipal League* (Berkeley, Calif., 1950); Bradley Rice, *Progressive Cities: The Commission Government Movement in America, 1901-1920* (Austin, Tex., 1977).

8. Charles and Mary Beard, *The Rise of American Civilization* (New York, 1927); Harold Faulkner, *The Quest for Social Justice, 1890-1914* (New York, 1931); Benjamin Parke DeWitt, *The Progressive Movement* (New York, 1915).

9. The word is the Beards', *Rise of American Civilization*, 543. See also the discussion of the Beards' work in William Anderson, "Progressivism: An Historiographical Essay," *History Teacher* 5 (1973): 427-28.

10. These contemporaneous authors tended to argue that to mobilize quickly, the national government turned to large corporations and abandoned its role of watchdog. Citizens, disillusioned at the end of the war they had thought would preserve democracy but instead seemed only to preserve secret European treaty systems, no longer could summon the zeal to crusade for a better society at home. See Anderson, "Progressivism," 428-29.

11. Richard Hofstadter, *The Age of Reform: From Bryan to F.D.R.* (New York, 1955). Strains of the argument also appear in Professor Hofstadter's later works, including *Anti-Intellectualism in American Life* (New York, 1963), and *The Progressive Historians: Turner, Beard, and Parrington* (New York, 1968).

12. George Mowry, *The California Progressives* (Berkeley, Calif., 1951); idem, *The Era of Theodore Roosevelt and the Birth of Modern America* (New York, 1958); Alfred Chandler, "The Origins of Progressive Leadership," in *The Letters of Theodore Roosevelt*, ed. Elting Morrison (Cambridge, Mass., 1963). See also the review of the consensus school in David Kennedy, "Overview: The Progressive Era," *Historian* 37 (1975): 455-58; However, these historians noted, that reform effort no longer emerged as such a clear victory for the forces of democracy. And the progressives, no longer that amorphous group "the people," showed their warts. Propelled by genuine religious fervor and a wish to tame industrial abuse, they were also stimulated by fear of immigrants and immigrant culture. They were intolerant, moralistic, and often racist. This view of progressivism did not long remain unchallenged. Their works appearing contemporaneously with those of Hofstadter, Mowry, and the others, scholars like Morton White and Eric Goldman attacked the idea that progressives sought to restore an idealized form of the nineteenth-century social order. Rather, progressives like Charles Beard, John Dewey, or Thorstein Veblen had begun to replace nineteenth-century values with a new intellectual framework, one that emphasized that neither

knowledge nor ethics could exist as absolutes. Instead, they were good if they served useful goals. That kind of logic, these scholars argued, could certainly not be labeled an intellectual yearning for the past. In fact many progressives were involved in a "revolt against formalism." See, for instance, Morton White, *Social Thought in America: The Revolt against Formalism* (Boston, 1949); Eric Goldman, *Rendezvous with Destiny: A History of Modern American Reform* (New York, 1952).

13. Scholars in the 1950s produced a variety of regional studies, often a blend of both the Hofstadter and Beard versions of progressivism. Russell Nye, for example, in his *Midwestern Progressive Politics: A History of Its Origins and Development, 1870-1958* (East Lansing, Mich., 1959) continued to interpret progressivism as a struggle for democracy against industrialism. He did agree, however, that progressive leaders were not those who had suffered most financially. There were not, for instance, embattled farmers.

14. Richard Sherman, "The Status Revolution and Massachusetts Progressive Leadership," *Political Science Quarterly* 78 (1963): 59-65; Daniel Potts, "The Progressive Profile in Iowa," *Mid-America* 47 (1965): 257-68; David Thelen, "Social Tensions and the Origins of Progressivism," *Journal of American History* 56 (1969): 328-41.

15. Gabriel Kolko, *Railroads and Regulation, 1877-1916* (Princeton, 1965); Gabriel Kolko, *The Triumph of Conservatism: A Reinterpretation of American History* (New York, 1963). William Appleman Williams, in his earlier *Contours of American History* (Cleveland, 1961), had argued along similar lines.

16. See, for instance, James Weinstein, *The Corporate Ideal in the Liberal State, 1900-1918* (Boston, 1968); Raymond Callahan, *Education and the Cult of Efficiency: A Study of the Social Forces That Have Shaped the Administration of the Public Schools* (Chicago, 1962).

17. See, for a summary of arguments, J. Joseph Huthmacher, "A Critique of the Kolko Thesis," in *From Roosevelt to Roosevelt: American Politics and Diplomacy, 1901-1941,* ed. Otis Graham (New York, 1971), 101-2.

18. Kolko, *Triumph of Conservatism,* 1.

19. Robert Wiebe, *The Search for Order, 1877-1920* (New York, 1967), 19; See also Robert Wiebe, *Businessmen and Reform: A Study of the Progressive Movement* (Cambridge, Mass., 1962); idem, *The Segmented Society: An Introduction to the Meaning of America* (New York, 1975); Samuel Hays, *The Response to Industrialism, 1885-1914* (Chicago, 1957); idem, *Conservation and the Gospel of Efficiency* (Chicago, 1959); idem, "The Politics of Reform in Municipal Government in the Progressive Era," *Pacific Northwest Quarterly* 55 (1968): 157-69.

20. Louis Galambos, *The Public and the Image of Big Business in America, 1880-1940* (Baltimore, 1975), 3.

21. For instance, see Louis Galambos, "The Emerging Organizational

Synthesis in Modern American History," *Business History Review* 44 (1970): 279-90; Robert Berkhofer, "Organizational Interpretation," 611-29; Galambos, "Technology, Political Economy, and Professionalization," 471-93; David Hounshell, "Commentary on the Discipline of the History of American Technology," *Journal of American History* 67 (1981): 854-65.

22. David Thelen, *The New Citizenship: Origins of Progressivism in Wisconsin, 1885-1900* (Columbia, Mo., 1972); Sheldon Hackney, *Populism to Progressivism in Alabama* (Princeton, 1969). Interestingly, as Hackney's title implies, these arguments also sometimes resurrected the arguments of early analysts that Populism and progressivism were connected. George Mowry, who traced the similarity of progressive and antebellum reformers' goals, declared in 1972, for instance, "Progressivism obviously had its political roots in Populism." *The Progressive Era, 1900-1920: The Reform Persuasion* (Washington, D.C., 1972), 5.

23. Albo Martin, *Enterprise Denied: Origins of the Decline of American Railroads, 1897-1917* (New York, 1971).

24. See, for instance, Arthur Link and Richard McCormick, *Progressivism* (Arlington Heights, Ill., 1983); John Buenker, John Burnham, and Robert Crunden, *Progressivism* (Cambridge, Mass., 1977).

25. Richard McCormick persuasively summarizes this argument in his "Discovery That Business Corrupts Politics: A Reappraisal of the Origins of Progressivism," *American Historical Review* 86 (1981): 247-74.

26. See, for example, Ellis Hawley, "The Discovery and Study of 'Corporate Liberalism,' " *Business History Review* 52 (1978): 309-21.

27. Ibid.

28. Daniel Rodgers, "In Search of Progressivism," *Reviews in American History* 10 (1982): 121.

29. Peter Buck, "Telephone Books and Party Lines," *Reviews in American History* 14 (1986): 341.

30. Ibid.

31. Charles Kettering, title to draft of speech, summarized in typescript copy, 1920, the Antiochiana Collection, uncatalogued files, Antioch College Library, Antioch College, Yellow Springs, Ohio.

32. See, for example, E.L. Shuey, "Model Factory Town," *Municipal Affairs* 3 (1899): 144-51; S. Rogers, "Putting Heart into Work," *Outlook* 125 (1920): 705-10; "Driving Politics out of Dayton," *Literary Digest* 48 (1913): 147-48; "Why It Pays Patterson to Be the Best Employer in America," *Current Opinion* 4 (1917): 322.

33. Good examples include Stuart Brandes, *American Welfare Capitalism, 1880-1940* (Chicago, 1976); Bradley Rice, *Progressive Cities: The Commission Government Movement in America, 1901-1920* (Austin, Tex., 1977); Joel Spring, *Education and the Rise of the Corporate State* (Boston, 1972).

34. For a summary of the arguments about chronology, see Buenker,

Burnham, and Crunden, *Progressivism,* 110-25; See also Arthur Link, "What Happened to the Progressive Movement in the 1920s?" *American Historical Review* 64 (1959): 833-51; Paul Glad, "Progressivism and the Business Culture of the 1920s," *Journal of American History* 53 (1966): 75-89.

35. Mansel Blackford, *The Politics of Business in California, 1890-1920* (Columbus, Ohio, 1977), 170.

36. Judith Papachristou, *Bibliography in the History of Women in the Progressive Era* (New York, 1985); Dennis Harrison, "The Consumers' League of Ohio: Women and Reform, 1909-1937" (Ph.D. diss., Case Western Reserve University, 1975); Kathryn Kish Sklar, "Hull House: A Community of Women Reformers," *Signs* 10 (1985): 658-77.

37. Bureau of the Census, *Statistical Abstract of the United States, 1930* (Washington, D.C., 1930), 22-26; Bureau of the Census, *Statistical Abstract of the United States, 1940* (Washington, D.C. 1942), 24-30; Bureau of the Census, *Abstract of the Fourteenth Census of the United States, 1920* (Washington, D.C., 1923), 128-31.

2. Employee Welfare at National Cash Register

1. Among such Dayton companies were S.N. Browne and Co., manufacturers of carriage wheels; Pierce and Coleman, wholesale dressers of lumber; the Dayton Furniture Co., maker of bedroom sets; the Dayton Wheel Works, makers of wagon wheels and spokes; the Dayton Machine Co., makers of hay rakes; J.W. Stoddard and Co., Printz and Kuhns, the Aughe Plow Works, the Farmers' Friend Manufacturing Co., and the Woodsum Machine Co., all makers of agricultural machinery, particularly threshers and plows; the Dayton Malleable Iron Works, the C.C. Morrison Co., and the Stilwell and Bierce Co., all makers of iron castings, carriage hardware, and iron fittings used in flour mills; the Banner Mills, Commercial Mills, Dayton City Mills, Dayton View Mills, Oregon Mills, and Ludlow Star Mills, all flour mills. See Joseph Sharts, *Biography of Dayton: An Economic Interpretation of Local History* (Dayton, 1922), 52-59; John C. Wait, "Car Building Industry in the United States," *Engineering Magazine* 9 (1895): 686; Carl Becker, "Economic and Technological Change in the Railroad Car Building Industry and the Response of the Barney and Smith Car Company, 1893-1926" (unpublished paper), pamphlet file, Archives and Special Collections Department, Wright State University (hereafter, WSU).

2. A partial list of the new kinds of firms that rapidly displaced the old includes the W.P. Callahan Co., manufacturers of gasoline engines; the Ohio Foundry, makers of electric generators; the Pasteur-Chamberland Co., making germproof water filters; the Egry Register Co.,

making autographic recording machines; the Dayton Manufacturing Co., makers of railroad hardware, lamps and electroliers; the New Era Gas Engine Co.; the Computing Scale Co.; the Speedwell Motor Car Co., which began manufacturing automobiles in the plant of the old Stoddard firm, which had made hay rakes; the Courier Motor Car Co., and finally, by 1909, the Wright Aeroplane Co. Sharts, *Biography of Dayton,* 63-68; A.W. Drury, *A History of Dayton and Montgomery County, Ohio* (Dayton, 1909), 456-60.

3. Samuel Crowther, *John H. Patterson: Pioneer in Industrial Welfare* (New York, 1923), 61-64.

4. Ibid.

5. Alfred Chandler has argued that the railroads were the first "modern" corporations. The NCR, however, certainly made many contributions to the development of this type of business enterprise, characterized, as again Chandler was the first to argue, by many distinct operating units and a hierarchy of salaried executives. See *The Railroads: The Nation's First Big Business* (New York, 1965); *The Visible Hand: The Managerial Revolution in American Business* (Cambridge, Mass., 1977).

6. Roy Johnson and Russell Lynch, *The Sales Strategy of John H. Patterson* (Chicago, 1932), 33.

7. Only a partial list of prominent business leaders who began their careers with the NCR includes Thomas Watson, president of IBM (then called the Computing-Tabulating-Recording Co.); Alvan Macauley, president of the Packard Motor Car Co.; E.S. Jordan, president of the Jordan Motor Car Co.; Harry Ford, president of the Saxon Motor Car Co.; Charles Kettering, creator of the electric self-starter and numerous other important inventions, later a prominent executive at General Motors; and dozens of others. For extensive lists of names see ibid.; Crowther, *John H. Patterson,* 231-32.

8. In the past ten years several scholars have investigated American welfare work. Among the best studies are Gerald Zahavi, "Negotiated Loyalty: Welfare Capitalism and the Shoeworkers of Endicott Johnson, 1920–1940," *Journal of American History* 71 (1983): 602-20; Stephen Meyer, *The Five-Dollar Day; Labor Management and Social Control in the Ford Motor Company, 1908-1921* (Albany, N.Y., 1981); Tamara K. Hareven, *Family Time and Industrial Time: The Relationship between the Family and Work in a New England Industrial Community* (Cambridge, England, 1982); Daniel Nelson, *Managers and Workers: Origins of the New Factory System in the United States, 1880-1920* (Madison, Wis., 1975); Brandes, *American Welfare Capitalism. Welfare work* was the name for the phenomenon very often used by its contemporaries. It is the term I will use most often, as the term with the greatest historical authenticity and as the term that partially at least avoids the implications of probusiness values in the term *welfare capitalism* and the implications of prounion values in the term

industrial paternalism. For discussion of similar company practices in England, see Charles Dellheim, "The Creation of a Company Culture: Cadburys, 1861-1931," *American Historical Review* 92 (1987): 13-45. There is evidence that John H. Patterson was aware of such practices, especially at Cadburys. He visited that company's plants on two of his European trips. See the Patterson Scrapbook Collection, European trips scrapbooks, the Corporate Archives, NCR World Headquarters, Dayton, Ohio (hereafter, NCR Head.).

9. The NCR continued many elaborate recreation programs well into the 1960s. Stanley Allyn, *My Half-Century with NCR* (New York, 1967), 150-52.

10. *The N.C.R.* (March 1905), 91-92. NCR Headquarters has an extensive collection of in-house publications.

11. Allyn, *My Half-Century,* 59.

12. "The Unfinished Autobiography of John H. Patterson," handwritten manuscript, NCR Head. This partial autobiography has apparently been kept at the NCR Headquarters since the 1940s. The author rediscovered it during the course of her research at the company archives. Apparently Patterson in 1920 hired Otto Nelson, a long-time NCR employee who worked in the company projection department, as his secretary and research assistant for the autobiography project. Installed at a desk in Patterson's home, Nelson spent the next two years transcribing Patterson's reminiscences and collecting copies of his talks, lectures, and published articles. When Patterson was in Dayton, which was not often, he "occasionally gave his attention to the autobiography." Not surprisingly, the project remained unfinished at the time of Patterson's death in 1922. In 1945 Nelson apparently tried to interest an agent in finding a publisher for the manuscript, which, though unfinished, was definitely not just a fragment. The portion at the NCR Archives is approximately ninety thousand words long. (Such a length estimate provides a better sense of the character of the manuscript, since many of the handwritten pages are not completely filled.) Apparently Nelson did not manage to secure an agent. The manuscript was not published but instead stored at the company office. (Hereafter it will be referred to as Patterson autobiography.) For discussion about the nature of the autobiography, see Otto Nelson to Edward Bodin, August 21, 1945, NCR Head.

13. Edwin Shuey, "A Model Factory Town," *Municipal Affairs* 3 (March 1899): 144-51; Carroll Fugitt, "The Truce between Capital and Labor," *Cassier's* 28 (Sept. 1905): 339-45; "Discussion of Palms in the Factory," Records of the Advance Club, meeting of April 23, 1897, 5-6, Patterson Collection Book 104, NCR Head. The Advance Club was composed of officers of the NCR, heads of departments, assistant heads, and

foremen. Fifty members of the rank and file at the company, chosen by lot and changing every month, also attended Advance Club meetings, which were held every Friday morning from 1896 probably until 1910. Records and Minutes of Advance Club meetings will hereafter be cited as Advance.

14. Or at least so thought Stanley Allyn, who came to the company as a young man in 1913 and rose to be president in 1940. Allyn, *My Half-Century*, 9.

15. "Discussion of the Bathing Privilege," remarks by George Grove, April 23, 1897, Advance, NCR Head.

16. See, for instance, *The N.C.R.* (June 1894): 148; *The N.C.R.* (May 1894): 121; NCR Head.

17. "The Health Pyramid," *The N.C.R.* (June 1907): 78.

18. Throughout the period here discussed, most NCR employees were men. The ratios between 1896 and 1927 usually averaged nine to one. See remarks of Mr. Griffith, April 23, 1897, 6, Advance; "A Ten Million Dollar Payroll," *The N.C.R.* (April 1927), NCR Head.

19. *The N.C.R.* (March 1905): 94.

20. See, for example: Sherman Rogers, "Putting Heart into Work," *Outlook* 112 (Aug. 1920): 705-10. Rogers called the NCR factory buildings "art palaces."

21. *Woman's Welfare* (March 1905): 10. *Woman's Welfare* was a pamphlet published quarterly by the Women's Century Club at the NCR, NCR Head.

22. Patterson autobiography, 184.

23. *The Boy Gardeners: Our Own Story,* pamphlet printed by the NCR Boys' Garden Company (1911?), NCR Head. See also Edwin Owen Greening, "Garden Progress in the Boys' Gardens in Dayton, Ohio," *One and All Gardening* (London, 1913). The gardens got wide publicity within the United States and even garnered some international attention, as indicated by the above citation from an English gardening annual. At a board of directors' meeting, May 31, 1902, the company agreed to order two clay and paper maché models of the gardens, one to be sent to Teachers College, Columbia University, for prominent display. Minutes, board of directors meeting, National Cash Register Company, Minutes Book 2, 119, NCR Head. (hereafter, minutes of the board of directors' meetings of the NCR Company will be cited as Board).

24. Lena Harvey Tracy, *How My Heart Sang: The Story of Pioneer Industrial Welfare Work* (New York, 1950), 133.

25. "The Camp of National Cash Register Employees at Michigan City, Indiana," *American Machinist* (Sept. 1906): 361-62.

26. *N.C.R. News* (May 1916): 8-9, NCR Head.

27. Shuey, "Model Town," 147.

28. For example, the profit-sharing plan in 1924 cost the company $1,490,711.26. *N.C.R. News* (June 1925): 33, NCR Head.

29. *N.C.R. News* (Jan. 1917): 19, NCR Head.

30. "Discussion of Effects of Privileges," April 23, 1897, 7, Advance, NCR Head.

31. For discussions of the connections between progressivism and scientific management, see Samuel Haber, *Efficiency and Uplift: Scientific Management in the Progressive Era, 1896-1920* (Chicago, 1964); Daniel Nelson, *Frederick W. Taylor and the Rise of Scientific Management* (Madison, Wis., 1980); David Noble, *America by Design* (New York, 1977); William Akin, *Technocracy and the American Dream* (Berkeley, Calif., 1974).

32. *N.C.R. News* (Jan. 1919): 31, NCR Head.

33. Certainly Taylorism and welfare work could coexist, if somewhat uneasily, as Daniel Nelson and Stuart Campbell have demonstrated in "Taylorism versus Welfare Work in American Industry: H.L. Gant and the Bancrofts," *Business History Review* 66 (1972): 1-11.

34. "Letters from a Workingman," *Outlook* 88 (March 1908): 552-55.

35. Rogers, "Putting Heart into Work," 707.

36. Patterson autobiography, 24.

37. Tracy, *How My Heart Sang*, 144-45; "Some First Steps in Welfare Work," *Woman's Welfare* (Jan. 1905): 131-35, NCR Head.

38. Similarly, Gerald Zahavi discovered a complex pattern of "negotiated loyalty" when he studied personnel relations at the Endicott Johnson Co. during a later time period. See "Negotiated Loyalty," 602-11.

39. Patterson autobiography, 25. Patterson exaggerated when he claimed "we forced [welfare work] upon industry," but he did become a prominent national spokesperson for the cause, tirelessly touring the country, lobbying and giving speeches. For files of news clippings that detail the numerous Patterson welfare work trips, see Patterson Scrapbook Collection, especially collection book 113, NCR Head.

40. The best summary of scholarly debate about welfare work can be found in Brandes, *American Welfare Capitalism*, 1-20.

41. Relations between the NCR Company and the Dayton Socialist party will be discussed at greater length in chap. 4. One note here will suffice. When Patterson died in 1922, the local Socialist party passed a public resolution of "deep regret." The party's treasurer received a letter from Edith McClure Patterson thanking "your entire organization for the resolution, expressed with such deep appreciation for Mr. Patterson's service." Letter from Edith McClure Patterson to Oscar Edelman, May 24, 1922, Oscar Edelman Papers, WSU.

42. Dayton *Herald*, June 16, 1903.

43. Issac Marcossen, "Fight for the Open Shop," *World's Work* (1905): 6951-59.

44. "A New Year's Letter to N.C.R. People from President Patterson," *The N.C.R.* (Jan. 1907): 5, NCR Head.

45. *World N.C.R.* (April 1906): 28, NCR Head.

46. See Daniel Nelson, "The New Factory System and the Unions: The National Cash Register Company Dispute of 1901," *Labor History* 15 (1974): 163-79. Nelson provides an excellent summary of the issues at stake during the strike and notes the reorganization at NCR that followed in its aftermath. He overstates the case, however, when he argues that "Patterson's basic commitment to welfare work was in no way altered."

47. "A Deplorable Strike," *Nation* 73 (July 1901): 6-7.

48. Along with Cyrus McCormick and Edward Filene, Patterson acted as a vice chairman of the federation's Welfare Committee and traveled very frequently on federation business at his own expense. Dayton *Journal*, Feb. 25, 1904.

49. Gordon Jensen, "The National Civic Federation: American Business in an Age of Social Change and Social Reform, 1900–1910 (Ph.D. diss., Princeton University, 1956).

50. James Weinstein, *The Corporate Ideal in the Liberal State, 1900-1918* (Boston, 1968), 6. For information about Kirby, see also A.W. Drury, *History of Dayton*, 609-12; Warren Deem, "The Employers' Association of Dayton," unpublished seminar paper written at Harvard University, 1953, pamphlet file, WSU.

51. A.O. Marshall, *The Benefits of Employers' Associations* (Dayton, 1903), 3.

52. Dayton *Daily News*, June 14, 1901; Dayton *Daily News*, Aug. 19, 1901; Employers' Association of Dayton, *Dayton Manufacturing Company vs. Metal Polishers, Etc.* (Dayton, 1901), 1-15.

53. There is no firm evidence that John H. Patterson ever joined either the Employers' Association of Dayton or the National Association of Manufacturers. His brother Frank may have. Hugh Chalmers, for a time the company's general manager, was an officer of the Employers' Association of Dayton. Warren Deem, "Employers' Association," 1-10.

54. *N.C.R. News* (Jan. 1917): 18, NCR Head.

55. Johnson and Lynch, *Sales Strategy of John H. Patterson*, 300.

56. *N.C.R. News* (Aug. 1916): 28, NCR Head.

57. Miss Harvey had not been asked back after the 1901 strike. Minutes book 1, May 25, 1901, 206, Board, NCR Head.

58. Allyn, *My Half-Century*, 148-49.

59. *N.C.R. News* (June 1925): 33, NCR Head. Moreover, company newsletters began to lecture workers about their "mutual responsibilities" in other areas with greater frequency as well. For example, a 1929 article about the NCR Medical Department scolded, "For instance, a young man who says that his work is too hard for him, and that he is on the verge of collapse, will, after a few questions, admit that he had been

up until two or three o'clock several nights attending a dance; that he had been eating liberally of hot dogs embalmed in mustard, sleeping with his windows closed, etc." *N.C.R. News* (March 1929): 37, NCR Head.

60. "Prison Cells for Trust Sinners," *Literary Digest* (March 1913): 444.

61. Hollister's comments summarized in "Doubts about Cash Register Sins," *Literary Digest* (March 1915): 678.

62. Patterson quoted in William Rodgers, *Think—A Biography of the Watsons and I.B.M.* (New York, 1969), 49.

63. *The Record: United States Circuit Court of Appeals, Sixth District, 1911-1913. John H. Patterson, Thomas J. Watson, Edward A. Deeds, Etc.* v. *the United States of America.*

64. Merle Thompson, *Trust Dissolution* (Boston, 1919), 194-201; "Bath-Tubs, Cash Registers, and the Trust Problem," *Outlook* (March 1913): 476-79; Thomas Watson's version of the affair appears in Thomas Watson, *Men, Minutes, Money* (New York, 1934).

65. Editorial in the Brooklyn *Eagle*, quoted in "Prison Cells for Trust Sinners," 445.

66. Ibid.

67. John Lewellyn, secretary of Dayton YMCA, to John H. Patterson, March 15, 1913, Patterson Collection scrapbook 195, NCR Head.

68. Fred Fansher, secretary, Dayton Chamber of Commerce, to John H. Patterson, Feb. 28, 1913, Patterson Collection scrapbook 195. These letters accurately reflect the tone of the many others pasted to the pages of scrapbooks in the archives of the NCR Corp. NCR Head.

69. Thompson, *Trust Dissolution*, 199.

70. Allyn, *My Half-Century*, 17.

71. Ibid., 25.

72. Minute book 2, April 2, 1902, 85, Board, NCR Head.

73. Allyn, *My Half-Century*, 41.

74. Johnson and Lynch, *Sales Strategy of John H. Patterson*, 306-7.

75. John H. Patterson, "Wives: Assistant Salesmen," *System: The Magazine of Business* 34 (July 1918): 34.

76. Johnson and Lynch, *Sales Strategy of John H. Patterson*, 300.

77. Patterson autobiography, 183.

78. Daniel Pope, *The Making of Modern Advertising* (New York, 1983), 112-227.

79. The phrase is Alfred Chandler's. *The Visible Hand*, 1-6.

80. Robert Wiebe, *Businessmen and Reform: A Study of the Progressive Movement* (Cambridge, Mass., 1962), 16; Hofstadter, *The Age of Reform*.

81. F.C. Kelley, "Dayton's 'Uncle Bountiful,' " *Collier's* 53 (Aug. 1914): 8.

82. Idem, "Business Genius and How He Works," *American Magazine* 81 (Feb. 1916): 50.

83. Patterson autobiography, 181-82. Patterson was a forty-four-year-old bachelor when he married Katharine Beck in 1888. After she died in 1894 Patterson never remarried. The two "small children" were his daughter, Dorothy, and his son, Frederick.

84. John H. Patterson to Lena Harvey Tracy, March 16, 1903; letter reproduced in Tracy, *How My Heart Sang*, 177. Ida Tarbell sent an autographed copy of her book, *New Ideals in Business* (New York, 1915), to Patterson. The book, liberally marked in Patterson's hand with marginal comments and underlining, now can be found in the Dayton Room at the Dayton Public Library. In his copy of Tarbell's book, Patterson frequently underlined or noted passages that discussed the moral obligations of business owners. See, for example, 67, 201-7, 310-17.

85. Crowther, *John H. Patterson*, 213.

86. Ibid., 214-47; Tracy, *How My Heart Sang*, 160-74; Edwin Wildman, "Morality in Business: John H. Patterson of Dayton, Ohio," *Forum Magazine* (Aug. 1919): 158-69.

87. Patterson's reputation for eccentricity was such that James Cox was apparently taken in by exaggerated versions of Patterson's fasting habits, which were strenuous enough even unvarnished. In his memoirs Cox reported that Patterson "at one time fasted for sixty days, dwindling to a shadow." *Journey through My Years* (New York, 1946), 44.

88. Brandes, *American Welfare Capitalism*, 37.

3. Flood Control in the Miami Valley

1. Merle Thompson, *Trust Dissolution* (Boston, 1919), 195-97. See also newspaper clippings collection describing the Patterson trial, Edward A. Deeds clippings file, v. 1 "Flood Prevention" scrapbooks, Records of the Miami Conservancy District, Archives and Special Collections, University Library, Wright State University, Dayton, Ohio. (Hereafter, MCD, WSU. In 1975 the Miami Conservancy District deposited the majority of its early records at the Wright State University Archives. Those records still housed at Conservancy headquarters, Dayton, Ohio, will be cited as MCD, D.)

2. Edward A. Deeds Clipping File, V. 1, 1913, "Flood Prevention" scrapbooks, MCD, WSU. See, for instance, *The Oklahoman* (Oklahoma City, Okla.), April 4, 1913; *The Telegram* (Portland, Oreg.), March 28, 1913; the *Johnston Democrat* (Johnston, Pa.), April 4, 1913. In these and dozens of other editorials, Patterson received praise as an extraordinary leader, a man who typified the best the "new business deals" could offer.

3. Typed transcript, Court Hearing on Official Plan, October 3 to November 23, 1916, Memorial Hall, Dayton, Ohio, subseries 5: John

McMahon Legal Files, bxs. 14-A and B, Cross-examination Testimony of Arthur Morgan, Oct. 26, 1916, transcript pp. 1286-99 (hereafter cited as Official Plan Hearings), MCD, WSU.

4. Dayton *Daily News*, April 2, 1913.

5. There are no scholarly accounts of the flood. The one book, Allan Eckert, *A Time of Terror: The Great Dayton Flood* (Boston, 1965), uses the names of real people and describes real events but offers the reader a heavily fictionalized summary, replete with the dying thoughts of "strapping hulks" caught in the icy waters on missions to save women and children. Arthur Morgan, *The Miami Conservancy District* (New York, 1951), 11-74, provides more accurate information. *The Miami Conservancy District* is Morgan's brief explanation and justification for his decisions made as chief engineer. It is the one book on the Conservancy District. Obviously Morgan favored his own creation but focused here on the technical details of construction. Instead of text, four chapters on the flood and its aftermath consist largely of reprinted letters, newspaper reports, government documents, useful as a kind of scrapbook. But the best sources for the great Miami Valley flood of 1913 are the genuine scrapbooks: Edward A. Deeds clipping file, v. 1-8, MCD, WSU; the Patterson flood scrapbooks, the NCR corporate archives, NCR World Headquarters, Dayton, Ohio (hereafter, NCR Head).

6. Testimony of Edward A. Deeds, October 26, 1916, transcript pp. 1381-87, Official Plan Hearings, MCD, WSU; Arthur Ruhl, "The Disaster at Dayton," *Outlook* 103 (April 12, 1913): 805-7.

7. See, for example, *Miami Valley Socialist* (Dayton, Ohio), August 15, 1913.

8. Dayton *Daily News*, March 29, 1913; Dayton *Daily News*, April 2, 1913.

9. Ruhl, "Disaster at Dayton," 808.

10. Ibid. See also, Minutes of the City Council of the City of Dayton, Record Books of the City Council, BK C, office of the City Commission, Dayton, Ohio. There is a lively scholarly debate on this question of progressive attitudes toward "the state," associationalism, and community organization. See, for instance, Jonathan Lurie, "Private Associations, Internal Regulation and Progressivism: The Chicago Board of Trade as a Case Study," *American Journal of Legal History* 16 (1972); 215-38; Peter Romanofsky, " 'The Public is Aroused': The Missouri Childrens' Code Commission, 1915–1919," *Missouri Historical Review* 28 (1973): 204-22; Thomas McGraw, "Regulation in America: A Review Article," *Business History Review* 49 (1975): 159-83; John V. Craven, ed., *Industrial Organization, Antitrust, and Public Policy* (Boston, 1983).

11. Dayton *Daily News*, April 2, 1913; James Cox, "Ohio After the Flood," *Hearst's Magazine* 23 (June 1913): 869-871.

12. Dayton *Journal*, April 3, 1913.

13. Ruhl, "Disaster at Dayton," 809.

14. Dayton *Daily News*, April 3, 1913.

15. Dayton *Journal*, April 23, 1913.

16. "Report of T.L. Rhoads, Major, Medical Corps, U.S. Army" (dated April 1913). Copy in Edward A. Deeds clippings file, v. 2. "Flood Prevention" scrapbooks, MCD, WSU.

17. Memberships lists, Articles of Incorporation, Dayton Citizens' Relief Commission Records, subseries 1, bx. 1-1, MCD, WSU.

18. Memo, John H. Patterson to Ezra Kuhns, April 14, 1913, Patterson Flood Clippings File, NCR Head.

19. "Report of T.L. Rhoads."

20. For information on rehabilitation efforts, see Constance Leupp, "The National Red Cross at Work," *Outlook* 103 (April 5, 1913): 766-68; Ray Stannard Baker, "The Valley That Found Itself," *World's Work* 31 (April 1916): 681-85; Edward Devine, "Flood Rehabilitation in a City," *Survey* 32 (May 1914): 147-51; J. Bojesen, "Red Cross Agent's Personal Experience," *Survey* 32 (May 1914): 143-46.

21. Devine, "Flood Rehabilitation." See also James Cebula, "The New City and the New Journalism: The Case of Dayton, Ohio," *Ohio History* 88 (1979): 278-89.

22. Devine, "Flood Rehabilitation," 149.

23. Ibid.; Resolutions, Dayton Citizens' Relief Commission Records, subseries 1, bx. 1-1, MCD, WSU.

24. Dayton *Journal*, April 4, 1913.

25. Devine, "Flood Rehabilitation," 150-51.

26. Dayton *Daily News*, April 2, 1913.

27. Resolutions, Dayton Citizens' Relief Commission Records, subseries 1, bx. 1-1, MCD, WSU.

28. Minutes, meetings of the Dayton Citizens' Relief Commission, May 2, 1913, subseries 1, bx. 1-2, MCD, WSU.

29. John H. Patterson, "How I Get My Ideas Across," *System* 33 (June 1918): 879; for further accounts of the fund-raising campaign, see *Dayton Daily News*, May 24, 1913; *Dayton Daily News*, May 28, 1913.

30. Dayton *Daily News*, Feb. 10, 1915.

31. Allyn, *My Half-Century*, 72.

32. The best biography of Charles Kettering is Stuart Leslie, *Boss Kettering* (New York, 1983). For information about Kettering's partnership with Deeds in the founding of Delco, see 38-69.

33. Testimony of Edward A. Deeds, Oct. 26, 1916, transcript pp. 1380-85, Official Plan Hearings, MCD, WSU.

34. Deeds's wartime service came under a cloud. In 1918 a Senate committee led by Charles Evans Hughes investigated charges of inefficiency and corruption in the administration of the aircraft procurement programs. When Deeds had accepted a commission as a colonel in the

Army, he resigned as president of the Dayton-Wright Co. and placed his stock in trust. But Dayton-Wright, as well as Delco and the United Motors Corp., all companies Deeds had led before the war and all companies in which he owned large blocks of shares, received lucrative wartime contracts. The Hughes investigation recommended that Deeds be court-martialed for conflict of interest, but a military appeals board later dropped the charges. Sixty-fifth Congress, 2d Session, Senate, Report 380, part I: "Investigation of the War Department—Aircraft Production", April 10, 1918; see also: Charles E. Hughes, "Abstract: Aircraft Investigation, with Subject Index and References to Hughes Investigation and Senate Subcommittee Investigation held in 1918" (Washington, D.C., 1919).

35. Arthur Morgan argued that Deeds's leadership was crucial. One story he told to illustrate his contention took place in 1915. Deeds took a vacation trip to the West Indies. After he had been gone several weeks, several members of the Citizens' Relief Commission visited Morgan to say that after reconsidering they decided the Morgan plans were too difficult and must be abandoned. Deeds, however, returned from vacation, in Morgan's account, in the nick of time, rallied the commission, and, to demonstrate his faith in the proposed Conservancy, donated the money from his own funds to build an imposing stone headquarters building in downtown Dayton. As Morgan told it, "I heard no further suggestion from his friends for abandonment." *Miami Conservancy District*, 146.

36. Articles of Incorporation, Dayton Citizens' Relief Commission Records, subseries 1, bx. 1-1, MCD, WSU.

37. Testimony of Edward A. Deeds, Oct. 26, 1916, transcript p. 1382, Official Plan Hearings, MCD, WSU.

38. Ibid., transcript p. 1383.

39. For information about the growth of technical and engineering education in the United States, see David Noble, *America by Design: Science, Technology, and the Rise of Corporate Capitalism* (New York, 1977). Two former Antioch College colleagues of Arthur Morgan have written privately published memoirs: Clarence Leuba, *A Road to Creativity: Arthur Morgan, Engineer, Education, Administrator* (North Quincy, Mass., 1971); Walter Kahoe, *Arthur Morgan, a Biography and Memoir* (Moylan, Pa., 1977). No scholarly biography of Morgan exists. The best source for Morgan's early life remains his voluminous handwritten diaries. The Arthur Morgan Papers, series I, diaries, the Olive Kettering Library, Antioch College, Yellow Springs, Ohio.

40. "Flood Prevention Report," typescript, June 11, 1915, submitted by Edward A. Deeds to the Citizens' Relief Commission. Dayton Citizens' Relief Commission Records, subseries 1, bx. 1-2, MCD, WSU. The original plan required the use of land in ten counties, but the official plan

of 1916, with slightly altered locations for two dams, omitted Logan County. The counties that became part of the Miami Conservancy District were Montgomery, Preble, Greene, Clark, Butler, Miami, Warren, Shelby, and Hamilton.

41. Ibid.

42. Opening Arguments for the District, by E.B.J. Schubring, J.D., Oct. 3, 1916, transcript p. 16, Official Plan Hearings, MCD, WSU.

43. Ibid., transcript pp. 16-34.

44. Ibid. Besides the central structures of the retarding basins, there were to be channel improvements and levees at Piqua, Troy, Tipp City, Dayton, West Carrollton, Franklin, Miamisburg, Middletown, and Hamilton.

45. The Conservancy Law: "To Prevent Floods, to Protect Cities, Villages, Farms, and Highways from Inundation, and to Authorize the Organization of Drainage and Conservation Districts" (passed, Feb. 6, 1914), printed copy, MCD, D.

46. Ibid.

47. The original plan required the use of land in ten counties; the counties that became part of the Miami Conservancy District were Montgomery, Preble, Greene, Clark, Butler, Miami, Warren, Shelby, and Hamilton. Therefore, in 1914 and 1915 the hearings held in Montgomery County to review issues raised about the proposed dams were conducted by a court of ten common pleas judges. The official plan of 1916, however, eliminated Logan County. So during the official hearing only nine common pleas judges sat as the Conservancy Court. After 1916, all Miami District Conservancy Courts consisted of nine judges, from the counties named above included in the official plan.

48. Morgan, *Miami Conservancy District*, 208.

49. For descriptions of the Garver-Quinlisk bills, see Urbana *Citizen*, (Urbana, Ohio), April 22, 1915. A list of the important cases in the four-year legal battle includes: (1) *Deeds* v. *Snyder*, 91 Ohio St. 407; *Miami Co.* v. *Dayton, et al.*, 92 Ohio St. 215; *Com'rs.* v. *Gates*, 83 Ohio St. 20, 34; *State ex rel. Franklin Co. Conservancy District* v. *Valentine*, 94 Ohio St. 440; (2) *Houck* v. *Little River District*, 239 U.S. 254, 262. The quotation cited appeared in the Dec. 9, 1918, U.S. Supreme Court Memorandum Opinion by the chief justice deciding *Orr* v. *Allen, et al.* Copies of all decisions in MCD, D.

50. Piqua *Leader Dispatch* (Piqua, Ohio), Jan. 21, 1914.

51. Troy *Record*, March 14, 1915.

52. Ibid.

53. *Miami Valley Socialist*, Feb. 12, 1915. For an analysis of the Dayton local of the Socialist party, see John Walker, "Socialism in Dayton, Ohio, 1912-1925: Its Membership, Organization, and Demise," *Labor History* 26 (1985): 384-405.

54. These charges were very widely circulated. Governor James Cox

received numerous letters of inquiry. Typical was one from W.L. Tobey, publisher of the Hamilton *Telegraph*. Tobey told Cox that "of course, we have written an article along the line that it would have made no difference if the Lewiston Dam had broken and emptied into the Miami Valley, that it would have made no impression as compared with the amount of water that poured through here." Nevertheless Tobey wanted the governor to tell him "the exact facts." W.L. Tobey to James Cox, May 24, 1913, folder 10, James M. Cox Papers, Ohio State Archives, Ohio State Historical Society, Columbus, Ohio (hereafter, Cox Papers). For quotation, see *Miami Valley Socialist*, Feb. 19, 1915.

55. William Shine to James Cox, Dec. 1, 1914, folder 36, Cox Papers.

56. This was the name the Troy *Record* persisted in attaching to Edward A. Deeds. Troy *Record*, March 1, 1915.

57. Typed transcript of anti-Conservancy meeting in Piqua, Ohio, St. George's Hall, April 8, 1916, Speech by L.A. Pearson, transcript p. 12, subseries 7, bx. 16-7, MCD, WSU (hereafter, Piqua meeting).

58. Conservancy Law, MCD, D. The controversial paragraph in Section 24 read as follows: "The rights of landowners, municipalities, corporations, and other users of water to the waters of the district for domestic use, water supply, industrial purposes, for water power, or for any other purposes shall extend only to such rights as were owned by them prior to the organization of the district, and to such use as could be made of such waters if the improvements of the district had not been made. Wherever the organization of, or the improvements made by the district make possible a greater, better, or more convenient use of, or benefit from, the waters of the district for any purpose, the right of such greater, better, or more convenient use of, or benefit from, such waters shall be the property of the district; and such rights may be leased, sold, or assigned by the district in return for reasonable compensation."

59. Testimony of Arthur Morgan for the District, Oct. 26, 1916, transcript pp. 1286-1311, Official Plan Hearings, MCD, WSU.

60. Arthur Morgan, speech in the Hall of Industrial Education, NCR, Dayton, Ohio (dated April 1913), typed copy of notes in Edward A. Deeds clippings file, v. 1, "Flood Prevention" scrapbooks, MCD, WSU (hereafter, Morgan NCR speech).

61. Troy *News*, Sept. 11, 1915.

62. Mead's testimony reproduced in the Piqua *Dispatch*, Feb. 12, 1915.

63. Testimony of Edward A. Deeds, Nov. 15, 1916, transcript p. 2595, Official Plan Hearing, MCD, WSU.

64. Ibid.

65. Ibid., transcript p. 2603.

66. Ibid.

67. As early as October 1913, a specialized engineering journal had

prophesied the future fight between urban and rural areas. Analyzing the first released draft of Morgan's report to the Relief Commission, the editors of the *New York Engineering News* speculated that "possibly the Dayton engineers realized that plans requiring radical alteration (ie; Channels) would have to meet the vast bulk of inertia which a city community can bring to bear—whereas most citizens would favor a scheme whose ideal is the complete subjugation of the river while placing the inconvenience on outside districts rather than city territory." *New York Engineering News*, Oct. 16, 1913, 771-72, copy in Edward A. Deeds clipping files, v. 1, "Flood Prevention" scrapbooks, MCD, WSU.

68. Speech by James Kite, transcript pp. 3-6, Piqua meeting, MCD, WSU.

69. Piqua meeting, Statement by Dr. Van Deaton, transcript p. 37.

70. Ibid., Statement by Attorney Thomas, transcript p. 39.

71. Marion *Star* (Marion, Ohio), March 19, 1915.

72. Closing arguments of P.R. Taylor, Nov. 16, 1916, transcript pp. 3066-95, Official Plan Hearings, MCD, WSU; statement of Attorney Thomas, transcript pp. 38-40, Piqua meeting, MCD, WSU.

73. Quoted in Dayton *Daily News*, Feb. 4, 1915.

74. *Miami Union* (Troy, Ohio), Feb. 4, 1926.

75. Testimony of Edward A. Deeds, Nov. 15, 1916, transcript pp. 2594-95, Official Plan Hearings, MCD, WSU. For another description of Rentschler, see Morgan, *Miami Conservancy District*, 310.

76. Copy of flyer inserted as supplement in Troy *Record*, Feb. 8, 1915.

77. The phrase "practical business judgment" was Deeds's, given in answer to a question asking him to describe his conception of the duties of the Conservancy's board of directors. Testimony of Edward A. Deeds, Nov. 15, 1916, transcript p. 2596, Official Plan Hearings, MCD, WSU.

78. Chicago *Herald*, Feb. 22, 1915, copy in Edward A. Deeds clipping files, v. 6, scrapbooks, MCD, WSU.

79. Among the nationally prominent experts were: T.W. Jaycox, state engineer of Colorado and head of numerous earth dam projects in Colorado and in the West; F.J. Fischer, construction engineer of the Los Angeles Water Supply Commission; Brig. Gen. William Bixby, former chief of engineers, U.S. Army; Daniel Mead, professor of hydraulic engineering at the University of Wisconsin; Brig. Gen. H.M. Chittenden, also former chief of engineers, U.S. Army, Sherman Woodward, professor of hydraulics at Iowa State University; Maj. Gen. O.H. Ernst, another former chief of engineers, U.S. Army; Col. J.A. Ockerson, president of the Mississippi River Commission; Charles H. Miller, head of flood control for the Missouri Pacific Railroad; William A. O'Brien, chief engineer, Little River Drainage District; J.H. Kimball, chief engineer, Louisville, Kentucky. These and other consultants' credentials are dis-

cussed in Brief of Defendants in Error, "Salus Populi Suprema Lex," Brown and Frank, John McMahon. Defense of the Ohio Conservancy Act. M.C.D. File H-123.011-O, MCD, D.

80. Sidney *Journal* (Sidney, Ohio), March 13, 1916.

81. Presentation of Alternative Plan by John Hill, Oct. 18, 1916, transcript pp. 709-1105, Official Plan Hearings, MCD, WSU.

82. Testimony of Arthur Morgan for the District, Nov. 1, 1916, transcript p. 1457, Official Plan Hearings, MCD, WSU.

83. Comment by Judge C.W. Murphy, Nov. 1, 1916, transcript p. 1455, Official Plan Hearings, MCD, WSU. The other members of the Conservancy Court for the Official Plan Hearings were Carroll Sprigg (presiding), Montgomery County; A.C. Risinger, Preble County; C.H. Kyle, Greene County; F.W. Geiger, Clark County; W.D. Jones, Miami County; H.C. Mathers, Shelby County; W.J. Wright, Warren County; O.J. Cosgrave, Hamilton County.

84. Closing Arguments of P.R. Taylor, Nov. 23, 1916, transcript p. 3136, Official Plan Hearings, MCD, WSU.

85. Speech by F.W. Sterrett, reprinted in Troy *Record*, Feb. 6, 1915.

86. For a classic victory statement by one of those experts, nationally known engineer Daniel Mead, see interview with Mead, in Piqua *Dispatch*, Feb. 13, 1915.

87. W.C. McAdoo to Edward A. Deeds, Dec. 6, 1917, subseries 7, correspondence files: E.A. Deeds, MCD, WSU.

88. The Conservancy records contain a file of such letters. All were anonymous. A typical one read, "If you force us to give away our homes, you will *lose* yours. We will have revenge!" Anonymous to Deeds, no date, stamped "received 1917," subseries 7, general subject files and correspondence, MCD, WSU.

89. See Technical Reports, subseries 11, files 32: 1-9, MCD, WSU. Important reports included *Report 3: Theory of the Hydraulic Jump and Backwater Curves* (1917); *Report 5: Calculation of Flow in Open Channels* (1918); *Report 6: Contract Forms and Specifications* (1918); *Report 9: Rainfall and Runoff in the Miami Valley* (1921).

90. For an excellent discussion of the development of this process, see Noble, *America by Design*, 110-257.

91. Morgan, *Miami Conservancy District*, 353. Moreover, the District used "practical business judgment" in its purchases, using only standard makes and sizes of equipment, permitting interchange in case of breakage during operation and reducing the need to keep supplies of spare parts. *Miami Conservancy Bulletin* 1 (March 1919): 126, subseries 3: publications, MCD, WSU.

92. Morgan, *Miami Conservancy District*, 277.

93. Arthur Morgan to C.W. Porter-Shirley, Jan. 14, 1918, subseries 10: camp labor files, general correspondence, 30-7, MCD, WSU.

94. "The Camps," *Miami Conservancy Bulletin*, 1 (Aug. 1918): 12-15, subseries 3: publications, MCD, WSU.

95. C.W. Porter-Shirley to the National Americanization Committee, June 10, 1918, subseries 10: camp labor files, general correspondence, 30-9, MCD, WSU. Porter-Shirley asked for advice about "how to do something in the way of Americanization of these people." He received packets of pamphlets on English and citizenship programs for the District's Eastern European and Mexican workers. The Conservancy's general correspondence files also contain many of Morgan's references to the need to get men involved in humanitarian and educational reform, at the camps and elsewhere.

96. "Bill of Sale for Materials," John E. Freudenberger, landscape gardener, 1918; also "Welfare Lecture Notes" (undated), subseries 10: camp labor files: camp gardens, 29-12, MCD, WSU.

97. "Six Months' Progress of the Camp Community Associations," *Miami Conservancy Bulletin*, 1 (June 1919): 172-74, subseries 3: publications, MCD, WSU.

98. Morgan to Porter-Shirley, Jan. 14, 1918.

99. "Six Months' Progress," 172.

100. Edward A. Deeds to Ezra Kuhns, Feb. 27, 1918, subseries 7: correspondence of E.A. Deeds, MCD, WSU.

101. Annual Report of the Board of Directors, 1922, typescript copy, Dec. 31, 1922, 14, subseries 2: annual reports, MCD, WSU.

102. Morgan, *Miami Conservancy District*, 480.

103. Ibid., 401.

104. "Faulty Labor Policy of the Miami Conservancy District," *Labor Review* (newsletter copy), July 19, 1918, subseries 10: camp labor files, MCD, WSU.

105. Troy *News*, July 11, 1918.

106. Hamilton *Journal* (Hamilton, Ohio), July 18, 1918.

107. Arthur Morgan to J.E. Barlow, city manager of Dayton, Feb. 13, 1919, subseries 10: camp labor files: general correspondence, 27-9, MCD, WSU.

108. Joseph Kugler to C.W. Porter-Shirley, July 2, 1918, subseries 10: camp labor files: general correspondence, 27-7, MCD, WSU.

109. *Miami Valley Socialist*, Jan. 24, 1919.

110. Dayton *Journal*, July 13, 1922.

111. Leupp, "National Red Cross," 766-68; Sally Stewart, "Sharing More Than Marble Palaces," *Daughters of the American Revolution Magazine* 115 (1981): 188-91; Patrick Gilbo, *The American Red Cross: The First Century* (New York, 1981).

112. Dayton *Journal*, April 15, 1922. The Miami River crested at twenty-nine feet during the flood of 1913.

113. Charles Bennett, "Does Flood Protection Pay?" *American City* 52

(March 1937): 57-59; see also rainfall records file, MCD, D. The total rainfall in 1937 was approximately equal to that which fell in 1913, but in 1937 that accumulation fell over a period of twelve days. In 1913 the rains fell for only five days, making the 1913 storm the more severe of the two over the Miami Valley.

114. That concensus had been reached as early as the 1930s and was not later challenged. Charles Bennett and C.H. Eiffert, "Sixteen Years of Flood Control in Miami Valley," *Civil Engineering* 8 (May 1938): 343-45; J.D. Justin, *Earth Dam Projects* (New York, 1932), 260-66.

115. Reports of the Board of Directors, Balance Sheets and Supporting Exhibits, 1919–1925, subseries 2, MCD, WSU.

116. Ruhl, "Disaster at Dayton," 808.

117. Speech of L.A. Pearson, transcript p. 12, Piqua meeting, MCD, WSU.

118. For an overview of the relocation of the entire village, see records of the Osborn Removal Co., WSU.

119. "Health and Sanitation Report," 29-9, subseries 10: camp labor files, MCD, WSU.

120. Morgan NCR speech.

4. City Manager Government for Dayton

1. Ray Stannard Baker, "The Valley That Found Itself," *World's Work* 31 (April 1916): 681.

2. *Ibid.*, 685.

3. John H. Patterson, "What Dayton, Ohio Should Do to Become a Model City," March 19, 1896, speech transcript, 22, NCR Head.

4. John H. Patterson, "An Address to a Mass Meeting of Citizens," March 4, 1907, handwritten notes for speech, NCR Head.

5. For summaries of the charges made by NCR, see scrapbook 204, NCR Head; see also Dayton *Daily News*, Jan. 22, 1907; *Dayton Daily News*, Feb. 1, 1907; *Dayton Daily News*, Feb. 8, 1907.

6. John H. Patterson, typed speech transcript (copy), undated (probably 1901), Patterson Collection scrapbook 204, NCR Head.

7. See explanatory note on printed copy of the "Model City" speech, NCR Head.

8. Dayton *Herald*, Oct. 11, 1902.

9. *Republican* (Cohoes, N.Y.), Jan. 29, 1907. For an extensive collection of newspaper clippings from around the country describing the progress of the tour, see Patterson Collection scrapbook 204, NCR Head.

10. *Post* (Bridgeport, Conn.), Jan. 15, 1907, in scrapbook 204, NCR Head.

11. See letters reprinted in Dayton *Journal*, Jan. 15, 1907.

12. John H. Patterson to Russell Johnston, Jan. 17, 1907, Patterson Collection scrapbook 204, NCR Head.

13. A.W. Drury, *A History of the City of Dayton and Montgomery County, Ohio* (Chicago, 1909), 539-40.

14. Dayton *Daily News*, March 1, 1907.

15. Dayton *Daily News*, Feb. 4, 1907.

16. Minutes, Board of Directors' Special Meeting, June 14, 1907, NCR Co., minutes book, 1907, 111, NCR Head. (hereafter, minutes of the Board of Directors' Meetings of the NCR Co. will be cited as Board).

17. Ibid., 111-12.

18. See Steward Frank Mann, *A Half Century of Municipal Reform: The History of the National Municipal League* (Berkeley, Calif. 1950); Alfred Willoughby, *The Involved Citizen: A Short History of the National Municipal League* (New York, 1969).

19. For information about the 1912 Ohio Constitutional Convention and the 1912 Home Rule Amendment, see Lloyd Sponholtz, "The 1912 Constitutional Convention in Ohio: The Call-up and Non-Partisan Selection of Delegates," *Ohio History* 79 (1970): 209-19; Charles Galbreath, *History of Ohio* (Chicago, 1925), 91-135.

20. Chicago *Tribune*, Feb. 1, 1914. For a review of an extensive clippings file describing the home rule campaign and the push for a new city charter, see Patterson Collection scrapbook 216, NCR Head. Discussions of Patterson's travels and activities in *Columbus State Journal*, Sept. 5, 1913; *Republic* (Rockport, Ill.), Aug. 12, 1913; *Citizen* (Columbus, Ohio), Oct. 8, 1913, in Patterson Collection scrapbook 216, NCR Head.

21. For information on the New York Bureau of Municipal Research, see Augustus Cerillo, "The Reform of Municipal Administration in New York City: From Seth Low to John Purroy Mitchel," *New York Historical Society Quarterly* 57 (1973): 52-57; Jane Dahlberg, *The New York Bureau of Municipal Research* (New York, 1966); Norman Gill, *Municipal Research Bureaus* (Washington, D.C., 1944), 14-15.

22. Upson was the Dayton bureau's first director, to be succeeded by Rightor. After the Dayton Bureau of Municipal Research ceased operations, Rightor went on to become head of the new Detroit, Michigan, Bureau of Governmental Research. Chester Rightor, *City Manager in Dayton: Four Years of Commission-Manager Government, 1914-1917 and Comparisons with Four Preceding Years under the Mayor-Council Plan, 1910-1913* (New York, 1919), vii-x.

23. Patterson, "Model City."

24. Margaret Morris and Elliott West, eds., *Essays on Urban America* (Austin, Tex., 1975); Rice, *Progressive Cities.*

25. Initially, in the enabling legislation passed by the Texas legislature in April 1901, the Texas governor appointed three of the five Galveston City Commissioners. Rice, *Progressive Cities*, 3-22; see also Herbert Ma-

son, *Death from the Sea: Our Greatest Natural Disaster, the Galveston Hurricane of 1900* (New York, 1972).

26. Richard Childs, "The Coming of the City Manager Plan," *National Municipal Review* 3 (Jan. 1914): 44-48.

27. Oswald Ryan, "The Real Problem of Commission Government," *Annals* 38 (Nov. 1911): 282; Dunbar Carpenter, "Some Defects of Commission Government," *Annals* 38 (Nov. 1911): 199; H.S. Gilbertson, "Some Serious Weaknesses of the Commission Plan," *American City* 9 (Sept. 1913): 237.

28. William Ringle, "The Businessman Who Brought the Pro to City Hall," *Nation's Business* 59 (Dec. 1971): 30-32; John Crosby, "Municipal Government Administered by a General Manager: The Staunton Plan," *Annals* 38 (Nov. 1911): 207-13; Richard Stillman, *The Rise of the City Manager: A Public Professional in Local Government* (Albuquerque, 1974), 1-50.

29. For discussions of the campaign see Patterson Collection scrapbook 216, NCR Head.

30. Besides Patterson, the Citizen's Committee charter candidates included E.C. Harley, wholesale grocer; Fred Rike, department store owner; John McGee, president of a wholesale millinery firm; J.C. Zehnder, furniture store owner; O.B. Kneisley, dentist; Fred Cappel, president of a furniture-making company; William Sparks, laborer; Lee Warren James, lawyer; E.E. Burkhart, lawyer; Charles Folkerth, lawyer; C.E. Bice, president of lumber company; E.T. Banks, painter and "colored representative"; Albert Mendenhall, union printer; and Leopold Rauh, wholesale merchant and contractor. Rightor, *City Manager in Dayton*, 12.

31. Ibid., 12-17.

32. Joseph Sharts, notes for speech, undated (probably 1911), Oscar Edelman Papers, Archives and Special Collections, University Collections, Wright State University (hereafter WSU).

33. Walker, "Socialism in Dayton, Ohio," 384-404. Interestingly, in this article, the one published study of Dayton socialism, Walker does not discuss the 1912 split but rather key characteristics of the Dayton local—the nature of its membership and financial structure. The most useful evidence for the internal problems of local Dayton in 1911-12 has not yet been published. That information can be gleaned from the extensive records of the local and from private papers of Miami Valley Socialist leaders like long-time party treasurer Oscar Edelman (all at WSU), as well as from the Socialist newspaper, the *Miami Valley Socialist*.

34. See, for example, *Miami Valley Socialist*, July 26, 1912; *Miami Valley Socialist*, Aug. 9, 1912.

35. Dayton *Journal*, Sept. 10, 1910. See also minutes for meetings of Jan. 20, 1911; May 5, 1911; May 19, 1911; July 28, 1911, minutes book 1,

Papers of the Local Dayton Socialist party. Archives and Special Collections, University Library, Wright State University (hereafter: SP, WSU).

36. See, for instance, *Miami Valley Socialist*, Aug. 23, 1912.

37. "An Address to Citizens," handwritten speech transcript, March 1907, 279, in Patterson autobiography, NCR Head. (see chap. 2 endnotes for a discussion of this document).

38. Dayton *Daily News*, May 21, 1913.

39. Dayton *Daily News*, Aug. 13, 1913.

40. *Miami Valley Socialist*, July 19, 1912.

41. See clippings file in Patterson Collection scrapbook 204, NCR Head.

42. Interview in Dayton *Daily News*, May 21, 1913.

43. For contemporary summaries of the charter, see L.D. Upson, "The City Manager Plan of Government for Dayton," *National Municipal Review* 2 (Oct. 1913): 639-44; Henry Waite, "The City Manager Plan: How It Operates in Dayton, Ohio, the Largest City Which Has Tried It," *Municipal Journal* 36 (1914): 822-84.

44. Carl Thompson, "The Vital Points in Charter-making from a Socialist Point of View," *National Municipal Review* 2 (July 1913): 416-26.

45. *Miami Valley Socialist*, June 25, 1913.

46. Ibid.

47. *Miami Valley Socialist*, Nov. 12, 1913.

48. *Miami Valley Socialist*, Oct. 17, 1913.

49. *Miami Valley Socialist*, Oct. 29, 1915.

50. *Miami Valley Socialist*, Aug. 6, 1915.

51. *Miami Valley Socialist*, Oct. 29, 1915.

52. *Miami Valley Socialist*, Jan. 15, 1915.

53. *Miami Valley Socialist*, Nov. 5, 1915.

54. *Miami Valley Socialist*, Nov. 12, 1915; see also Official Election Returns: 1915 Files, Board of Elections, Dayton, Ohio.

55. Printed pamphlet, Aug. 1917, Oscar Edelman Papers, WSU.

56. Election flyer, dated 1917 (probably Oct. 1917), Oscar Edelman Papers, WSU.

57. Ibid.

58. *Miami Valley Socialist*, Oct. 4, 1918. A version of this satire circulated in pamphlet form during the election of 1917.

59. Rightor, *City Manager in Dayton*, 220-24.

60. Ibid., 228-29,

61. Walker, "Socialism in Dayton, Ohio," 395-404. See also, for an overview of the pressures facing the socialist movement nationally, Bruce Stave, ed., *Socialism and the Cities* (Port Washington, N.Y., 1975), 30-45; Charles Leinenweber, "The Class and Ethnic Bases of City Socialism, 1904-1915," *Labor History* 22 (1981): 31-56; David Shannon, *The Socialist Party of America: A History* (Chicago, 1967).

62. Rice, *Progressive Cities*, 107-8; number of city manager cities obtained from information desk, Office of the City Manager, Dayton, Ohio.

63. *Miami Valley Socialist*, Oct. 14, 1921.

64. Quoted in "Dayton's Unique Charter," *Literary Digest* (Aug. 1913): 308.

65. William Renwick, "Democracy Chooses an Autocrat," *Technical World Magazine* 212 (March 1914): 13-19.

66. Richard Childs, "The Coming of the City Manager Plan," Minority and Majority Reports of the National Municipal League's Committee on the Commission Form of Government, *National Municipal Review* 3 (Jan. 1914): 44-48.

67. *Dayton for the People*! pamphlet, printed by the Local Dayton Socialist party, Aug. 1915, Oscar Edelman Papers, WSU. See also petitions files, 1914-1917, Office of the City Commission, Dayton, Ohio; minutes of the meetings of Feb. 18, 1914, Feb. 16, 1914, and March 25, 1914, minutes of the City Commission of the City of Dayton, minutes book D-1, Office of the City Commission, Dayton, Ohio (hereafter: Commission Minutes, CC).

68. Herman James, "Defects in the Dayton Charter," *National Municipal Review* 3 (Jan. 1914): 97.

69. Arthur Morgan, "Professional Public Service," *Antioch Notes* (Oct. 15, 1927), Antiochiana Manuscripts Collection, Antioch College, Yellow Springs, Ohio.

70. *Miami Valley Specialist*, March 28, 1919.

71. For biographical information on Flotron, see Patterson Collection scrapbook 216, NCR Head.

72. Dayton *Daily News*, Aug. 21, 1913.

73. *Miami Valley Socialist*, April 1, 1921.

74. For generalizations about the composition of commissions, 1900–20, see Rice, *Progressive Cities*, 76-111.

75. See, for instance, resolutions passed at meetings of Feb. 12, 1915, Oct. 22, 1915, Dec. 10, 1915, Oct. 27, 1916, minutes of meetings, minutes book 1, SP, WSU.

76. Richard Childs, "How the Commission-Manager Plan Is Getting Along," *National Municipal Review* 4 (July 1915): 379.

77. Isaac Marcosson, "Business-Managing a City," *Colliers* 52 (Jan. 1914): 5.

78. Dayton Bureau of Research, Bulletin No. 8-3, Nov. 23, 1916, microfilm roll 17, file 8-D, Records of the Office of the City Manager, Dayton, Ohio, Archives and Special Collections, University Library, Wright State University (hereafter, CM, WSU).

79. Fred Rike, "Speech in Favor of Charter," Aug. 7, 1913, copy in Patterson Collection scrapbook 216, NCR Head.

80. Richard Bernard and Bradley Rice, "Political Environment and

the Adoption of Progressive Municipal Reform," *Journal of Urban History* 1 (1975): 149-74; Otis Pease, "Urban Reformers in the Progressive Era: A Reassessment," *Pacific Northwest Quarterly* 62 (1971): 49-58; Rice, *Progressive Cities*, 90-107.

81. For reviews of the Health Division's work, 1914-24, see memo, Dec. 8, 1926, "Welfare Department," microfilm roll 54, file 5BF, CM, WSU; Warren Babcock, "Abstracts from the Survey of Miami Valley Hospital," microfilm roll 51, file 5B4, CM, WSU; minutes, "Conference on City Health Matters, Jan. 5, 1917, microfilm roll 22, file 5F, CM, WSU; Edward Stoecklain, memo, "Public Welfare," Oct. 8, 1923, microfilm roll 45, file 5B5, CM, WSU.

82. For discussion of conditions in the workhouse prior to 1914, see minutes of Dayton City Council, book B-1, Feb. 12, 1912, 449-50, Office of the City Commission, Dayton, Ohio.

83. For discussions of post-1914 changes, see "Report from D.F. Garland to H.M. Waite," Dec. 1915, microfilm roll 16, file 5C1, CM, WSU; "Conference Minutes," Dec. 1916, microfilm roll 16, file 5F, CM, WSU; J.E. Barlow to Walter Richards, March 6, 1929, microfilm roll 48, file 5AA, CM, WSU.

84. J.E. Barlow to City Commission members, April 2, 1918, microfilm roll 26, file 5E6, CM, WSU; D.F. Garland to J.E. Barlow, April 12, 1918, microfilm roll 21, file 5E, CM, WSU; "Report on Garden Work for the Annual Meeting to be Held January 31, 1916," microfilm roll 16, file 5E9, CM, WSU.

85. Henry Waite to Ellsworth Kelley, March 18, 1916, microfilm roll 16, file 5B3, CM, WSU.

86. F.O. Eichelberger to Walter Richards (city manager, Columbus, Georgia), March 6, 1924, microfilm roll 48, file 5AA, CM, WSU.

87. "Report to F.O. Eichelberger of the Department of Public Welfare," Jan. 19, 1923, microfilm roll 43, file 2A, CM, WSU.

88. "Report to Mr. Eichelberger on the Door of Hope," Nov. 23, 1921, microfilm roll 38, file 5B1, CM, WSU.

89. Minutes of the City Commission, minutes book F-1, meeting of Dec. 12, 1917, "Discussion of Petition of Dr. E.M. Huston, Representing Associations of the Medical Profession of the City in Support of Dr. A.L. Light," Commission Minutes, CC.

90. "Records of the Department of Finance," Microfilm roll 2, CM, WSU. See also Henry Waite, speech transcript, 4-6, *Proceedings of the First Annual Convention of the City Managers' Association*, held in Springfield, Ohio, Dec. 2-4, 1914 (Niagara Falls, N.Y., 1915) (hereafter, 1914 *Proceedings*).

91. Transcript of discussion: "Municipal Cost Data," Nov. 15, 1915, 41-52; "Report of Mr. Waite," Nov. 16, 1915, 69-73, *Proceedings of the Second Annual Meeting of the City Managers' Association*, held at Dayton, Ohio,

Nov. 15-17, 1915 (Niagara Falls, N.Y., 1916) (hereafter, 1915 *Proceedings*).

92. Upson, "The City Manager Plan of Government for Dayton," 639-44, 1915 Proceedings.

93. "Report of Bert Klopfer, Secretary, Public Health League, Dayton, Ohio," Nov. 16, 1922, 187-89, *Proceedings of the Ninth Annual Meeting of the City Managers' Association*, held in Kansas City, Missouri, Nov. 14-16, 1922 (Niagara Falls, N.Y., 1923) (hereafter, 1922 *Proceedings*).

94. *Miami Valley Socialist*, Oct. 24, 1919.

95. John Andriot, ed., *Population Abstract of the United States* (McLean, Va., 1980).

96. "Report of Bert Klopfer," 187-89, 1922 *Proceedings*. In 1914, for instance, the largest sources of city taxes were as follows: street railways, $25,500.00; workhouse, $20,000.00; liquor tax, $121,210.00; general tax, $604,000.00. Minutes of the City Commission, book D-1, meeting of Jan. 19, 1914, Commission Minutes, CC.

97. "Report from Dayton, Ohio," 69-71, 1915 *Proceedings*.

98. "Remarks of J.E. Barlow," Nov. 8, 1918, 141-44, *Proceedings of the Fifth Annual Meeting of the City Managers' Association*, held in Roanoke, Virginia, Nov. 6-8, 1918 (Niagara Falls, N.Y., 1919) (Hereafter, 1918 *Proceedings*).

99. Rightor, *City Manager in Dayton*, 188.

100. "Report of Bert Klopfer," 187-89, 1922 *Proceedings*.

101. Patterson, "Model City."

102. "Report of Bert Klopfer," 188-89, 1922 *Proceedings*.

103. Clinton Rogers Woodruff, speech transcript, Nov. 7, 1918, 65, 1918 *Proceedings*.

104. "Remarks of C.C. Hoag," 77-81, 1918 *Proceedings*.

105. "Remarks of Harry Freeman," 83, 1918 *Proceedings*.

106. *Miami Valley Socialist*, March 21, 1913; *Miami Valley Socialist*, May 7, 1915.

107. For a summary of such arguments, see "Remarks of Charles Fassett," Nov. 16, 1922, 177-78, 1922 *Proceedings*.

108. "Remarks of Delos Wilcox," Nov. 16, 1922, 169, 1922 *Proceedings*.

109. See debate transcript, "Should Managers Ever Campaign for Policies?" "Remarks of Henry Waite," Nov. 15, 1920, 210, *Proceedings of the Seventh Annual Meeting of the City Managers' Association*, Held in Cincinnati, Ohio, Nov. 15-17, 1920 (Niagara Falls, N.Y., 1921)

110. "Remarks of Edwin Fort," Nov. 15, 1920, 210, 1920 *Proceedings*.

111. See municipal election statistics, 1907-29, for the city of Dayton, Board of Elections, Dayton, Ohio. (The 1913 flood destroyed many city records prior to 1907, including most municipal election results, making comparisons with voting records in the late nineteenth century impossible.)

112. "Remarks of A.R. Hatton at the Annual Dinner of the City Man-

agers' Association," City Club of Chicago, Nov. 14, 1921, 157, *Seventh Yearbook of the City Managers' Association* (Clarksburg, W.Va., 1921).

5. Educational Engineering

1. Patterson, "How I Get My Ideas Across," 875.

2. See, for instance, diaries and notebooks of Arthur Morgan, series I, Arthur Morgan Papers, Antioch College, Yellow Springs, Ohio (hereafter, AEM); Kelley, "Dayton's 'Uncle Bountiful,' " 8.

3. Given the importance of the phenomenon, there is still a great need for additional serious scholarly attention to be paid to the rise of public education in the late nineteenth century. Even the most recent monographs still focus narrowly on the same few large city systems, like Chicago's or New York's, which, in important ways, may not be typical of national patterns. But among the best of the still-too-few monographs that provide analyses of patterns in American education in the late nineteenth and early twentieth centuries are Michael Katz, *Class, Bureaucracy, and the Schools: The Illusion of Educational Change in America* (New York, 1975); Marvin Lazerson, *Origins of the Urban School: Public Education in Massachusetts, 1870-1915)* (Cambridge, Mass., 1971); Edward Krug, *The Shaping of the American High School, 1880-1920* (New York, 1964); Patricia Graham, *Community and Class in American Education* (New York, 1974); Selwyn Troen, *The Public and the Schools: Shaping the St. Louis System* (Columbia, Mo., 1975); David Tyack, *The One Best System: A History of American Urban Education* (Cambridge, Mass., 1974); Paul Mattingly, *The Classless Profession: American Schoolmen in the Nineteenth Century* (New York, 1975); Paul Peterson, *The Politics of School Reform, 1870-1940* (Chicago, 1985); David Hogan, *Class and Reform: School and Society in Chicago, 1880-1930* (Philadelphia, 1985).

4. See, for example, E.T. Armstrong, "Is Our Present High School System Efficient?" *American School Board Journal* 62 (July 1910): 394; "Some Defects in Our Public School System," *Educational Review* 63 (March 1911): 238-44; Ella Lynch, "Is the Public School a Failure?" *Ladies' Home Journal* 29 (Aug. 1912): 3-5; William Mearns, "Our Medieval High Schools," *Saturday Evening Post* 184 (March 1912): 18-19.

5. Frederic Burk, "Are We Living in B.C. or A.D.?" *Ladies' Home Journal* 29 (Sept. 1912): 7.

6. Proceedings of the Progressive Education Association, convention held at Dayton, Ohio, April 8-9, 1921, typed transcript, series VIII-D, AEM (hereafter, 1921 Proceedings).

7. The standard work tracing the development of the progressive education movement is Lawrence Cremin, *The Transformation of the School: Progressivism in American Education* (New York, 1962).

8. The best book on the Gary experiment is Ronald Cohen and Raymond Mohl, *The Paradox of Progressive Education: The Gary Plan and Urban Schooling* (Port Washington, N.Y., 1979).

9. 1921 Proceedings.

10. For an example of such complaints, see Joseph McKee, "The Gary System," *Catholic World* 102 (Jan. 1916): 513.

11. Upton Sinclair, *The Goosestep: A Study of American Education* (Pasadena, Calif., 1923).

12. Sinclair, who visited twenty-five cities and interviewed "thousands" of teachers and administrators before writing *The Goosestep,* charged that the country's schools and universities had become stooges of powerful business patrons. A process of "Fordization" had corrupted education and produced school administrators devoted, not to academic freedom, but to cost-accounting and business values. The University of Michigan had become the "University of Automobiles." The University of Chicago had always been the "University of Standard Oil." Ibid., 456.

13. Nearing was fired in 1915 by the University of Pennsylvania for his radical views and activities. He studied 131 school systems in cities having more than forty thousand residents. In almost every one, he charged, businessmen dominated. See, for instance, Scott Nearing, "Who's Who on Our Boards of Education," *School and Society* 5 (Jan. 1917): 89-90; idem, "Who's Who Among College Trustees," *School and Society* 6 (Sept. 1917): 297-99.

14. Cremin, *Transformation of the School.*

15. Joel Spring, *Education and the Rise of the Corporate State* (Boston, 1972), 163; Other inheritors of the Upton Sinclair legacy include Raymond Callahan, *Education and the Cult of Efficiency: A Study of the Social Forces That Have Shaped the Administration of the Public School* (Chicago, 1962); Krug, *Shaping of the American High School;* Lazerson, *Origins of the Urban School;* Paul Violas, *The Training of the Urban Working Class: A History of Twentieth Century American Education* (Chicago, 1978); Katz, *Class, Bureaucracy, and the Schools.*

16. Cohen and Mohl, *Paradox of Progressive Education,* 10-35.

17. Katz, *Class, Bureaucracy, and the Schools,* 114.

18. Arthur Morgan to Vici Neff, April 6, 1968, series VIII-C, AEM.

19. For discussion of the board and its work, see Arthur Morgan to Lloyd Marcus, Sept. 29, 1947, series VIII-C, AEM.

20. Quoted in Thomas Boyd, *Professional Amateur* (New York, 1957), 89.

21. *After a Year,* bulletin from the Moraine Park School, printed at the school, 1917, 6-7, series VIII-C, AEM.

22. "Personal Notes on Candidates," handwritten and typed notes, "Interview with Arthur Sides: December 23, 1916," series VIII-C, AEM.

23. Arthur Morgan to Vici Neff, April 6, 1968.

24. "Personal Notes on Candidates," handwritten and typed notes, "Interview with Leslie Cummings: December 21, 1916," series VIII-C, AEM.

25. "Personal Notes on Candidates," typed note, Dec. 21, 1916, series VIII-C, AEM.

26. "Personal Notes on Candidates," handwritten and typed notes, "Interview with Frank Slutz: December 10, 1916," series VIII-C, AEM.

27. Ibid. See also "Enrollment Records of the Moraine Park School, 1917-1925," series VIII-C, AEM.

28. *After a Year,* i-ii. With the exception of this foreword by Slutz the remainder of this Moraine Park School bulletin was written by the students.

29. After 1919 the board would also include Adam Schantz, owner of Dayton's largest brewery, and Charles Paul, soon to be Morgan's replacement as chief engineer of the Miami Conservancy District. Arthur Morgan to Lloyd Marcus, Sept. 29, 1947.

30. Alfred Jones, "The Government of the School," *After a Year,* 9.

31. Robert Kennedy, "Junior Government," *After a Year,* 9.

32. "Trains," *Self-Measurements,* pamphlet written by the teachers of the Moraine Park School, printed at the school, 1921, unpaginated, series VIII-C, AEM.

33. *Citizens in the Making,* pamphlet written by the students at the Moraine Park School, printed at the school, 1920, 11, series VIII-C, AEM.

34. Ibid., 12-13.

35. Ibid., 10-13.

36. Ibid., 13.

37. The Moraine Park School used a system of evaluation that listed ten categories, in which students earned ratings of excellent, satisfactory, or unsatisfactory. The categories were as follows: body building, spirit building, society serving, man conserving, opinion forming, truth discovery, thought expression, wealth production, comrade seeking, and life refreshing. See "Reports of Progress," copy of evaluation report sent to parents, series VIII-C, AEM.

38. Frank Slutz, "The Life Occupations," *Self-Measurements,* 38.

39. Charles Kettering, remarks, typed transcript, unpaginated, fundraising dinner at the Engineers Club, Dayton, Ohio, Jan. 19, 1921, series V-A, AEM (hereafter, Engineers Club Dinner).

40. See the pamphlets, bulletins, and student newspapers covering the years 1917–25 in series VIII-C, AEM.

41. Frank Slutz to Arthur Morgan, Aug. 16, 1926, series VIII-C, AEM.

42. Between 1917 and 1923, the years for which most detailed records exist, enrollment reports included the names, addresses, and occupa-

tions of parents. More than half of the students were the children of company presidents or important executive officers. "Enrollments at the Moraine Park School," 1917-23, series VIII-C, AEM.

43. Martha Chryst, "Cooking," *The Arts of Life*, 26, pamphlet written by the students of the Moraine Park School, printed at the school, 1919, series VIII-C, AEM.

44. Engineers Club Dinner.

45. "Our Orphans," *The Arts of Life*, 25. These children of the Wright, Kettering, Schantz, Deeds, Rike, and other prominent Dayton business families were, by the mid-1980s, themselves elderly, but several still appeared regularly in local newspaper articles featuring community campaigns—to revitalize downtown Dayton, to build a new arts center, to improve the local schools, among others.

46. Arthur Morgan to Lloyd Marcus, Sept. 29, 1947.

47. For discussion of nineteenth-century urban schools, see Carl Kaestle, *The Evolution of an Urban School System: New York City, 1750-1850* (Cambridge, Mass., 1973); William Bullough, *Cities and Schools in the Gilded Age: The Evolution of an Urban Institution* (Port Washington, N.Y., 1974); Tyack, *One Best System*. For a summary of conditions in the Dayton Schools, see *Annual Report of the Dayton Board of Education, 1897-1898* (Dayton, Ohio, 1898), 135-48. The printed and transcript *Annual Reports* are at Archives and Special Collections, University Collections, Wright State University (hereafter, the *Annual Reports of the Dayton Board of Education* will be cited, Education, WSU).

48. Ibid., 142.

49. Ibid., 59-60, 1926–27, Education, WSU.

50. Ibid., 90-99.

51. Callahan, *Education and the Cult*, 244.

52. J.J. Burns, "Report of the Superintendent," 1884-85, 128-31, Education, WSU.

53. Ibid., 131.

54. For a brief history of these activities, see "Special Report of the Superintendent," 1912-13, 85-96, Education, WSU.

55. "Special Report of Col. W.J. White," 1898-99, Education, WSU. The *Annual Reports* for the period 1898-1908 provide listings for board members. For further information about particular individuals, see R.L. Polk, ed. *Williams Dayton, Ohio City Directory* (Taylor, Mich.) for the years 1890-1929.

56. "Report of Superintendent Brown," 1913-14, 115, Education, WSU.

57. Dayton *Daily News*, Jan. 11, 1916.

58. Ibid.

59. The only school in the system that was integrated was the school

for juvenile delinquents and other wards of the court. The best available summaries of Brown's work appear in the yearly "Reports of the Superintendent," 1909-15, Education, WSU.

60. Anna Littell, "Report of the Supervisor of Kindergartens," 1913-14, 108, Education, WSU.

61. The system continued into the 1920s. For an evaluation of it written by new Superintendent Paul Stetson, see "Report of the Superintendent," 1921-22, 52-53, Education, WSU.

62. "Rules for Social Centers," 1912-13, 95-96, Education, WSU.

63. Stetson published regularly on such subjects as efficiency in schools and had earned a wide audience among educators by the time he came to the Dayton system in 1921. See, for instance, Paul Stetson, "Some Examples of Efficiency in School Business Management," *American School Board Journal* 55 (Dec. 1917): 17-18.

64. William McAndrew, "Rapid Review of an American School System," *Educational Review* 75 (Jan. 1928): 1.

65. "Business Department of the Dayton Board of Education Reorganizes," *American School Board Journal* 73 (Dec. 1926): 70-71.

66. Introduced by William Wirt into the Gary schools in 1908, the system assigned students to groups called platoons that worked alternately at different subjects, thus maximizing building use. The playgrounds of an elementary school, for instance, would be useful all day long, rather than simply during recesses shared by an entire grade or class. Meanwhile, since classrooms, music rooms, and science laboratories could be used more intensively by the platoons of students moving from activity to activity, platoon schools could accommodate larger numbers of students within the same space than could traditional schools. See Cohen and Mohl, *Paradox of Progressive Education*, 24-34.

67. Paul Stetson, "The School Building Program of Dayton, Ohio," *American School Board Journal* 70 (March 1923): 67-69.

68. "Report of the Superintendent," 1926-27, 65-72, Education, WSU.

69. McAndrew, "Rapid Review," 3.

70. "Report of the Superintendent," 1926-27, 73-74, Education, WSU.

71. "Report of the Superintendent," 1928-29, 67-80, 81, 83, Education, WSU.

72. "Report of the Superintendent," 1927-28, 75-80, Education, WSU.

73. Dayton *Daily News*, Nov. 9, 1927.

74. Dayton *Daily News*, Jan. 11, 1916.

75. "Report of the Superintendent," 1916-17, 96, Education, WSU.

76. McAndrew, "Rapid Review," 2-3.

77. For one description of the drill, see L.F. Bucher, "Report of the Medical Inspector," 1914-15, 162, Education, WSU.

78. "Report of the Superintendent," 1916-17, 88, Education, WSU.

79. Dayton *Daily News,* Jan. 11, 1916.

80. Ibid. For accounts of teacher conflict with a business-dominated board in another larger city, see David Hogan, *Class and Reform: School and Society in Chicago, 1880-1930* (Philadelphia, 1985), 157-219. Hogan's portrait of Chicago school politics depicts teachers, especially those in the Chicago Teachers' Foundation, and board members almost perpetually at odds, as the board sought to diminish teachers' mobility and professional autonomy. Hogan's analysis of the motives of many of the businessmen on the business-dominated Chicago board is a strongly negative one. In fact he asserts that some were "little more than greedy, avaricious opportunists interested in tapping the revenues of the board (or the teachers' pension fund) to line their own pockets" (218). Teacher–board conflict, however, was not a uniform constant. Jeffrey Mirel paints a very different picture. In his work on the Detroit school system, he too found the common pattern of business domination of the board by the late 1920s. But in the case of Detroit, those businessmen were the leaders of a fight to maintain teachers' salaries in 1930 and 1931 in the wake of the terrible financial crises caused by the onset of the Depression. See Jeffrey Mirel, "The Politics of Educational Retrenchment in Detroit, 1929-1935," *History of Education Quarterly* 24 (1984): 323-58.

81. Scholars have not paid a great deal of attention to Antioch College, despite its role as a pioneer in several educational movements over the decades. The most important work is Burton Clark, *The Distinctive College: Antioch, Reed, and Swarthmore* (Chicago: 1970). Two unpublished dissertations should be mentioned: Roy Talbert, "Beyond Pragmatism: The Story of Arthur E. Morgan" (Ph.D. diss., Vanderbilt University, 1973); George Newman, "The Morgan Years: Politics of Innovative Change: Antioch College in the 1920s" (Ph.D. diss., University of Michigan, 1978). Talbert focuses on Morgan's life, not on Antioch College per se. The two other works direct their attention narrowly, to narratives of curricular change, personalities, and campus atmosphere. None of these works seeks to place changes at Antioch in the 1920s within the larger contexts of the developments of progressive education and business-progressivism. It should be noted that Talbert has used a portion of his dissertation as one basis for his book *FDR's Utopian: Arthur Morgan and the TVA* (Jackson, Miss., 1987). As the title indicates, however, the book focuses on Morgan's work for Roosevelt's New Deal and mentions the Antioch years only briefly.

82. Lucy Morgan, *Pioneering Days at Antioch* (Yellow Springs, Ohio, 1947), 1.

83. Morgan made such statements in an interview with Antioch student Maury Waters. Handwritten interview transcript, June 6, 1951, Antiochiana Manuscripts Collection, Antioch Library, Antioch College,

Yellow Springs, Ohio. (College records and publications, as well as a wide variety of manuscript materials relating to Antioch College, form a special, totally uncatalogued archive, known as Antiochiana, within the Antioch College Library. Hereafter these materials will be cited as A, A.)

84. For a series of speeches Morgan gave to major national Unitarian meetings, see series III-B, AEM.

85. Arthur Morgan, speech transcript, meeting of the Association of College and Preparatory Schools, Nov. 30, 1923, Drown Hall, Lehigh University, A, A (hereafter the transcript of this meeting will be cited as Lehigh Meeting, ACPS).

86. Arthur Morgan, "The Antioch Plan: Education for Symmetry," typescript, 4, marked by handwritten note, "1921 or 1922," series V-A, AEM.

87. Ibid., 11.

88. Lehigh Meeting, ACPS.

89. Minutes of Antioch College faculty meetings, Dec. 8, 1926, typed transcript, individual speakers not identified; those participating in discussion noted as Professors Nash, Swinnerton, Kennedy, and Mathewson, A, A.

90. George Roberts, "An Experiment in Education," *National City Bank Bulletin* (Feb. 1923): 28.

91. For a summary of Antioch's health program as it developed, see George Paul, "Health Provisions of Antioch College," *Nation's Health* 5 (Feb. 1923): 63.

92. Letter to parents and teachers of prospective students, signed "A.E.M., 1921," series V-A, AEM.

93. Arthur Morgan, "Almus Pater," *Antioch College Bulletin* 26 (Nov. 1929): 1-5.

94. Arthur Morgan to Charles Eliot, Sept. 27, 1916, series II, AEM.

95. The minutes of meetings of the Board of Trustees, 1921–29, list names and occupations of trustees for each year, A, A; Arthur Morgan to Angelo Patri, July 14, 1920, series V-A, AEM.

96. The exact figure was $2,222,141.32. For a complete list of major patrons of Antioch College during the period here studied, see "People Who Have Contributed to Antioch College in the Amount of $5,000. or More Since 1921," May 1, 1933, A, A.

97. Daniel Wren, "American Business Philanthropy and Higher Education in the Nineteenth Century," *Business History Review* 57 (Autumn 1983): 342-46.

98. Mayo quoted by Arthur Morgan in "Question and Answer Session: Morning Session, April 9, 1921," 1921 Proceedings.

99. Engineers Club Dinner.

100. Roberts, "Experiment in Education," 28.

101. Engineers Club Dinner.

102. The total yearly enrollment by men and women at Antioch between 1921 and 1929 was as follows:

YEAR	MEN	WOMEN	TOTAL
1921–22	164	39	203
1922–23	311	82	393
1923–24	377	140	517
1924–25	444	154	598
1925–26	468	172	640
1926–27	532	187	719
1927–28	509	197	706
1928–29	459	205	664
1929–30	467	213	680

Statistics from J.D. Dawson file, A, A.

103. See student budgets detailed in Angelo Patri, "The Strangest College in the U.S.," *Liberty Magazine* (Oct. 1924): 57-58.

104. Charles Eliot, "Address Given at a Meeting in the Interest of Antioch College, Hotel Somerset, Boston," reprinted in *School and Society* 18 (July 1923): 35-37.

105. Charles Francis Potter, notes for article to be titled "The New American Education," typescript, handwritten date on document marked "1925?" A, A.

106. Ida Clyde Clarke, "Antioch, an Adventure in Education," *Pictorial Review* (Jan. 1924): 20.

107. "Enrollment Summaries," *Antioch Notes* 5 (Dec. 1, 1927): 1, A, A. A very interesting contemporary demographic profile of the college student population in the 1920s can be found in O.E. Reynolds, *The Social and Economic Status of College Students* (New York, 1927).

108. Algo Henderson, "The Extramural School," Oct. 26, 1933, typescript, 1-9, A, A.

109. Algo Henderson typed notes labeled "Quotations Concerning the Antioch Experience from Mrs. Sontag," (no date; probably late 1932, early 1933): 5-6, A, A.

110. Ibid., 5.

111. Henderson, "Extramural School," 6.

112. Typed flyer, "Antioch Industrial Service," 1923, A, A.

113. Philip Nash, "Antioch Fund Campaign Starts: Dean Reviews Moves That Lead to Establishment of Lumber Department at Antioch College," *Wood Construction* (March 1925): 10.

114. *Journal* (Dayton, Ohio), July 8, 1926.

115. "The Antioch Industrial Research Institute of Antioch College," July 22, 1931, typed report, 1, A, A.

116. "Institute Activities," 1931, typed report, 2-3, A, A.

117. Patri, "Strangest College," 57.

118. Clarke, "Antioch, an Adventure," 20.

119. *Los Angeles Times*, April 11, 1926, clipping in A, A.

120. George Marvin, "The Answer of Antioch," *Outlook* (February 1926): 212.

121. In 1923, for instance, salaries ranged from one thousand dollars for part-time teaching to five thousand dollars for heads of departments. See R.M. Hughes, "Conditions at Antioch College," March 1923, typed report, A, A.

122. Arthur Morgan to Homer Corry, Feb. 4, 1921, series V-A, AEM.

123. Marvin, "The Answer of Antioch." For a review of the educational climate in American colleges during the decade, see William Learned, "The Quality of the Educational Process in the United States and Europe," *Bulletin No. 20* (Carnegie Foundation for the Assessment of Teaching, New York, 1927), 1-75.

124. For a perceptive assessment of the nature of American college faculties in the early decades of the twentieth century, see David Levine, *The American College and the Culture of Aspiration, 1915-1940* (Ithaca, N.Y., 1986).

125. For a representative list of faculty members, containing brief biographies and summaries of credentials, see "The Officers of Instruction," *General Catalogue of Antioch College* 5 (1925-26): 11-20.

126. Arthur Morgan, "Memorandum to the Faculty: An Inventory and Appraisal," Nov. 1, 1931, A, A (hereafter this document will be cited as Letter from Portugal).

127. "Minutes of Regular Faculty Meeting," Sept. 21, 1921, typed notes, A, A.

128. "Minutes of Regular Faculty Meeting," Nov. 13, 1925, typed transcript, A, A.

129. "Minutes of Special Faculty Meeting," Dec. 8, 1926, typed transcript, A, A.

130. See, for example, the interpretations in Clark, *Distinctive College*, 39-41; Talbert, "Beyond Pragmatism," 116-28. Talbert, in particular, misinterprets the Letter from Portugal. Morgan, he argues, had changed his objectives for the college in midstream, had "moved from building enlightened proprietors to remaking human life" and in the process had "lost the faculty." In fact, a key to understanding Morgan is the realization that in some ways all his projects sought to reshape and remake human life. He did not first wish, as Talbert suggests, to create a trade school for business administrators, only gradually endowing his plans with loftier objectives. They had always been there.

131. Letter from Portugal, 3.

132. Ibid., 9.

133. O.F. Mathiasen, typed memo, untitled, Jan. 4, 1932, A, A.

134. Ibid.

135. "Report of the Autonomous Course Plan Committee, 1927–1928," typescript, 1928, 8 (Professors P.S. Dwyer, R.E. Hiller, and O.F. Mathiasen comprised the faculty committee during the year 1927-28), A, A.

136. Ibid.

137. William Leiserson to Arthur Morgan, typed memo, undated (probably 1928?), A, A.

138. Lucy Morgan, speech, printed transcript of speeches given at an Open Forum held during November 1931, Antioch College, A, A (hereafter this transcript will be cited as Open Forum).

139. The charges about the faculty wives appeared in a lengthy memo defending his father written from Europe by Ernest Morgan. See Ernest Morgan to Dr. Henderson, Mr. Chatterjee, Mr. Horton, and Bishop Jones, dated Dec. 1931, A, A. (Another shorter copy of this memo is in series V-A, AEM.)

140. Open Forum.

141. Lehigh Meeting, ACPS.

142. "Proposed Statement of Russell Steward," typed memo, Nov. 20, 1947, series V-B, AEM; Charles Kettering to Arthur Morgan, Oct. 29, 1947, series V, AEM.

143. The speech was quoted in *Springfield News* (Springfield, Ohio), Feb. 7, 1928.

144. Open Forum.

145. See minutes of the Executive Committee of the Board of Trustees of Antioch College, 1926-29, A, A.

146. Marvin, "Answer of Antioch," 211. Available NCR Board Meeting minutes for the relevant years do not corroborate Marvin's story.

147. Engineers Club Dinner.

148. Ibid.

149. Ibid.

150. Ibid.

151. Cremin, *Transformation of the School*, 89.

152. Katz, *Class, Bureaucracy, and the Schools*, 125.

153. The account of the University of Cincinnati's influence appeared in Clarke, "Antioch, an Adventure," 211, and in many other contemporary publications.

154. A list of school board members with a note on changed numbers and election practices appears in Charlotte Conover, *Dayton and Montgomery County: Resources and People* (New York, 1932), 456-59.

155. O.F. Mathiasen, typed memo, Jan. 4, 1932.

156. Arthur Morgan to Morris Keeton, Feb. 6, 1965, series III, AEM.

157. Letter from Portugal, 14.

158. Arthur Morgan to Algo Henderson, typed memo, Jan. 9, 1932, A, A.

6. Conclusion

1. Wiebe, *Businessmen and Reform*, 217.
2. Patterson, "Model City."
3. McAndrew, "Rapid Review," 1.
4. Rightor, *City Manager in Dayton*, vii.
5. Morgan, "Almus Pater," 5.
6. Richard Hofstadter, quoted in Wiebe, *Businessmen and Reform*, 217.
7. Arthur Morgan, "Almus Pater," 1.
8. Typed session transcript, "Morning Session of Meeting of the Progressive Education Association," held at Engineers Club, Dayton, Ohio, April 9, 1921, series VIII-D, AEM.
9. Ibid.
10. Ibid.
11. For a comprehensive listing of historical scholarship about women's activities and influence during this period, see Papachristou, *Bibliography in the History of Women*. For discussion of the work of female progressive reformers in Ohio, see Harrison, "The Consumers' League of Ohio."
12. "Remarks of Frank Slutz," meeting of Progressive Education Association, April 9, 1921, AEM.
13. For discussions of the major themes addressed by organizational history, see Samuel Hays, "The New Organizational Society," in *Building the Organizational Society: Essays on Associational Activities in Modern America*, ed. Jerry Israel (New York, 1972), 1- 15; Galambos, "Emerging Organizational Synthesis," 279-90; idem, "Technology, Political Economy, and Professionalization," 471-93; Cuff, "American Historians," 19-31; Berkhofer, Organizational Interpretation," 611-29; Wiebe, *Segmented Society;* Stephen Skowronek, *Building a New American State: The Expansion of National Administrative Capacity, 1877-1920* (Cambridge, Mass., 1982); Alfred Chandler, "The Emergence of Managerial Capitalism," *Business History Review* 58 (Winter 1984): 473-503; Chandler and Tedlow, eds., *Coming of Managerial Capitalism;* Thomas McCraw, *Prophets of Regulation, Charles Francis Adams, Louis D. Brandeis, James M. Landis, Alfred E. Kahn* (Cambridge, Mass., 1984), 80-143. Useful unpublished dissertations include Guy Alchon, "Technocratic Social Science and the Rise of Managed Capitalism, 1910-1933" (Ph.D. diss., University of Iowa, 1982); Martin Sklar, "The Corporate Reconstruction of American Society, 1896-1914:

The Market and the Law" (Ph.D. diss., University of Rochester, 1982); Jack Bernardo, "The Organizational Republic: Societal Corporatism in the United States" (Ph.D. diss., University of Tennessee, 1982).

14. Arthur Morgan, "The Point System," *Antioch Notes* (Oct. 1927), A, A.

15. Minutes of city council meeting, April 9, 1913, Records Books of the City Council, bk. C-1, 435, Office of the City Commission, Dayton, Ohio.

16. Ibid.

17. Arthur Morgan, "Factors in Engineering Accomplishment," *Antioch College Bulletin* 19 (April 1923): 53, A, A.

18. Ibid.

19. Kelley, "Dayton's 'Uncle Bountiful,' " 8.

20. Dayton *Daily News*, Nov. 1, 1927.

Bibliography

Manuscript Collections

PRIVATE ARCHIVES

Archives of Antioch College, Antiochiana, Antioch College, Yellow
 Springs, Ohio. (This collection, which includes personal correspondence files from many individuals, college records, college publications, among a wide variety of other materials illuminating the history
 of Antioch College, is unprocessed and uncatalogued. It is housed in
 separate quarters from other manuscript materials held by the Antioch Library, but to date no finding aids or guides to the collection have
 been issued. Records from this archives used here have been cited as
 Antiochiana.)
Archives of the NCR Corporation, World Headquarters, Dayton, Ohio.
 (This very extensive archive occupies rooms in a four-story warehouse in the NCR headquarters complex of buildings. Including
 company business records, publications, correspondence files for
 many individuals, hundreds of scrapbooks and newspaper files,
 among other materials, it is largely uncatalogued and unprocessed.
 Through the generous intervention of Steve Ward of the NCR Patent
 Division, the author received permission to do research in this archive. In general, however, it remains a resource that, to date, the
 company reserves for its own use and closes to the public. The NCR
 archivist's primary job has been and is to help company lawyers
 research patent infringement cases, not to make collections accessible
 to scholars.)

RECORDS GROUPS

Annual Reports of the Dayton Board of Education, 1897-1930, Archives
 and Special Collections, University Library, Wright State University,
 Dayton, Ohio.

Records of the Charter Party, Cincinnati Historical Society, Cincinnati, Ohio. (Progressive era municipal reform efforts in Cincinnati, the largest city in southern Ohio, and Dayton's nearest big-city neighbor, influenced municipal reform in Dayton. These records shed light on the "good government" cause in southwest Ohio, not just Cincinnati, and provide reports, correspondence, and memos from such figures as Murray Seasongood, Henry Bentley, Victor Heintz, and Charles P. Taft.)

Records of the Dayton City Commission, 1914-1930, Offices of the City Commission, Municipal Building, Dayton, Ohio. (These records, important to an understanding of the city manager campaign and the development of a new form of municipal government, include extensive minutes of city commission meetings, financial papers, ordinances, and legal documents.)

Records of the Dayton City Council, 1890-1913, Offices of the City Commission, Municipal Building, Dayton, Ohio. (The most important of these records are the oversized bound books containing the handwritten secretary's minutes for meetings of the Dayton City Council.)

Records of Local Dayton, Socialist Party, 1898-1956; Wright State University. (These records, including extensive minutes, membership lists, financial records, and other materials, may be one of the best collections for a Socialist party local to be found anywhere in the country, useful especially for information about the city manager fight.)

Records of the Miami Conservancy District, Wright State University, and Miami Conservancy District Headquarters Building, Dayton, Ohio. (This very extensive organizational record group is divided. Location of the individual records cited here is noted where appropriate. These records include not only court records and transcripts, minutes, financial documents, memos, correspondence, reports, diaries, and numerous other materials for the Miami Conservancy District, but also the organizational records of the Dayton Citizens' Relief Commission and the Dayton Flood Prevention Commission, as well as files from the Arthur Morgan Engineering Company.)

Records of the Office of the City Manager, Dayton, Ohio, 1914-1930, Wright State University. (Rediscovered in a Dayton warehouse in 1975 by an archivist with the Ohio Historical Society, these records have recently been microfilmed. They are very extensive and include memos, reports, speeches, correspondence, legal documents, and numerous other materials illuminating the workings of both the city manager's office and the divisions of city government during this period.)

Records of the Osborn Removal Company, 1920-1928, Wright State University. (These records supplement those of the Miami Conservancy District itself, which organized the Osborn Removal Company to relocate the village of Osborn. The maps, tax information, and correspondence in this record group shed further light on issues generated by the establishment of the District.)

PERSONAL PAPERS

Cox, James. Papers. Ohio Historical Society, Columbus, Ohio. (James Cox, later to be the Democratic party's candidate in the presidential campaign of 1920, was elected governor of Ohio in 1912, defeated in 1914, and reelected in 1918. Cox's roots were in Dayton, and his papers help illuminate issues surrounding flood relief, city manager campaigning, and the construction of the Conservancy District.)

Edelman, Oscar. Papers. Wright State University. (Edelman was a longtime leader of the Socialist party in Dayton. His papers include much useful correspondence and supplementary party records.)

Morgan, Arthur. Papers. Manuscripts Collections, Antioch College, Yellow Springs, Ohio. (This huge and well-catalogued collection provides a rich source for the study of the Conservancy District, as well as progressive educational reform. The Morgan Papers also house the Records of the Moraine Park School.)

Willis, Frank. Papers. Ohio Historical Society. (Frank Willis defeated James Cox in the Ohio gubernatorial race of 1914. Flood relief and the Conservancy District were major issues in that campaign.)

Newspapers

DAYTON, OHIO

Court Reporter, 1917-1937
Daily News, 1889-
Daily Times, 1890-1898
Evening Item, 1890
Evening Press, 1892-1905
Forum, 1913-1939
Gross-Daytoner Zeitung, 1914-1937
Herald, 1878-1949
Herald and Empire, 1869-1897
Independent, 1923-1925
Journal, 1847-1949
Labor Review, 1916-1929
Labor Union, 1927-1929
Liberator, 1890-1894
Miami Valley Socialist, 1912-1929
Ohio Fiery Cross, 1924

Press, 1932-1955
Religious Telescope, 1834-1946
Review, 1929-1934
Shopping News, 1927-
Tattler, 1890-1891
University of Dayton News, 1926-1955
Watchword, 1893-1946
Weekly Journal, 1826-1904
Weekly Times-News, 1890-1897

LIMA, OHIO

Advertiser, 1889-1916
Allen County Republican-Gazette, 1877-1918
Clipper, 1889-1898
Courier, 1877-1918
Daily Herald, 1899-1900
Independent Observer, 1899-1900
Morning Star, 1924-1933
News, 1897-
Printer, 1899
Republican-Gazette, 1882-1926
Times-Democrat, 1855-1912

MIDDLETOWN, OHIO

Butler County Signal, 1874-1907
Journal, 1857-1912
News-Journal, 1891-
News-Signal, 1905-1932
Signal, 1888-1907

SIDNEY, OHIO

Daily Journal, 1909-1928
Daily News, 1891-
Gazette, 1891-1905
Journal-Gazette, 1856-1909
Shelby County Democrat, 1852-1940
Weekly Progress, 1915-1917
Weekly Republican, 1908-1928

SPRINGFIELD, OHIO

Beacon, 1886-1897
Daily News, 1905
Daily Times, 1908-1911
Gazette, 1879-1908
National New Era, 1884-1904
Ohio Rural Times, 1898-1900
Press-Republican, 1899-1905
Republic-Times, 1865-1900
Rural Times, 1900
Times, 1911-1914
Times, 1895-1898
Tribune, 1909-1945
Weekly Gazette, 1873-1908
Weekly Republic, 1839-1905

YELLOW SPRINGS, OHIO

News, 1894-
Review, 1895-1899
Torch, 1894-1895
Weekly Citizen, 1891-1894

PIQUA, OHIO

Citizen, 1904
Correspondent, 1878-1894
Daily Call, 1883-
Daily Dispatch, 1886-1901
Daily Headlight, 1899
Helmet, 1874-1911
Journal, 1865-1901
Leader-Dispatch, 1888-1919
Leader-Journal, 1882-1912
Press-Dispatch, 1915-1922

TROY, OHIO

Buckeye, 1876-1909
Daily News, 1909-
Democrat, 1880-1948
Miami Union, 1864-1953

Dissertations and Unpublished Papers

Adelman, Nancy. "The Study of Educational Change and Its Application to Three New Jersey Communities in the Progressive Era." Ed.D. diss., Columbia, University, 1985.

Alchon, Guy. "Technocratic Social Science and the Rise of Managed Capitalism, 1910-1933." Ph.D. diss., University of Iowa, 1982.

Becker, Carl. "Economic and Technological Change in the Railroad Car Building Industry and the Response of the Barney and Smith Car Company, 1893-1926." Pamphlet File, Archives, Wright State University.

Bower, Stephen. "The Child, the School, and the Progressive Educational Concept of Community, 1890-1920." Ph.D. diss., Indiana University, 1980.

Bremer, William Walling. "New York City's Family of Social Servants and the Politics of Welfare: A Prelude to the New Deal, 1928-1933." Ph.D. diss., Stanford University, 1973.

Buroher, Robert L. "From Voluntary Association to Welfare State: The Development of Public Social Services in Illinois, 1890-1920." Ph.D. diss. University of Chicago, 1973.

Deem, Warren. "The Employers' Association of Dayton." Pamphlet File, Wright State University.

Dilla, Somlar. "Romanticism, Cultural Transmission and Progressivism as Rationales for the Choice of Educational Goals and Practices: A Historical-Pedagogical Perspective." Ph.D. diss., University of South Africa, 1979.

Dunek, Robert. "The Citizen-Administrator: A Role Integration Study of City Managers in Southern California." Ph.D. diss., University of Southern California, 1985.

Finfer, Laurence A. "Leisure as Social Work in the Urban Community: The Progressive Recreation Movement, 1890-1920." Ph.D. diss., Michigan State University, 1974.

Finn, Mary E. "Schools and Society in Buffalo, New York, 1918-1936: The Effects of Progressivism." Ph.D. diss., State University of New York, Buffalo, 1980.

Flanagan, Maureen Anne. "Charter Reform in Chicago, 1890-1915: Community and Government in the Progressive Era." Ph.D. diss., Loyola University of Chicago, 1981.

Grenier, Judson A. "The Origins and Nature of Progressive Muckraking." Ph.D. diss., University of California, Los Angeles, 1965.

Harrison, Dennis Irven. "The Consumer's League of Ohio: Women and Reform, 1909-1937." Ph.D. diss., Case Western Reserve University, 1975.

Hillsey, Judy Arlene. " 'The Way to Win': A Search for Success in the New Industrial Order, 1870-1910." Ph.D. diss., Rutgers University, 1980.

Hirschhorn, Bernard. "In the Practice of Democracy: Richard Spencer Childs, Political Reformer, 1882-1978." Ph.D. diss., Columbia University, 1981.

Hurst, Steven Melvin. "Progressive Government: Administrative Reorganization and Bureaucratic Transition in Ohio, 1880-1921." Ph.D. diss., Miami University, 1977.

Javersak, David Thomas. "The Ohio Valley Trades and Labor Assembly: The Formative Years, 1882-1915." Ph.D. diss., West Virginia University, 1977.

Jensen, Gordon M. "The National Civic Federation: American Business in an Age of Social Change and Social Reform, 1900-1910." Ph.D. diss., Princeton University, 1956.

Jones, Regina. "An Inquiry into the Classroom Discipline Legacy from the Progressive Education Movement." Ed.D. diss., Temple University, 1981.

Kelly, David Harvey. "Labor Relations in the Steel Industry: Management's Ideas, Proposals, and Programs, 1920-1950." Ph.D. diss., Indiana University, 1976.

Kent, John. "The Scientific Curriculum: Progressive Reform in an Age of Progressivism, 1914-1926." Ed.D. diss., Boston University, 1984.

Klein, John William. "The Role and Impact of Rockefeller: Philanthropy during the Progressive Era." Ph.D. diss., Fordham University, 1980.

Lagemann, Ellen Condliffe. "A Generation of Women: Studies in Educational Biography." Ph.D. diss., Columbia University, 1978.

Lange, Juliann. "The Decline of the Teaching of Rhetoric and the Rise of Progressivism in the American Secondary Schools, 1893-1940." Ph.D. diss., University of Akron, 1985.

Lamoreaux, Naomi Raboy. "Industrial Organization and Market Behavior: The Great Merger Movement in American Industry." Ph.D. diss., John Hopkins University, 1979.

Leckie, Shirley Anne. "Parks, Planning, and Progressivism in Toledo, Ohio: 1890-1929." Ph.D. diss., University of Toledo, 1981.

McCarthy, Michael Patrick. "Businessmen and Professionals in Municipal Reform: The Chicago Experience, 1887-1920." Ph.D. diss., Northwestern University, 1970.

McQuaid, Kim. "A Response to Industrialism: Liberal Businessmen and the Evolving Spectrum of Capitalist Reform, 1886-1960." Ph.D. diss., Northwestern University, 1975.

Meyer, Stephen, III. "Mass Production and Human Efficiency: The Ford Motor Company, 1908-1921." Ph.D. diss., Rutgers University, 1977.

232   Bibliography

Miggins, Edward Michael. "Businessmen, Pedagogues, and Progressive
    Reform: The Cleveland Foundation's 1915 School Survey." Ph.D.
    diss., Case Western Reserve University, 1975.
Newman, George. "The Morgan Years: Politics of Innovative Change:
    Antioch College in the 1920's." Ph.D. diss., University of Michigan,
    1978.
Noble, David Franklin. "Science and Technology in the Corporate Search
    for Order: American Engineers and Social Reform, 1900-1929." Ph.D.
    diss., University of Rochester, 1974.
Pennoyer, John Christian. "The Harper Report of 1899: Administrative
    Progressivism and the Chicago Public Schools." Ph.D. diss., Univer-
    sity of Denver, 1978.
Quillen, Isaac James. "Industrial City: A History of Gary, Indiana, to
    1929." Ph.D. diss., Yale University, 1942.
Ramirez, Bruno Santi. "Collective Bargaining and the Politics of Indus-
    trial Relations in the Progressive Era, 1898-1916." Ph.D. diss., Univer-
    sity of Toronto, 1975.
Raucher, Alan Richard. "The Emergence of Public Relations in Business,
    1900-1929." Ph.D. diss., University of Pennsylvania, 1964.
Reese, William John. "Progressivism and the Grass Roots: Social Change
    and Urban Schooling, 1840-1920." Ph.D. diss., University of Wiscon-
    sin, Madison, 1980.
Ross, Steven Joseph. "Workers on the Edge: Work, Leisure and Politics in
    Industrializing Cincinnati, 1830-1890." Ph.D. diss., Princeton Univer-
    sity, 1980.
Shirffer, Isobel C. "Ida M. Tarbell and Morality in Big Business: An
    Analysis of a Progressive Mind." Ph.D. diss., New York University,
    1967.
Sklar, Martin. "The Corporate Reconstruction of American Society, 1896-
    1914: The Market and the Law." Ph.D. diss., University of Rochester,
    1982.
Talbert, Roy. "Beyond Pragmatism: The Story of Arthur Morgan." Ph.D.
    diss., Vanderbilt University, 1971.
Travis, Anthony Raymond. "The Impulse toward the Welfare State:
    Chicago, 1890-1932." Ph.D. diss., Michigan State University, 1971.
Vaughn, Courtney Ann. "The Politics of Progressive Higher Education:
    As Seen through the Career of Henry Garland Bennett." Ed.D. diss.,
    Oklahoma State University, 1980.
Warner, Hoyt L. "Ohio's Crusade for Reform, 1897-1917." Ph.D. diss.,
    Harvard University, 1951.
Wachter, Daniel. "Vertical Integration in Late Nineteenth Century U.S.
    Industry." Ph.D. diss., Purdue University, 1983.
Zahavi, Gerald. "Workers, Managers, and Welfare Capitalism: The

Shoeworkers and Tanners of Endicott Johnson, 1880-1950." Ph.D. diss., Syracuse University, 1983.

Zaretsky, Eli Sherman. "Progressive Thought on the Impact of Industrialization on the Family and Its Relation to the Emergence of the Welfare State, 1890-1920." Ph.D. diss., University of Maryland, 1979.

Primary Sources

ARTICLES

Abbott, L. "Big Business and Bad Business." *Outlook* 101 (June 1912): 355-58.

Adams, C.S. "Antioch Plan of Cooperative Education as It Affects Students in Chemistry." *Journal of Chemical Education* 2 (Oct. 1925): 1-15.

Akin, J.W. "A Mayor's View of City Managership." *Public Management* 12 (March 1930): 190-91.

Albright, H.F. "How We Manage to Guess Right 90% of the Time." *System* 30 (Aug. 1916): 148-56.

Alden, P. "Humanizing of Industry." *Contemporary* 111 (Feb. 1917): 164-71.

Allen, J. "Running a Modern Town." *Collier's* 56 (Oct. 1915): 9-10.

"Antioch College." *School* 37 (Sept. 10, 1925): 1.

"Antioch Continues Its Experimentation." *New Student* 7 (April 4, 1928): 1.

"The Antioch Plan." *New Republic* 27 (July 20, 1921): 205.

"Aspects of Scientific Management." *Nation* 92 (May 11, 1911): 464-65.

Babcock, D. "How We Increased Quality and Reduced Prices 30%." *System* 30 (Oct. 1916): 419-22.

———. "Taylor System of Management in the Franklin Shops." *Engineering Magazine* 51 (Sept.–Oct. 1916): 843-48, 1-9.

Baker, Frederick. "The Commission Plan vs. the Municipal Business Manager Plan." *Pacific Municipalities* 27 (Dec. 1913): 669-81.

Ballard, P. "Scientific Management and Science." *Cassier's* 41 (May 1912): 425-30.

Banning, K. "Short Cuts in Executive Work: Ingenious Devices to Save Time and Effort." *System* 23 (June 1913): 602-9.

Barstow, M. "Lakeland Votes for Manager Plan." *American City* 27 (Oct. 1922): 356.

Bates, Frank G. "Commission Government Law of New Jersey." *American Political Science Review* (Aug. 1911): 431-32.

Bates, Frank. "Forms of City Government." *Bulletin No. 5, Indiana Bureau of Legislative Information* (1916).

"Bathtubs, Cash Registers, and the Trust Problem." *Outlook* 103 (March 1913): 476-78.

Bauman. A.A. "Business Man as God." *Contemporary* 110 (Dec. 1916): 741-48.

Beard, Charles A. "Politics and City Government." *National Municipal Review* 6 (March 1917): 205-10.

Becker, O.M. "Auxiliary Methods of Successful Labor Employers." *Engineering Magazine* 31 (April 1906): 38-59.

Beeks, Gertrude. "Employees' Welfare Work." *Independent* 55 (Oct. 1903): 2515-18.

"Big Business and the People." *World's Work* 20 (Sept. 1910): 13356-58.

"Big Business in a Quandary." *Current Literature* 51 (Dec. 1911): 627-29.

Bingham, C.A.; Brownlow, Louis; Carr, O.E.; Otis, H.G.; and Ridley, Clarence E. "Management Problems of the City Manager." *Public Management* 11 (March 1929): 210-21.

Bjorkman, E. "What Industrial Civilization May Do to Man." *World's Work* 17 (April 1909): 11479-98.

Bloomfield, M. "Scientific Management: Co-operative or One-sided?" *Survey* 28 (May 18, 1912): 312-13.

Boggs, T.H. "Certain Social Effects of Individualistic Industry." *American Journal of Sociology* 21 (Nov. 1915): 360-81.

Bojesen, J. "Red Cross Agent's Personal Experience." *Survey* 32 (May 1914): 143-46.

Bond, A.R. "Good Housekeeping in the Factory; Effect of Esthetic Surroundings upon the Man at the Machine." *Scientific American* 119 (Sept. 14, 1918): 208-9.

Bope, H.P. "Welfare Work of the Steel Corporation." *Survey* 29 (Feb. 1913): 1-5.

Boyton, W.E. "Proportional Manager." *Independent* 92 (Oct. 1917): 135.

Bradford, Ernest S., and Gilbertson, H.S. "Commission Form vs. City Manager Plan." *American City* 10 (Jan. 1914): 37-40.

Brewer, B. "Scientific Management in the Army and Navy." *World's Work* 23 (Jan. 1912): 311-17.

Brodke, M.B. "Leisure Time Program for Workers." *Playground* 22 (Dec. 1928): 526-27.

Brower, I.C. "The City Manager and the City Press." *Public Management* 9 (March 1927): 194-205.

Brownell, A. "Business Reduced to a Science." *World's Work* 9 (Dec. 1904): 5596-601.

Brownlow, Louis. "The City Manager in the United States." *Public Administration* 9 (Oct. 1931): 393-416.

———. "Co-ordination of Municipal Administration under the City Manager." *Public Management* 12 (March 1930): 106-13.

Bruere, Robert W. "Antioch and the Going World." *Survey Graphic* 11 (June 1927): 259.

"Building for Business at College." *Visual Education* 5 (Nov. 1924): 378-79.

Burnett, V.E. "Peculiarities of Welfare Work." *Industrial Management* 61 (June 1921): 439-40.

Burns, W. "Time-saving Arrangements." *Cassier's* 39 (Jan. 1911): 228-31.

"Business Extension Not Criminal Monopoly." *Outlook* 109 (April 7, 1915): 796-97.

"By Consent of the Scientifically Managed." *Survey* 35 (Dec. 1915): 342.

Calkings, R. "Social Needs of Wage Earners." *Independent* 54 (July 1902): 1716-18.

Callaway, H.R. "Efficiency and the Worker." *Engineering Magazine* 45 (Aug. 1913): 715-17.

Carlton, F.T. "Scientific Management and the Wage-Earner." *Journal of Political Economics* 20 (Oct. 1912): 834-45.

Carpenter, C.U. "Concrete Example of Successful Administration." *Engineering Magazine* 22 (March 1902): 822-28.

Carr, O.E. "Council-Manager Government at Niagara Falls." *American City* 14 (May 1916): 494-95.

———. "Progress, Prospects and Pitfalls of the New Profession of City Manager." *Canadian Engineer* 35 (1918): 513-14, 519.

———. "Should City Managers Defend Themselves against Attacks in Political Campaigns." *City Manager Yearbook* (1932): 112-15.

Carran, A. "Eleven Years of Progress under the Commission-Manager Plan in a Small City." *American City* 40 (April 1929): 138-39.

Carter, J. "Wanted (and Won): A City Manager." *Woman Citizen* 12 (Nov. 1927): 22-23.

"Cash Register Care." *Outlook* 110 (June 23, 1915): 398.

Casson, H.N. "Efficiency in the Intellectual Life." *Independent* 70 (May 11, 1911): 999-1001.

Catchings, W. "If Business Were All in the Open." *World's Work* 27 (March 1914): 540-47.

Childs, Richard S. "Along the Governmental Battle Front." *National Municipal Review* 19 (Jan. 1930): 5-6.

———. "Best Practice under the City Manager Plan." *National Municipal Review* 22 (Jan. 1933): 41-44.

———. "Citizen Organization for Control of Government." *Annals of the American Academy of Political and Social Science* 292 (March 1954): 129-35.

———. "City Manager Government." *National Municipal Review* 25 (Feb. 1936): 50-51.

———. "Half Century of Municipal Reform." *American Journal of Economics and Sociology* 15 (April 1956): 321-26.

———. "How the Commission-Manager Plan Is Getting Along." *National Municipal Review* (Jan. 1917): 69-73.

———. "It's a Habit Now in Dayton." *National Municipal Review* 38 (Sept. 1948): 421-27.

———. "League's Second Stretch." *National Municipal Review* 33 (Nov. 1944): 514-19.

———. "Lockport Proposal to Improve the Commission Plan." *American City* 4 (June 1911): 285-87.

———. "Looking Back at City Managers Twenty Years Hence." *Public Management* 19 (March 1937): 79-83.

———. "A New Civic Army." *National Municipal Review* 10 (June 1921): 327-30.

———. "New Profession of City Manager." *New Republic* 8 (Sept. 1916): 135-37.

———. "No Tenure for City Managers." *National Municipal Review* 38 (April 1949): 167-70.

———. "A Theoretically Perfect County." *Annals of the American Academy of Political and Social Science* 47 (May 1913): 274-78.

Chipman, M. "Mere Efficiency." *Harper's Weekly* 62 (Jan. 29, 1916): 119-20.

Church, A.H. "Meaning of Scientific Management." *Engineering Magazine* 41 (April 1911): 97-101.

"Cincinnati Reformed and Contented." *Literary Digest* 88 (Jan. 1926): 10-11.

"City Manager—and the Next Step." *American City* 12 (Jan. 1915): 1-2.

"City Manager Municipalities." *American City* 22 (April 1920): 376-78.

"City Manager Plan." *American Municipalities* 26 (Jan. 1914): 113-14.

"City Manager Plan." *Outlook* 104 (Aug. 1913): 887-89.

"City Manager Plan." *World's Work* 61 (May 1932): 18.

"City Manager Plan in Forty-five Cities." *American City* 12 (June 1915): 499-507.

"City Manager Plan—The Application of Business Methods to Municipal Government." *American City* 11 (July 1914): 11-13.

"City Manager: Victim of Politics in Knoxville." *Literary Digest* 89 (June 1926): 18.

"City Managers (Dayton, Springfield, Ohio)." *Municipal World* 24 (April 1914): 84.

"City Manager's Contact with the Public." *Public Management* 13 (July 1931): 235-38.

"City Managing—A New Profession." *Independent* 80 (Dec. 1914): 433-34.

Cohen, Joseph A. "City Managership as a Profession." *National Municipal Review* 13 (July 1924): 391-411.

Coher, F.W. "Charter Revisions." *American Political Science Review* 16 (Feb. 1922): 89-93.

———. "Philadelphia's New Charter (1920)." *American Political Science Review* 13 (Nov. 1919): 645-47.

Collins, F.W. "Causes of Failures in Efficiency Work." *Engineering Magazine* 45 (Sept. 1913): 862-66.

Collins, W. "Industrial Paternalism." *Commonweal* 13 (April 22, 1931): 687-89.

"Comment on the Proposed Efficiency Experiment Station." *Engineering Magazine* 42 (Oct. 1911): 6-24.

"The Commission Form of Government." *World's Work* 27 (Jan. 1914): 254-55.

"Commission-Manager Form with Proportional Representation." *American City* 22 (Jan. 1920): 24-26.

Commons, R. "Organized Labor's Attitude toward Industrial Efficiency." *American Economic Review* 1 (Sept. 1911): 463-72.

"Complete List of City Manager Cities." *American City* 20 (Jan. 1919): 22.

Comstock, S. "Woman of Achievement: Miss Gertrude Beeks." *World's Work* 26 (Aug. 1913): 444-48.

Conover, Charlotte R. "John Henry Patterson, 1844-1922." *Builders in New Fields* (1939): 132-139.

Cooke, M.L. "Scientific Management as a Solution of the Unemployment Problem." *Annals of the American Academy of Political and Social Science* 61 (Sept. 1915): 146-64.

Copley, F.B. "Frederick W. Taylor, Revolutionist." *Outlook* 111 (Sept. 1915): 41-48.

Cottrell, Edwin A. "The Controlled Executive in Municipal Government." *City Manager Yearbook* (1933): 91-98.

Crandall, S. "Attempt to Wreck the Dayton Charter." *American City* 12 (June 1915): 509-10.

Crane, F. "Defense of the President of the National Cash Register Company." *Independent* 74 (April 1913): 861-62.

Cranston, M.R. "Social Science in Business." *Reader Magazine* 10 (June 1907): 1-9.

Daniel, Hawthorne. "Arthur E. Morgan's New Type of College." *World's Work* 41 (Feb. 1921): 405.

Darlington, P.J. "Bathing Facilities in Industrial Plants: Physiological Benefits of Hot and Cold Baths." *Engineering Magazine* 46 (Dec. 1913): 428-30.

Darlington, P.J. "Principles of Works Management." *Engineering Magazine* 34, 35 (March, April 1908): 1029-38; 57-67.

Darmstadter, D. "The Cleveland Charter Threatened Again." *American Political Science Review* 23 (Aug. 1929): 632-35.

Davis, J.C. "Welfare Work—Pseudo or Real." *Industrial Management* 59 (Jan. 1920): 48.

"Davison and Patterson, Farm Boys Who Rose." *Literary Digest* 73 (May 1922): 38-40.

Day, Willard, F. "Management Principles and the Consulting Engineer." *Engineering Magazine* 41 (April 1911): 133-40.

———. "The City Manager's Relation to Political Organizations." *Public Management* 12 (March 1930): 120-22.

"Dayton's Step Forward in City Government." *World's Work* 26 (Oct. 1913): 614.

"Dayton's Uncle Bountiful." *Collier's* 53 (Aug. 1, 1914): 8.

"Dayton's Unique Charter." *Literary Digest* 47 (Aug. 30, 1918): 308.

"Deplorable Strike." *Nation* 73 (July 1901): 6.

Devine, E.T. "Flood Rehabilitation in a City." *Survey* 32 (May 1914): 147-51.

"Doubts about Cash Register Sins." *Literary Digest* 50 (March 1915): 678.

Douglas, O.W. "Industrial Recreation." *American City* 17 (Oct. 1917): 365-69.

"Driving Politics out of Dayton." *Literary Digest* 48 (Jan. 1913): 147-48.

Droke, M. "Say We Say Farewell to Welfare?" *Industrial Management* 66 (Oct. 1923): 206-8.

Drury, H.D. "Scientific Management: A History and Criticism." *Nation* 101 (Oct. 1915): 520-21.

D'Unger, G. "Spirit of Neighborliness in a Great Corporation." *World To-Day* 17 (Dec. 1909): 1285-92.

Dunlap, J.R. "Dangerous Labor Legislation Now before Congress—A Call for Prompt Action." *Engineering Magazine* 51 (April 1916): 1-11.

"Efficiency in the Arsenals." *Survey* 36 (June 1916): 266.

"Efficiency Program." *Independent* 70 (April 1911): 739-40.

Emerson, H. "Philosophy of Efficiency." *Engineering Magazine* 41 (April 1911): 23-26.

"Enlightened Selfishness—The New Cue of Big Business." *Current Opinion* 56 (Feb. 1914): 144.

Epstein, A. "Employee's Welfare: An Autopsy." *American Mercury* 25 (March 1932): 335-42.

———. "Industrial Welfare Movement Sapping American Trade Unions." *Current History Magazine, New York Times* 24 (July 1926): 516-22.

Farnham, D.T. "Scientific versus Intuitive Administration." *Engineering Magazine* 51 (Sept. 1916): 849-54.

Farrell, J.A. "Profit Sharing: When? Why? How?" *System* 29 (March 1916): 226-32.

"Father of Scientific Management: Frederick W. Taylor." *Outlook* 109 (March 31, 1915): 755-56.

"Fight to Purify Big Business: Reckoning Up the Gains." *Century* 83 (Feb. 1912): 630-31.

"Fighting Waste with Movies: At the Plant of the National Cash Register Company." *Literary Digest* 65 (May 1, 1920): 36-37.

Fitch, J.A. "Mutual Misunderstanding of Efficiency Experts and Labor Men." *Survey* 32 (April 1914): 92-93.

Flanders, R.E. "Scientific Management from a Social Standpoint." *Scientific American Supplement* 73 (June 22, 1912): 391.

Fleisker, A. "Welfare Service for Employees." *Annals of the American Academy of Political and Social Science* 69 (Jan. 1917): 50-57.

Foster, H.S. "Cities Having City Managers Overwhelmingly Favor the Plan." *American City* 32 (April 1925): 397.

Frighy, C.E. "Welfare Work and Industrial Stability." *Industrial Management* 58 (Nov. 1919): 413-14.

French, L.H. "Welfare Manager." *Century* 69 (Nov. 1904): 61-71.

Frind, H.O. "Company Recreation for Employees; Summary of Discussions, 18th Recreation Congress." *Recreation* 25 (Dec. 1931): 523-24.

Fugitt, C.T. "Work of the National Cash Register Company." *Cassier's* 28 (Sept. 1905): 339-59.

"Further Comment on the Possibilities of the City Manager Plan in Municipal Government." *Engineering and Contracting* 40 (Dec. 31, 1913): 729.

Gairns, J.E. "Promotion of Employees." *Cassier's* 32 (Sept. 1907): 420-26.

"Garbage Collection Costs in Dayton, Ohio." *American City* 29 (July 1923): 31.

Gilbreth, F.B., and Gilbreth, L.M. "What Scientific Management Means to America's Industrial Position." *Annals of the American Academy of Political and Social Science* 61 (Sept. 1915): 208-16.

Glenn, J.M. "Industrial Recreation." *Playground* 18 (Sept. 1924): 337-39.

Going, C.B. "Efficiency of Labor." *Review of Reviews* 46 (Sept. 1912): 329-38.

"Growing Powers and Responsibilities of Business Men." *American City* 9 (Aug. 1913): 105-6.

Hachtel, Edward. "Where Education and Industry Cooperate to Make Men." *Forbes* 20 (Aug. 1927): 12.

Hadley, A.T. "Ethics of Corporate Management." *North American Review* 184 (Jan. 1907): 120-34.

Hall, B. "What Is Wrong with Welfare." *Industrial Management* 67 (June 1924): 355.

Halsey, Frederick. "The National Cash Register Company's Experiment." *American Machinist* 24 (June 1901): 688-89.

Hammett, M.L. "Proof of the Pudding Is in the Eating." *American City* 18 (May 1918): 424-26.

Hanchett, David Scott. "Students Who Must Work." *Personality* 1 (Nov. 1927): 79.

Hatton, A.R. "Pitfalls of Our Profession." *Public Management* 9 (March 1927): 230-40.

"Health and Recreation in Industrial Establishments." *Playground* 22 (March 1929): 689-90.

Healy, Patrick, III. "Should City Managers Be Community Leaders?" *Public Management* 15 (July 1933): 219.

Hendrick, Burton J. "Fitting the Man to His Job: A New Experiment in Scientific Management." *McClure's* 41 (June 1913): 50-59.

———. "Taking the American City out of Politics." *Harper's* 137 (1918): 106-13.

Hiden, R.G. "Running a Town as a Business: A General Manager in Staunton." *Harper's Weekly* 54 (May 21, 1910): 13-14.

Hoag, C.G. "How Proportional Representation Would Strengthen the City Manager Plan." *American City* 7 (Nov. 1912): 441-42.

———. "The Representative Council Plan of City Government: The City Manager Plan Improved by the Applications of Proportional Representation to the Election of the Council." *American City* 8 (April 1913): 373-80.

Holden, A.M. "The City-Manager Plan." *American Political Science Review* 10 (May 1916): 337-40.

"How a Thirty-Million Dollar Business Man Keeps His Workers Happy." *Literary Digest* 64 (March 1920): 118-22.

"Humanitarianism as a Business Investment." *Current Literature* 53 (Dec. 1912): 653-56.

"Indictment of the New Science of Management." *Current Literature* 50 (June 1911): 622-24.

"Indoor Recreation for Industrial Employees." *Monthly Labor Review* 25 (Sept. 1927): 465-78.

"Industrial Efficiency in Welfare Work." *Charities and the Commons* 16 (July 1906): 444-46.

Irwin, W. "Awakening of the American Business Man." *Century* 81 (March–April 1911): 689-92, 946-51.

"Is the City Manager Plan a Success? Excerpts from Letters from Cities Where the Plan Is in Operation." *American City* 24 (Jan. 1921): 6-8.

James, H.G. "Defects in the Dayton Charter." *National Municipal Review* 3 (Jan. 1914): 95-97.

Jordan, E. "Welfare Worker's Human Side." *North American Review* 216 (Oct. 1922): 535-42.

Kammerer, Gladys M. "Is the Manager a Political Leader?—Yes." *Public Management* 44 (Feb. 1962): 26-29.

Keir, M. "Scientific Management and Socialism." *Scientific Monthly* 5 (Oct. 1917): 359-67.

Kelley, F.C. "Business Genius and How He Works." *American Magazine* 81 (Feb. 1916): 50-51.

Keys, C.M. "New Morals of Business." *World's Work* 27 (April 1914): 620-25.

Kilpatrick. W. "City Manager Charters Analyzed." *American City* 31 (Oct.–Nov. 1942): 331-34, 449-51.

Kimball, D.S. "Industrial Organization and the Technical Schools." *Engineering Magazine* 52 (Oct. 1916): 104-8.

Kingsley, D.P. "Boundaries of Business." *System* 24 (Dec. 1913): 620-21.

Laist, T.F. "Young Folk Antioch Objective." *Wood Construction* 11 (Nov. 1, 1925): 9.

————. "Antioch Short Courses Ready." *Wood Construction* 12 (Jan. 1, 1926): 11.

"Larger Profits from Happier Workers." *Literary Digest* 76 (Feb. 1923): 22-24.

Lee, G.S. "Good News and Hard Work." *Outlook* 104 (May 1913): 251-54.

Lee, J. "Dayton Cash Register Village." *Charities Review* 10 (Jan. 1901): 543-48.

LeMont, F.H. "Making Savings out of the Payroll." *System* 29 (April–May 1916): 434-37.

Lewis, Eleanor. "Seventy-five Years of an Ideal—Antioch College." *Dearborn Independent* 26 (Nov. 1925): 2.

Lewis, J.S. "Works Management for Maximum Production." *Engineering Magazine* 19 (May 1900): 211-20.

Lewis, L. "Uplifting 17,000 Employees." *World's Work* 9 (March 1905): 5939-50.

Lippincott, C.A. "Promoting Employee Teamwork and Welfare without Paternalism." *Industrial Management* 71 (March 1926): 146-50.

Long, C.F. "Emergency Sanitation Work in the Flooded District." *American City* 8 (May 1913): 520-21.

Lowrie, S.G. "Ohio Model Charter Law." *American Political Science Review* 7 (Aug. 1913): 422-24.

McAndrew, William. "Rapid Review of an American School System." *Educational Review* 75 (Jan. 1928): 1-4.

McCleary, J.T. "Big Business and Labor." *Annals of the American Academy of Political and Social Science* 42 (July 1912): 25-37.

Mcfarlane, C. "In Stricken Dayton." *Collier's* 51 (April 1913): 8-9.

"Making the Cities' Business Businesslike." *Nation* 121 (Dec. 1925): 703.

Manville, M.F. "City Manager Plan Exposed: Satire." *American City* 23 (Nov. 1920): 491-92.

Marcosson, Isaac F. "Business-Managing a City." *Collier's* 102 (Jan. 3, 1914): 5-6, 24-25.

"More Than All the Comforts of a Home for These Fellow Workers." *Literary Digest* 65 (May 15, 1920): 112-17.

Morgan, Arthur E. "The Advancement of Latent Human Powers." *School and Society* 15 (Jan. 21, 1922): 80.

————. "An Adventure in Education." *Journal of Education* 107 (June 11, 1928): 695.

————. "A Budget for Your Life." *Woman's Home Companion* 54 (March 1927): 27.

————. "Cooperative Education." *School and Society* 22 (Oct. 1925): 557.

————. "Individuality without Individualism." *Christian Register* 107 (Jan. 1928): 46.

————. "Is the College a Menace to Education?" *Christian Leader* (Sept. 1926): 6.

————. "Newer Aspects of College Education." *Progressive Education* (July 1928): 270.

————. "The Spirit of Antioch." *Friend's Intelligences* 85 (Aug. 1928): 653.

————. "Tobacco and Scholarship." *The No-Tobacco Educator* 7 (Dec. 1925): 6.

————. "Traveling in New Educational Territory." *North Central Association Quarterly* 2 (Dec. 1927): 279.

————. "What's the Matter with Modern Collegiate Education—and Antioch's Answer." *National Magazine* 50 (July–Aug. 1921): 165.

Mount, Harry A. "Solvent College Students." *Popular Finance* (March 1924): 29.

Munroe, Paul. "A Unique Manufacturing Establishment." *American Machinist* 20 (March 25, 1897): 225-31.

"National Cash Register Company." *Fortune* (Aug. 1930): 67-71.

"Notable American." *Outlook* 131 (May 17, 1922): 94.

Orb, G. "Industrial Welfare Work in Akron." *Review* 2 (March 1920): 228.

Otey, Elizabeth L. "Employer's Welfare Work." *B.L.S. Bulletin* 123 (1913): 1-80.

Otis, H.G. "City Manager Movement—Facts and Figures." *American City* 20 (June 1919): 611-13.

————. "City Manager Plan Thrives under Handicaps." *American City* 21 (Sept. 1919): 281.

Parrott, F. "Conservancy Cottages near Dayton, Ohio." *House Beautiful* 44 (Nov. 1918): 320-22.

Parsons, J. "Prisoners of the Flood." *McClure's* 41 (July 1913): 39-48.

Patri, Angelo. "The Strangest College in the United States." *Liberty Magazine* (Oct. 25, Dec. 1, 1924): 57-59.

————. "Where You Must Work Your Way through College." *Liberty* 30 (Nov. 29, 1924): 11.

Patterson, John H. "Altruism and Sympathy as Factors in Works Administration." *Engineering Magazine* 20 (Jan. 1902): 579-80.

————. "How I Get My Ideas Across." *System* 33 (June 1918): 875-79.

Paul, George. "A College That Teaches Health." *Literary Digest* 27 (April 1923): 27.

Perkins, G.W. "Corporations in Modern Business." *North American Review* 187 (March 1908): 388-98.

Pfiffner, John M. "The City Manager and the Courts." *Public Management* 12 (Aug. 1930): 425-29.

———. "Why Not License City Managers?" *Public Management* 12 (Aug. 1930): 441-42.

"Prison Cells for Trust Sinners." *Literary Digest* 46 (March 1913): 444-45.

"Protecting Dayton against Floods." *Technical World* 19 (Aug. 1913): 932-33.

Radcliffe, H. "Educational Bureau in Industrial Corporations." *Engineering Magazine* 42 (Dec. 1911): 400-402.

Rayburn, C.C. "Welfare Work from the Employee's Standpoint." *Chautauquean* 43 (June 1906): 332-34.

"Rehabilitation Work at Dayton." *Survey* 30 (April 26, 1913): 129-30.

"Remington Cash Register Co. Rings Up a Sale to National." *Business Week* (Sept. 1931): 11.

Renwick, William T. "Democracy Chooses an Autocrat." *Technical World* 21 (March 1914): 13-19.

"Report on Outdoor Recreation for Industrial Workers." *Monthly Labor Review* 23 (Sept. 1926): 521-22.

"Reports from Other Cities Regarding the City Manager Plan." *American City* 12 (June 1915): 507.

"Responsibility of Industry for Recreation." *Playground* 28 (April 1928): 8-10.

Richmond, I.S. "Cooperation in Dayton." *Religious Education* 18 (April 1925): 124-25.

Richter, A.E. "Keeping Workers Fit." *System* 36 (Oct. 1919): 622-26.

Riddle, Kenyon. "The Managers Plan of Municipal Government." *Engineering News* 71 (April 16, 1914): 831-32.

———. "The Town Manager as City Engineer." *American City* 9 (Dec. 1913): 523-25.

Rightor, E. "City Manager and the Municipal Budget." *American City* 24 (May 1921): 527-33.

Rike, H. "Need for and Value of Physical Examination of Employees as Illustrated in the Work of the Rike-Kumler Company." *Annals of the American Academy of Political and Social Science* 65 (May 1916): 223-28.

Roe, Joseph W. "How the College Can Train Managers." *Engineering Magazine* 51 (July 1916): 537-42.

Rogers, S. "Tell the Truth Papers: Putting Heart into Work." *Outlook* 125 (Aug. 1920): 705-10.

Rossy, M.S. "Cost of an Employee Service Department." *Industrial Management* 70 (July 1925): 4-5.

Ruhl, Arthur. "Disaster at Dayton." *Outlook* 103 (April 1913): 805-9.

Ryan, O. "The Commission Plan of City Government." *American Political Science Review* 5 (Feb. 1911): 38-56.

"Sanitation at Dayton." *Survey* 30 (April 19, 1913): 120-23.

"Science versus Systems." *Engineering Magazine* 40 (March 1911): 952.

Shepherd, G. "This City Upset the Mayor's Chair." *Collier's* 75 (Feb. 1925): 9.

Sherwood, H.F. "How the Gem City Plan Worked." *Outlook* 133 (Aug. 1916): 805-8.

Shuey, E.L. "Model Factory Town." *Municipal Affairs* 3 (March 1899): 144-51.

"Standardized Operations and Scientific Management." *Scientific American* 104 (June 1911): 600.

Stevens, Myra. "A College That Really Trains Students for Life." *Other Peoples' Money* 6 (June 1928): 8.

Stote, A. "Ideal American City." *McBride's* 97 (April 1916): 89-92.

"System in the City Manager's Office." *American City* 39 (Nov. 1928): 86.

"Systems of Payment in Factories." *Scientific American Supplement* 83 (Jan. 13, 1917): 18-19.

Tarbell, Ida M. "Fear of Efficiency." *Independent* 91 (July 7, 1917): 19-20.

——. "Good Homes Make Good Workmen." *American Magazine* 80 (July 1915): 39-43.

Taylor, Frederick W. "New Science of Business Management." *American Magazine* 71 (Feb. 1911): 479-80.

——. "Principles of Scientific Management." *American Magazine* 71, 72 (March–May 1911): 570-81, 785-93; 101-13.

Taylor, G.R. "Norwood and Oakley: How Cincinnati Factories Have Turned Two Residential Suburbs Topsy Turvy." *Survey* 29 (Dec. 1912): 287-301.

Tead, O. "Industrial Counselor, a New Profession." *Independent* 88 (Dec. 1916): 393-95.

Thompson, Carl D. "The Vital Points in Charter Making from a Socialist Point of View." *National Municipal Review* 2 (1913): 416-26.

Thompson, H. "Big Business and the Citizen." *Review of Reviews* 46 (July 1912): 49-58.

"Those Who Can Afford Welfare Work." *World's Work* 36 (June 1918): 131-32.

Towne, R. "Engineer as an Economist." *Engineering Magazine* 51 (April 1916): 12-16.

Townsend, A. "Character Sketch." *Cosmopolitan* 33 (Sept. 1902): 526-30.

"Training for the Profession." *City Manager's Magazine* 7 (March 1925): 156-64.

Trick, E.H. "Put It in the Pay Envelope." *Factory and Industrial Management* 75 (March 1928): 524-25.

Truxton, Iwalke. "One City Manager's Personal Code." *Public Management* 10 (Jan. 1928): 15-16.

Turner, Julia Emery. "Antioch's Experiment." *Vassar Quarterly* 8 (Nov. 1922): 1.

———. "Institutional Management: Training at Antioch College." *Nation's Health* (June 1924): 63-64.

Upson, L.D. "City Manager Plan in Ohio." *American Political Science Review* 9 (Aug. 1915): 496-503.

———. "The City Manager Plan of Government for Dayton." *National Municipal Review* 2 (Oct. 1913): 639-44.

———. "Dayton's Exhibit of City Manager Government." *American City* 13 (Dec. 1915): 538-39.

———. "How Dayton's City-Manager Plan Is Working." *American Review of Reviews* 49 (June 1914): 714-17.

"Vocational Guidance: A Study in the Predicament of Public Education." *Nation* 114 (1922): 529.

Waite, Henry M. "City Manager Plan—The Application of Business Methods to Municipal Government." *American City* 11 (July 1914): 11- 13.

———. "The City Manager Plan: How It Operates in Dayton, Ohio." *Municipal Journal* 26 (June 1914): 822-23.

———. "Engineer as City Manager." *Engineering Magazine* 48 (March 1915): 894-96.

———. "Legislative Body in City Manager Government." *National Municipal Review* 12 (1923): 66-69.

"Waite, Master of Efficiency." *Independent* 88 (Nov. 20, 1916): 300.

Wallis, Rolland S. "The Trend of City Managers' Salaries." *City Managers' Magazine* (March 1925): 51-53.

Webster, A.G. "Scientific Management and Academic Efficiency." *Nation* 93 (Nov. 2, 1911): 416-17.

Weisenberg, M. "Labor's Defense against Employer's Welfare Tactics." *Current History* 25 (March 1927): 803-8.

"Welfare or Hell Fare?" *Review* 2 (March 13, 1920): 245.

Wells, Bert C. "A City Manager's Relation to Civic Organizations." *Public Management* 12 (March 1930): 118-20.

"What the City Managers Are Expected to Do." *American City* 12 (June 1915): 508-9.

"What the Men Are Thinking." *System* 28 (Sept. 1915): 230-37.

"What They Are Doing for Employees These Days." *Illustrated World* 33 (March 1920): 62-64.

White, L.D. "Four Hazards to Success and Progress in City Manager Government." *American City* 37 (Dec. 1927): 747-50.

"Why It Pays Patterson to Be the Best Employer in America." *Current Opinion* 64 (May 1918): 322.

"Why There Was Not Another Dayton Flood." *Literary Digest* 73 (June 1922): 21-22.

Wilder, E.M. "Commission and Commission-Manager Forms Contrasted." *Pacific Municipalities* 27 (Dec. 1913): 689-93.

Wildman, E. "Morality in Business; John Henry Patterson of Dayton, Ohio." *Forum* 62 (Aug. 1919): 158-68.

Wilhelm, D. "Big Businessman as a Social Worker." *Outlook* 107, 108 (Aug., Sept. 1914): 1005-9; 196-201.

Wilson, R. "Cincinnati Shows the Way." *Review of Reviews* 85 (May 1932): 33-34.

Work, E.W. "Trouble in the Cash Register Works." *Independent* 53 (June 1901): 1371-73.

Zelt, W.H. "Antioch Students in Demand." *Wood Construction* 11 (July 1925): 9.

Primary Sources

BOOKS

Allyn, Stanley C. *My Half-Century with NCR*. New York, 1967.

Bagley, William Chandler. *Classroom Management*. New York, 1925.

———. *The Educative Process*. New York, 1924.

Baker, Ray Stannard. *American Chronicle*. New York, 1945.

———. *The New Industrial Unrest: Reasons and Remedies*. Garden City, 1920.

Bloomfield, Meyer. *Readings in Vocational Guidance*. Boston, 1915.

Boettiger, L. *Employer Welfare Work*. New York, 1923.

Bromage, Arthur W. *A Councilman Speaks*. Ann Arbor, 1951.

———. *Councilmen at Work*. Ann Arbor, 1954.

Bruere, Henry; Childs, Richard S.; Donnelly, Frederick W.; Gilbertson, H.S.; and James, H.G. *Commission Government and the City Manager Plan*. Philadelphia, 1914.

Cadbury, Edward. *Experiments in Industrial Organization*. London, 1912.

Cherington, Paul T. *Advertising as a Business Force: A Compilation of Experience Records*. Garden City, 1913.

———. *The First Fifty Years of the Council-Manager Plan of Municipal Government*. New York, 1965.

Clute, William K. *The Law of Modern Municipal Charters*. Detroit, 1920.

Conover, Charlotte. *Dayton and Montgomery County*. New York, 1932.

———. *Some Dayton Saints and Prophets*. Dayton, 1907.

———. *The Story of Dayton*. Dayton, 1917.

Conover, Frank. *Centennial Portrait and Biographical Record of the City of Dayton and of Montgomery County, Ohio*. Dayton, 1897.

Counts, George. *The Social Composition of Boards of Education: A Study in the Social Control of Public Education.* Chicago, 1927.

Cronson, Bernard. *Pupil Self-Government.* New York, 1907.

Crowther, Samuel. *John H. Patterson, Pioneer in Industrial Welfare.* New York, 1923.

Curtis, Henry S. *The Play Movement and Its Significance.* New York, 1917.

Dewey, John, and Dewey, Evelyn. *Schools of Tomorrow.* New York, 1915.

Driscoll, D.W. *Clubmen of Dayton in Caricature.* Dayton, 1912.

Drury, Augustus Waldo. *History of the City of Dayton and Montgomery County, Ohio.* Dayton, 1909.

Dutton, Samuel T. *Social Phases of Education in the School and the Home.* New York, 1899.

Foster, Charles R. *Extra-Curricular Activities in the High School.* Richmond, 1925.

Galvin, Eileen H., and Walker, Eugenia M. *Assemblies for Junior and Senior High Schools.* New York, 1929.

Gantt, H.L. *Industrial Leadership.* New Haven, 1916.

Gill, Wilson L. *Manual of the School Republic.* Madison, Wis., 1932.

———. *A New Citizenship.* Hanover, N.H., 1913.

Gladden, Washington. *Recollections.* Boston, 1909.

Goldmark, Josephine. *Fatigue and Efficiency.* New York, 1912.

Hotchkiss, Willard Eugene. *Higher Education and Business Standards.* Boston, 1909.

Hoxie, Robert F. *Scientific Management and Labor.* New York, 1915.

James, Herman G., *Applied City Government.* New York, 1914.

Johnson, Ray W., and Lynch, Russell W. *The Sales Strategy of John H. Patterson, Founder of the National Cash Register Company.* New York, 1932.

Johnston, Charles R. *The Modern High School.* New York, 1914.

Kilpatrick, William Heard. *The Project Method.* New York, 1918.

King, Irving. *Education for Social Efficiency.* New York, 1913.

Lee, Joseph. *Constructive and Preventive Philanthropy.* New York, 1906.

Leuba, Clarence. *A Road to Creativity: Arthur Morgan, Engineer, Educator, Administrator.* North Quincy, Mass., 1971.

Lewis, Elias St. Elmo. *Financial Advertising.* Indianapolis, 1908.

Lipman, Frederick L. *Creating Capital, Money-making as an Aim in Business.* Boston, 1918.

Mabie, Edward Charles. *City Manager Plan of Government.* New York, 1918.

MacDonald, Susanne Rike. *The Backward Look: Memoirs of Susanne Rike MacDonald.* New York, 1957.

Marcosson, Isaac F. *Colonel Deeds, Industrial Builder.* New York, 1947.

———. *Wherever Men Trade: The Romance of the Cash Register.* New York, 1945.

Maxey, C.C. *Outline of Municipal Government*. Garden City, 1924.
———. *Readings in Municipal Government*. Garden City, 1920.
Nichols, Egbert R. *Intercollegiate Debates*. New York, 1917.
O'Shea, Michael. *Social Development and Education*. Cambridge, Mass., 1909.
Patterson, John H. *Letters from Abroad*. New York, 1902.
Perry, Clarence A. *The High School as a Social Centre*. New York, 1914.
———. *The School as a Factor in Neighborhood Development*. New York, 1914.
———. *Wider Use of the School Plant*. New York, 1910.
Puffer, J. Adams. *The Boy and His Gang*. Boston, 1912.
———. *Vocational Guidance*. Chicago, 1913.
Rainwater, Clarence E. *The Play Movement in the United States*. Chicago, 1922.
Rightor, Chester E. *The City Manager in Dayton*. New York, 1919.
Robbins, Charles L. *The Socialized Recitation*. New York, 1920.
Roemer, Joseph, and Allen, Charles F., eds. *Readings in Extra-Curricular Activities*. New York, 1929.
Shuey, Edwin L. *Factory People and Their Employers*. New York, 1900.
Sinclair, Upton. *The Goose-Step: A Study of American Education*. Pasadena, 1922.
———. *The Goslings: A Study of the American Schools*. Pasadena, 1924.
Tarbell, Ida. *All in a Day's Work*. New York, 1939.
———. *New Ideals in Business*. New York, 1916.
Tart, Frank. *Dayton Power and Light*. New York, 1953.
Thompson, Merle. *Trust Dissolution*. Boston, 1919.
Tolman, William H. *Industrial Betterment*. New York, 1900.
———. *Municipal Reform Movements in the United States*. New York, 1895.
———. *Social Engineering*. New York, 1909.
Toulmin, Harry A., Jr. *The City Manager: A New Profession*. New York, 1915.
Tracy, Lena Harvey. *How My Heart Sang*. New York, 1950.
Ward, Edward J. *The Social Center*. New York, 1913.
White, Leonard D. *The City Manager*. Chicago, 1927.
Whitlock, Brand. *Forty Years of It*. New York, 1914.
Wildman, Edwin. *Morality in Business: John Henry Patterson of Dayton, Ohio*. New York, 1919.
Winter, Ella, and Hicks, Granville, eds. *The Letters of Lincoln Steffens*. New York, 1938.
Witmer, Lightner. *The Nearing Case*. New York, 1915.
Woodruff, C.R., ed. *A New Municipal Program*. New York, 1919.

Secondary Sources

ARTICLES

Aduddell, Robert M., and Cain, Loris P. "Public Policy toward 'The Greatest Trust in the World,' " *Business History Review* 55 (Summer 1981): 217-42.

Alanen, Arnold R., and Peltin, Thomas J. "Kohler, Wisconsin: Planning and Paternalism in a Model Industrial Village." *Journal of the American Institute of Planners* 44 (1978): 145-59.

Allen, Howard W. "Geography and Politics: Voting on Reform Issues in the U.S. Senate, 1911-16." *Journal of American History* 27 (1961): 216-28.

Anderson, Fenwick. "Hail to the Editor-in-Chief: Cox vs. Harding, 1920." *Journalism History* 1974 1 (2): 46-49.

Anderson, William G. "Progressivism: An Historiographical Essay." *History Teacher* 5 (1973): 427-52.

Antler, Joyce. "Female Philanthropy and Progressivism in Chicago." *History of Education Quarterly* 21 (1981): 461-69.

Auerbach, Jerold S. "Progressives at Sea: The LaFollette Act of 1915." *Labor History* 2 (1961): 344-60.

Bailyn, Bernard. "The Challenge of Modern Historiography." *American Historical Review* 87 (1982): 9-11.

Berkhofer, Robert. "The Organizational Interpretation of American History: A New Synthesis." *Prospects* 4 (1979): 611-29.

Berkowitz, Edward D., and McQuaid, Kim. "Businessman and Bureaucrat: The Evolution of the American Social Welfare System, 1900-1940." *Journal of Economic History* 38 (1978): 120-42.

Bernard, Richard M., and Rice, Bradley R. "Political Environment and the Adoption of Progressive Municipal Reform." *Journal of Urban History* 1 (1975): 149-74.

Blackford, Mansel G. "Businessmen and the Regulation of Railroads and Public Utilities in California during the Progressive Era." *Business History Review* 44 (1970): 307-19.

———. "Scientific Management and Welfare Work in Early Twentieth Century American Business: The Buckeye Steel Casting Company." *Ohio History* 90 (1981): 238-58.

Buenker, John. "The Progressive Era: A Search for a Synthesis." *Mid-America* 51 (1969): 175-93.

———. "Urban Liberalism and the Federal Income Tax Amendment." *Pennsylvania History* 36 (1969): 192-215.

Bunting, David, and Barborer, Jeffrey. "Interlocking Directorates in Large American Corporations, 1896-1964." *Business History Review* 45 (1971): 317-35.

Castrovinci, J.L. "Prelude to Welfare Capitalism: The Role of Business in the Enactment of Workmen's Compensation Legislation in Illinois, 1905-1912." *Social Service Review* 50 (1976): 80-102.

Cebula, James E. "The New City and the New Journalism: The Case of Dayton, Ohio." *Ohio History* 88 (1979): 277-90.

Chandler, Alfred D. "The Beginnings of Big Business in American Industry." *Business History Review* 33 (1959): 1-31.

———. "The Emergence of Managerial Capitalism." *Business History Review* 58 (1984): 473-503.

———. "Management Decentralization: An Historical Analysis." *Business History Review* 30 (1956): 111-74.

———. "The Railroads: Pioneers in Modern Corporate Management." *Business History Review* 39 (1965): 16-40.

———. "The Role of Business in the United States: A Historical Essay." *Daedalus* 98 (Winter 1969): 35-38.

Chessman, G. Wallace. "Town Promotion in the Progressive Era: The Case of Newark, Ohio." *Ohio History* 87 (1978): 253-75.

Chipperfield, G.H. "The City Manager and Chief Administrative Officer." *Public Administration* 42 (1964): 123-31.

Coelko, Philip R., and Shepherd, James. "The Impact of Regional Differences in Prices and Wages on Economic Growth: The United States in 1890." *Journal of Economic History* 39 (1979): 69-86.

Cuff, Robert. "American Historians and the 'Organizational Factor,' " *Canadian Review of American Studies* 4 (1973): 19-31.

Davidson, Chandler. "At-large Elections and Minority-Group Representation: A Reexamination of Historical and Contemporary Evidence." *Journal of Politics* 43 (1981): 982-1005.

Davis, Lance, and North, Douglas. "Institutional Change and American Economic Growth: A First Step towards a Theory of Institutional Innovation." *Journal of Economic History* 30 (1970): 131-49.

Dawson, Andrew. "The Paradox of Dynamic Technological Change and the Labor Aristocracy in the United States, 1880-1914." *Labor History* 20 (Winter 1979): 325-51.

Dubofsky, Melvyn. "Success and Failure of Socialism in New York City, 1900-1918." *Labor History* 9 (Fall 1968): 361-75.

Eilbert, Henry. "The Development of Personnel Management in the United States." *Business History Review* 33 (Fall 1959): 347.

Felt, Jeremy. "The Progressive Era in America, 1900-1917." *Societas* 3 (1973): 103-14.

Filene, Peter. "An Obituary for the 'Progressive Movement.' " *American Quarterly* 22 (1970): 20-34.

Gaffield, Chad. "Big Business, the Working-Class, and Socialism in Schenectady, 1911-1916." *Labor History* 19 (Summer 1978): 350-72.

Galambos, Louis. "The Agrarian Image of the Large Corporation,

1879-1920: A Study in Social Accommodation." *Journal of Economic History* 28 (Sept. 1968): 341-62.

————. "Business History and the Theory of the Growth of the Firm." *Explorations in Entrepreneurial History* 4 (1966–67): 3-16.

————. "The Emerging Organizational Synthesis in Modern American History." *Business History Review* 44 (1970): 279-90.

————. "Technology, Political Economy, and Professionalization: Central Themes of the Organizational Synthesis." *Business History Review* 57 (1983): 471-93.

Gatewood, Willard B., Jr. "Progressivism: From the Old Style to the New." *Journal of Interdisciplinary History* 10 (1979): 147-53.

Ghent, Joyce Maynard, and Jaher, Frederic Cople. "The Chicago Business Elite: 1830-1930: A Collective Biography." *Business History Review* 50 (1976): 288-328.

Goob, Gerald. "Reflections on the History of Social Policy in America." *Reviews in American History* 7 (Sept. 1979): 293-305.

Goodenow, Ronald K. "Educating the Masses and Reforming the City: Another Look at the Gary Plan." *Teachers College Record* 83 (1982): 467-73.

Grant, Philip A., Jr. "Congressional Campaigns of James M. Cox, 1908 and 1910." *Ohio History* 81 (1972): 4-14.

Greenberg, Stephanie W. "Neighborhood Change, Radical Transition and Work Location: A Case Study of an Industrial City, Philadelphia, 1880-1930." *Journal of Urban History* 7 (May 1981): 267-314.

Haukins, Daniel F. "The Development of Modern Financial Reporting Practices among American Manufacturing Corporations." *Business History Review* 37 (1963): 135-68.

Hawley, Ellis. "The Discovery and Study of 'Corporate Liberalism,' " *Business History Review* 52 (1978): 309-20.

Hays, Samuel P. "The Politics of Reform in Municipal Government in the Progressive Era." *Pacific Northwest Quarterly* 55 (1964): 157-69.

Hobson, Wayne K. "Professionals, Progressives and Bureaucratization: A Preassessment." *Historian* 39 (1977): 639-58.

Kennedy, David M. "Overview: The Progressive Era." *Historian* 37 (1975): 453-68.

Kirshner, Don S. "The Ambiguous Legacy: Social Justice and Social Control in the Progressive Era." *Historical Reflections* 2 (1975): 69-88.

Kleppner, Paul, and Baker, Stephen C. "The Impact of Voter Registration Requirements on Electoral Turnout, 1900-16." *Journal of Political and Military Sociology* 8 (1980): 205-26.

Kousser, J. Morgan. "Progressivism for Middle Class Whites Only: North Carolina Education 1880-1910." *Journal of Southern History* 46 (1980): 169-94.

Lewis, Frank D. "Explaining the Shift of Labor from Agriculture to

Industry in the United States, 1869-1899." *Journal of Economic History* 39 (1979): 681-98.

Lineberry, Robert L., and Fowler, Edmund P. "Reformism and Public Policies in American Cities." *American Political Science Review* 61 (Sept. 1967): 701-16.

Link, Arthur S. "What Happened to the Progressive Movement in the 1920s?" *American Historical Review* 64 (1959): 833-51.

Livesay, Harold C., and Porter, Patrick B. "Vertical Integration in American Manufacturing 1899-1948." *Journal of Economic History* 29 (Sept. 1969): 494-500.

McCormick, Richard L. "The Discovery That Business Corrupts Politics: A Reappraisal of the Origins of Progressivism." *American Historical Review* 86 (1981): 247-74.

McCraw, Thomas K. "Regulation in America: A Review Article." *Business History Review* 49 (1975): 159-83.

McLean, Joseph E. "Wedding Big-City Politics and Professional Management." *Public Administration Review* 14 (Winter 1954): 55-62.

McQuaid, Kim. "Corporate Liberalism in the American Business Community, 1920-1940." *Business History Review* 52 (1978): 342-68.

———. "Young, Swope and General Electric's 'New Capitalism': A Study in Corporate Liberalism, 1920-33." *American Journal of Economics and Sociology* 36 (1977): 323-34.

Marcus, Alan I. "Professional Revolution and Reform in the Progressive Era: Cincinnati Physicians and the City Elections of 1897 and 1900." *Journal of Urban History* 5 (1979): 183-208.

Margulies, Herbert. "Recent Opinion on the Decline of the Progressive Era." *Mid-America* 45 (1963): 250-68.

Martin, Albro. "Uneasy Partners: Government Business Relations in Twentieth Century American History." *Prologue: Journal of the National Archives* (Summer 1979): 91-105.

Massouh, Michael. "Technological and Managerial Innovation: The Johnson Company, 1883-1898." *Business History Review* 50 (1976): 46-68.

Mitchel, J. Paul. "Boss Speer and the City Functional: Booster and Businessmen vs. Commission Government in Denver." *Pacific Northwest Quarterly* 63 (1972): 155-64.

Mohl, Raymond, and Betten, Neil. "Paternalism and Pluralism: Immigrants and Social Welfare in Gary, Indiana, 1906-1940." *American Studies* 15 (1974): 5-30.

Muraskin, William. "The Social Control Theory in American History." *Journal of Social History* 9 (1975-76): 559-69.

Neal, Larry. "Trust Companies and Financial Innovation, 1897-1914." *Business History Review* 45 (1971): 35-51.

Nelson, Daniel. "The Company Union Movement, 1900-1937: A Reexamination." *Business History Review* 56 (1982): 335-57.
————. "The Making of a Progressive Engineer: Frederick W. Taylor." *Pennsylvania Magazine of History and Biography* 103 (1979): 446-66.
————. "The New Factory System and the Unions: The National Cash Register Company Dispute of 1901." *Labor History* 15 (1974): 163-78.
————. "Scientific Management, Systematic Management, and Labor, 1880-1915." *Business History Review* 48 (1974): 479-500.
Oster, Donald B. "Reformers, Factionalists and Kansas City's 1925 City Manager Charter." *Missouri Historical Review* 72 (1978): 296-327.
Passer, Harold C. "Development of Large Scale Organization: Electrical Manufacturing around 1900." *Journal of Economic History* 12 (1952): 378-410.
Penrose, Edith T. "The Growth of the Firm—A Case Study: The Hercules Powder Company." *Business History Review* 34 (1960): 1-23.
Radosh, Ronald. "The Corporate Ideology of American Labor Leaders from Gompers to Hillman." *Studies on the Left* 6 (1966): 66-88.
Reese, William J. "Progressive School Reform in Toledo, 1898-1921." *Northwest Ohio Quarterly* 47 (1975): 44-59.
Rice, Bradley R. "The Galveston Plan of City Government by Commission: The Birth of a Progressive Idea." *Southwestern Historical Quarterly* 78 (1975): 365-408.
Richardson, James R. "Urban Political Change in the Progressive Era." *Ohio History* 87 (1978): 310-21.
Salisbury, Robert H., and Black, Gordon. "Class and Party in Partisan and Nonpartisan Elections: The Case of Des Moines." *American Political Science Review* 57 (Sept. 1963): 584-92.
Schacht, John N. "Toward Industrial Unionism: Bell Telephone Workers and Company Unions, 1919-1937." *Labor History* 16 (1975): 5-36.
Scheinberg, Stephen J. "Progressivism in Industry: The Welfare Movement in the American Factory." *Canadian Historical Association Papers* (1967): 184-97.
Schleppi, John R. " 'It Pays': John H. Patterson and Industrial Recreation at the National Cash Register Company." *Journal of Sport History* 6 (1979): 20-28.
Seltzer, Alan L. "Woodrow Wilson as a 'Corporate Liberal': Toward a Reconsideration of Left Revisionist Historiography." *Western Political Quarterly* 30 (1977): 183-212.
Sevitch, Benjamin. "The Rhetoric of Paternalism: Elbert H. Gary's Arguments for the Twelve-Hour Day." *Western Speech* 35 (1971): 15-23.
Sponholtz, Lloyd. "The Initiative and Referendum: Direct Democracy in Perspective, 1898-1920." *American Studies* 14 (1973): 43-64.
Stevens, George. "The Cincinnati Post and Municipal Reform, 1914-1941." *Ohio History* 79 (Summer–Autumn 1970): 231-42.

Stone, Alan. "A Spectre is Haunting America: An Interpretation of Progressivism." *Journal of Libertarian Studies* 3 (1979): 239-60.

Thelen, David P. "Social Tensions and the Origins of Progressivism." *Journal of American History* 56 (1969): 323-41.

Thompson, George V. "Intercompany Technical Standardization in the Early American Automobile Industry." *Journal of Economic History* 14 (March 1954): 1-20.

Trattner, Walter I. "Progressivism and World War I: A Reappraisal." *Mid-America* 44 (1962): 131-45.

Walker, John. "Socialism in Dayton, Ohio, 1912-1925: Its Membership, Organization, and Demise." *Labor History* 26 (1985): 384-404.

Walker, Kenneth K. "The Era of Industrialization: Capital and Labor in the Midwest in 1901." *Northwest Ohio Quarterly* 37 (1965): 49-60.

Warner, Landon. "Henry T. Hunt and Civic Reform in Cincinnati." *Ohio State Archaeological and Historical Quarterly* 62 (1953): 146-61.

Weinstein, James. "Big Business and the Origins of Workmen's Compensation." *Labor History* 8 (1967): 156-74.

———. "Organized Business and the Commission and Manager Movements." *Journal of Southern History.* 28 (1962): 166-82.

White, G. Edward. "The Social Values of the Progressives: Some New Perspectives." *South Atlantic Quarterly* 70 (1971): 62-76.

Williamson, Oliver. "The Modern Corporation: Origins, Evolution, Attributes." *Journal of Economic Literature* 19 (Dec. 1981): 1537-68.

Wyman, Roger. "Middle-Class Voters and Progressive Reform: The Conflict of Class and Culture." *American Political Science Review* 68 (1974): 488-504.

Zercan, Paul. "Understanding the Anti-Radicalism of the National Civic Federation." *International Review of Social History* 19 (1974): 194-210.

BOOKS

Allswong, John. *Bosses, Machines, and Urban Votes: An American Symbiosis.* Port Washington, N.Y., 1977.

Bannister, Robert C., Jr. *Ray Stannard Baker.* New Haven, 1966.

Barnard, John. *From Evangelicalism to Progressivism at Oberlin College, 1866-1917.* Columbus, Ohio, 1967.

Barritz, Loren. *The Servants of Power: A History of the Use of Social Science in American Industry.* Middletown, Conn., 1960.

Bates, Leonard. *The United States, 1898-1928: Progressivism and a Society in Transition.* New York, 1976.

Bendix, Reinhard. *Work and Authority in Industry: Ideologies of Management in the Course of Industrialization.* New York, 1963.

Bernstein, Irving. *The Lean Years: A History of the American Worker, 1920-1933.* Boston, 1960.

Blackford, Mansel G. *The Politics of Business in California, 1890-1920*. Columbus, Ohio, 1977.

Bonnett, Clarence E. *History of Employers' Associations in the United States*. New York, 1956.

Booth, David A. *Council-Manager Government in Small Cities*. Washington, D.C., 1968.

Brandes, Stuart D. *American Welfare Capitalism, 1880-1940*. Chicago, 1970.

Braverman, Harry. *Labor and Monopoly Capital: The Degradation of Work in the Twentieth Century*. New York, 1974.

Bremner, Robert H. *From the Depths: The Discovery of Poverty in the United States*. New York, 1956.

Brownell, Blaine A., and Stickle, Warren E., eds. *Bosses and Reformers*. Boston, 1973.

Bruder, Stanley. *Pullman: An Experiment in Industrial Order and Community Planning, 1880-1930*. New York, 1967.

Buenchner, John C. *Differences in Role Perceptions in Colorado Council-Manager Cities*. Boulder, 1965.

Caine, Stanly P. *The Myth of Progressive Reform: Railroad Regulation in Wisconsin, 1903-1910*. Madison, 1970.

Callahan, Raymond. *Education and the Cult of Efficiency*. Chicago, 1962.

Cavallo, Dominick. *Muscles and Morals: Organized Playgrounds and Urban Reform, 1880-1920*. Philadelphia, 1981.

Chambers, Clark A. *Seedtime of Reform: American Social Service and Social Action, 1918-1933*. Minneapolis, 1963.

Chambers, John W., II. *The Tyranny of Change: America in the Progressive Era, 1900-1917*. New York, 1980.

Chandler, Alfred D. *Giant Enterprise: Ford, General Motors, and the Automobile Industry*. New York, 1964.

———. *The Railroads: The Nation's First Big Business*. New York, 1965.

———. *The Visible Hand: The Managerial Revolution in American Business*. Cambridge, Mass., 1977.

Chandler, Alfred, and Tedlow, Richard, eds. *The Coming of Managerial Capitalism: A Casebook on the History of American Economic Institutions*. Homewood, Ill., 1985.

Clark, Burton. *The Distinctive College: Antioch, Reed and Swarthmore*. Chicago, 1970.

Clawson, Dan. *Bureaucracy and the Labor Process: The Transformation of U.S. Industry, 1860-1920*. New York, 1980.

Coben, Stanley, and Ratner, Lorman, eds. *The Development of an American Culture*. Englewood Cliffs, N.J., 1970.

Cochran, Thomas. *American Business in the Twentieth Century*. Cambridge, Mass., 1972.

Cohen, Ronald D., and Mohl, Raymond A. *The Paradox of Progressive*

Education: The Gary Plan and Urban Schooling. Port Washington, N.Y., 1979.

Cohen, Sol. *Progressive and Urban School Reform.* New York, 1964.

Condit, Carl W. *The Railroad and the City: A Technological and Urbanistic History of Cincinnati.* Columbus, Ohio, 1977.

Cremin, Lawrence A. *The Transformation of the School: Progressivism in American Education.* New York, 1961.

Curti, Merle. *The Social Ideas of American Educators.* Paterson, N.J., 1963.

Dworkin, Martin, ed. *Dewey on Education.* New York, 1959.

East, John Porter. *Council-Manager Government: The Political Thought of Its Founder, Richard S. Childs.* Chapel Hill, N.C., 1965.

Ebner, Michael, and Tobin, Eugene, eds. *The Age of Urban Reform: New Perspectives on the Progressive Era.* Port Washington, N.Y., 1977.

Eckert, Allan. *A Time of Terror: The Great Dayton Flood.* Boston, 1965.

Edwards, Richard. *Contested Terrain: The Transformation of the Workplace in the Twentieth Century.* New York, 1979.

Fox, Kenneth. *Better City Government: Innovation in American Urban Politics, 1850-1937.* Philadelphia, 1977.

Fragnoli, Raymond R. *The Transformation of Reform: Progressivism in Detroit—and After, 1912-1933.* New York, 1982.

Galambos, Louis. *The Public Image of Big Business in America, 1880-1940: A Quantitative Study in Social Change.* Baltimore, 1975.

Galambos, Louis, and Chandler, Alfred. *The Changing Economic Order: Readings in American Business and Economic History.* New York, 1968.

Garnet, Robert. *The Telephone Enterprise: The Evolution of the Bell System's Horizontal Structure, 1876-1909.* Baltimore, 1985.

Graham, Patricia. *Community and Class in American Education.* New York, 1974.

Green, Marguerite. *The National Civic Federation and the American Labor Movement, 1900-1925.* Washington, D.C., 1956.

Greenfield, Sidney M.; Strieken, Arnold; and Aubrey, Robert T., eds. *Entrepreneurs in Cultural Context.* Albuquerque, 1979.

Greenleaf, William. *Monopoly on Wheels: Henry Ford and the Selden Auto Patent.* Detroit, 1961.

Griffith, Ernest S. *A History of American City Government: The Progressive Years and Their Aftermath, 1900-1920.* New York, 1974.

Hogan, David. *Class and Reform: School and Society in Chicago, 1880-1930.* Philadelphia, 1985.

Israel, Jerry, ed. *Building the Organizational Society: Essays on Associational Activities in Modern America.* New York, 1972.

Kakir, Sudhir. *Frederick Taylor: A Study in Personality and Innovation.* Cambridge, Mass., 1970.

Katz, Michael. *Class, Bureaucracy, and the Schools: The Illusion of Educational Change in America.* New York, 1975.

Kennedy, David, ed. *Progressivism: The Critical Issues*. Boston, 1971.

Kerr, Clark; Dunlop, John T.; and Harbison, Frederick H. *Industrialization and Industrial Man: The Problems of Labor and Management in Economic Growth*. Cambridge, Mass., 1960.

Kirschner, Don. *City and County: Rural Response to Urbanization in the 1920s*. Westport, Conn., 1970.

Kneier, C.M. *City Government in the United States*. New York, 1957.

Kolko, Gabriel. *Railroads and Regulation, 1877-1916*. Princeton, 1965.

———. *The Triumph of Conservatism*. Chicago, 1963.

Krooss, Herman. *Executive Opinion: What Business Leaders Said and Thought on Public Issues, 1920s-1960s*. Garden City, 1971.

Krug, Edward A. *The Shaping of the American High School*. New York, 1964.

Lazerson, Marvin. *Origins of the Urban School: Public Education in Massachusetts, 1870-1915*. Cambridge, Mass., 1971.

Leiby, James. *A History of Social Welfare and Social Work in the United States*. New York, 1978.

Livesay, Harold, and Porter, Glenn. *Merchants and Manufacturers: Studies in the Changing Structure of Nineteenth Century Marketing*. Baltimore, 1971.

Lowi, Theodore J. *The End of Liberalism: Ideology, Policy and the Crisis of Public Authority*. New York, 1969.

Lubove, Roy. *The Professional Altruist: The Emergence of Social Work as a Career, 1880-1930*, Cambridge, Mass., 1965.

McClymer, John F. *War and Welfare: Social Engineering in America, 1890-1925*. Westport, Conn., 1980.

McCormick, Richard L. *From Realignment to Reform: Political Change in New York State, 1893-1910*. Ithaca, 1981.

McGraw, Thomas, ed. *Regulation in Perspective*. Cambridge, Mass., 1981.

Martin, Albro. *Enterprise Denied: Origins of the Decline of American Railroads, 1897-1917*. New York, 1971.

May, Henry. *Protestant Churches and Industrial America*. New York, 1949.

Mayhew, Katherine Camp, and Edwards, Anna Camp. *The Dewey School: The Laboratory School of the University of Chicago, 1896-1903*. New York, 1936.

Meyer, Stephen. *The Five Dollar Day: Labor Management and Social Control in the Ford Motor Company, 1906-1921*. Albany, 1981.

Michelman, Irving S. *Business at Bay: Critics and Heretics of American Business*. New York, 1969.

Miller, Zane L. *Boss Cox's Cincinnati: Urban Politics in the Progressive Era*. New York, 1968.

Montgomery, David. *Worker's Control in America: Studies in the History of Work Technology and Labor Struggles*. New York, 1979.

Mowry, George. *The California Progressives*. Berkeley, 1951.

————. *The Era of Theodore Roosevelt and the Birth of Modern America, 1900-1912*. New York, 1958.

Nadwormy, Milton J. *Scientific Management and the Unions, 1900-1932*. Cambridge, Mass., 1955.

Nelson, Daniel. *Frederick W. Taylor and the Rise of Scientific Management*. Madison, Wis., 1980.

————. *Managers and Workers: Origins of the New Factory System in the United States, 1880-1920*. Madison, Wis., 1975.

Niemi, Albert W., Jr. *State and Regional Patterns in American Manufacturing, 1860-1900*. Westport, Conn., 1974.

Noble, David F., *America by Design: Science, Technology, and the Rise of Corporate Capitalism*. New York, 1977.

Nye, Russell B. *Midwestern Progressive Politics: A Historical Study of Its Origins and Development, 1870-1950*. East Lansing, Mich., 1951.

O'Neill, William. *The Progressive Years: America Comes of Age*. New York, 1975.

Ozanne, Robert A. *Century of Labor-Management Relations at McCormick and International Harvester*. Madison, Wis., 1967.

Pease, Otis A., and Penick, James, Jr. *Progressivism in America: A Study of the Era from Theodore Roosevelt to Woodrow Wilson*. New York, 1974.

Peterson, Paul. *The Politics of School Reform: 1870-1940*. Chicago, 1985.

Philpott, Thomas L. *The Slum and the Ghetto: Neighborhood Deterioration and Middle-Class Reform in Chicago, 1890-1930*. New York, 1978.

Porter, Glenn. *The Rise of Big Business, 1860-1910*. Arlington Heights, Ill., 1973.

Quandt, Jean B. *From the Small Town to the Great Community: The Social Thought of Progressive Intellectuals*. New Brunswick, N.J., 1970.

Ransom, Roger L. *Coping with Capitalism: The Economic Transformation of the United States, 1776-1980*. Englewood Cliffs, N.J., 1981.

Rice, Bradley R. *Progressive Cities: The Commission Government in America, 1901-1920*. Austin, Tex., 1977.

Ross, Dorothy. *G. Stanley Hall*. Chicago, 1973.

Rucker, Darnell. *The Chicago Pragmatists*. Minneapolis, 1969.

Salvatti, Richard A. *The Role of the Manager in Communicating to the Public*. Ann Arbor, Mich., 1966.

Schiesl, Martin J. *The Politics of Efficiency: Municipal Administration and Reform in America, 1880-1920*. Berkeley, 1977.

Schwartz, Joel, and Prosser, Daniel, eds. *Cities of the Garden State: Essays in Urban and Suburban History of New Jersey*. Dubuque, Iowa, 1977.

Semonche, John B. *Ray Stannard Baker*. Chapel Hill, N.C., 1969.

Shergold, Peter R. *Working Class Life: The "American Standard" in Comparative Perspective, 1899-1913*. Pittsburgh, 1982.

Smith, George. *The Anatomy of a Business Strategy: Bell, Western Electric, and the Origins of the American Telephone Industry*. Baltimore, 1985.

Spring, Joel. *Educating the Worker-Citizen: The Social, Economic, and Political Foundations of Education.* New York, 1980.

———. *Education and the Rise of the Corporate State.* Boston, 1972.

Stave, Bruce M., ed. *Urban Bosses, Machines, and Progressive Reformers.* Lexington, Ky., 1972.

Steigerwalt, Albert K. *The National Association of Manufacturers, 1895-1914: A Study in Business Leadership.* Ann Arbor, Mich., 1964.

Stene, Edwin O. *The City Manager: Professional Training and Tenure.* Lawrence, 1966.

Stewart, Frank M. *A Half-Century of Municipal Reform: The History of the National Municipal League.* Berkeley, 1950.

Stewart, Ward, and Honey, John C. *University-sponsored Executive Development Programs in the Public Service.* Washington, D.C., 1966.

Talbert, Roy. *FDR's Utopian: Arthur Morgan of the Tennessee Valley Authority.* Jackson, Miss., 1987.

Thelen, David P. *The New Citizenship: Origins of Progressivism in Wisconsin, 1885-1900.* Columbia, Mo., 1972.

Tishler, Hace Sorel. *Self-Reliance and Social Security, 1870-1917.* Port Washington, N.Y., 1971.

Troen, Selwyn. *The Public and the Schools: Shaping the St. Louis System.* Columbia, Mo., 1975.

Tyack, David B., *The One Best System: A History of American Urban Education.* Cambridge, Mass., 1974.

Tyack, David, and Monsot, Elizabeth. *Managers of Virtue: Public School Leadership in America, 1820-1980.* New York, 1982.

Vatter, Harold G. *The Drive to Industrial Maturity: The U.S. Economy, 1860-1914.* Westport, Conn., 1975.

Warner, Hoyt, L. *Progressivism in Ohio, 1897-1917.* Columbus, 1964.

Weinberg, Julius. *Edward Alsworth Ross and the Sociology of Progressivism.* Madison, Wis., 1972.

Weinstein, James L. *The Corporate Ideal in the Liberal State: 1900-1918.* Boston, 1968.

White, Morton. *The Origin of Dewey's Instrumentalism.* New York, 1943.

———. *Social Thought in America: The Revolt against Formalism.* Boston, 1957.

Wiebe, Robert H. *Businessmen and Reform: A Study of the Progressive Movement.* Cambridge, Mass., 1962.

———. *The Search for Order, 1877-1920.* New York, 1967.

———. *The Segmented Society: An Introduction to the Memory of America.* New York, 1975.

Wilson, Harold S. *McClure's Magazine and Muckrakers.* Princeton, 1970.

Wilson, R. Jackson. *In Quest of Community.* New York, 1969.

———, ed. *Darwinism and the American Intellectual.* Homewood, Ill., 1967.

Index